RECIPES *and* RECIPROCITY

RECIPES *and* RECIPROCITY

BUILDING RELATIONSHIPS IN RESEARCH

Edited by HANNAH TAIT NEUFELD
and ELIZABETH FINNIS

UNIVERSITY OF MANITOBA PRESS

Recipes and Reciprocity: Building Relationships in Research

26 25 24 23 22 1 2 3 4 5

University of Manitoba Press
Winnipeg, Manitoba, Canada
Treaty 1 Territory
uofmpress.ca

Cataloguing data available from Library and Archives Canada
ISBN 978-0-88755-291-5 (PAPER)
ISBN 978-0-88755-293-9 (PDF)
ISBN 978-0-88755-295-3 (EPUB)
ISBN 978-0-88755-297-7 (BOUND)

Cover image by Karine Gagné
Cover and interior design by Jess Koroscil

Printed in Canada

The University of Manitoba Press acknowledges the financial support for its publication program provided by the Government of Canada through the Canada Book Fund, the Canada Council for the Arts, the Manitoba Department of Sport, Culture, and Heritage, the Manitoba Arts Council, and the Manitoba Book Publishing Tax Credit.

Funded by the Government of Canada | Canada

This book is dedicated to our families.
Thank you for introducing us to our first recipes
and contributing toward our ongoing fascination with
food as a shared reciprocal experience.

Contents

Acknowledgements

This book was made possible through the contributions of many who shared their time, energy, and food knowledge. We would like to extend our gratitude to the book's reviewers for their shared enthusiasm for this topic, and to Laura Peach for her detailed work in helping to prepare and format the manuscript. We are grateful to everyone at the University of Manitoba Press for their support and enthusiasm. In particular, we thank Jill McConkey for her editorial encouragement throughout the process of proposing and developing our volume. Many thanks to Maureen Epp for her fantastic, meticulous copy-editing of the manuscript. And we thank Glenn Bergen and Stephanie Paddey for all of their production and marketing work. Lastly, we could not have assembled this collection without the contributions of those who submitted their work. Thank you to all of the authors for your patience, dedication, and efforts over the duration of this writing project.

As avid consumers of food and knowledge through stories, we also wish to acknowledge the communities and people profiled in this volume for everything they have brought to our lives and scholarship through our collective food practices and experiences of cooking and eating together.

Introduction

Elizabeth Finnis
and Hannah Tait Neufeld

This book brings together authors from various disciplines, working in diverse geographical and cultural contexts, to discuss the ways that food and recipe sharing intersect in researchers' and participants' everyday lives. The project grew out of our conversations around developing an interdisciplinary writing project: Elizabeth was interested in exploring how food questions and experiences could emerge in unexpected ways in anthropological fieldwork, regardless of whether food was at the centre of a research program, while Hannah wanted to incorporate issues related to recipes and cooking within the reciprocal nature of Indigenous food sovereignty practices. The more we talked, the clearer it became that we were both interested in using food and recipes as lenses to consider intersectoral research practices and learning, along with interpersonal relationships and reflexivity. What can acts of cooking and sharing food and culinary traditions tell us about the relationships we build as part of our research processes?

Ultimately, we came to the idea for this volume, which focuses on exploring reciprocity, recipes, cooking, and research experiences from different disciplinary perspectives. A central goal of our volume is to bring to the forefront reflections on how food as a process—from choosing ingredients to preparing them to eating—can bridge field or community-based research and lived experience, transcending the potentially unobservable boundaries of difference and diversity. The contributors to this book use food preparation and consumption and/or recipe sharing as lenses through which to consider topics such as identity; resistance and reclaiming traditional foodways; ancestral connections; social and political change; ethical food and authenticity; language and food preparation; healthy eating; and the reflexive experiences of being a researcher. Some of the chapters in this volume (Classen, Finnis, Gagné, Kawano, Moffat, and Van Esterik) draw on anthropological, ethnographic approaches to research. Participant observation, through living and working with communities, is at the core of ethnographic fieldwork.[1] Methods such as semi-structured interviews and oral histories can be integrated within the ethnographic approach; however, it is the embodied participation in everyday life and the engagement of the senses that are key.[2] This approach to research "raises issues of obligation, reciprocity, trust and the formation of friendships" while building longer-term engagements with individuals and communities.[3] Other chapters (Cyr, Neufeld, Phillipps and Skinner) highlight perspectives the authors gained through community-based participatory research (CBPR) and shared in relation to research partnerships and learning using the seven principles of community engagement with Indigenous communities: Relationality, Responsibility, Reflexivity, Respect, Reverence, Responsivity, and Reciprocity.[4] The flexible nature of CBPR permits methodological adaptations depending on community and partner needs and interests, and use of the most effective research practices that embody community priorities, identities, strengths, and aspirations. Several chapters (Cyr, Kawano, and Xavier and Lickers) focus on self-reflective experiences with food traditions, including their own individual as well as social and cultural connections.

An additional goal of the volume is to encourage researchers to think about their own food- and cooking-related research experiences. Some of the contributions to this volume come from authors whose research agendas specifically address aspects of nutrition, food security, food preparation, production, and consumption. Other contributors conduct research that is not necessarily focused on food issues but whose experiences nevertheless highlight the complex ways that food is embedded in everyday research processes. The varied approaches and wealth of insights in these chapters demonstrate why food "is such an apt medium for purely social symbolism, from private hospitality to great ceremonial dramas,"[5] and show how cuisines and dishes are shaped by local, ecological, seasonal, and cultural contexts,[6] as well as by political and historical contexts and social changes.[7]

Given the symbolic, practical, and contested meanings of food, food production, and distribution, it is no surprise that there is a diverse and rich body of volumes that explore issues of food and foodways from a range of disciplinary perspectives and geographic locales, drawing on history,[8] nutrition,[9] local and global practices,[10] changes in food production practices and food system governance,[11] food, culture, and ethnographic encounters,[12] everyday foods and baking,[13] and discussions around the ethics of consuming animals[14]—to name just some themes. Recipe elements have also been incorporated into academic writing, both in terms of cookbooks or ideas of cuisine and in the inclusion of recipes as part of academic discussions of the socio-cultural and the political, the local and the global, and everyday practice. For example, in *Home Cooking in the Global Village: Caribbean Food from Buccaneers to Ecotourists*, Richard Wilk integrates recipes to help illustrate national identity and globalization at different points in Belize's history. Devon Mihesuah's revised edition (2020) of her 2003 book *Recovering Our Ancestors' Gardens: Indigenous Recipes and Guide to Diet and Fitness* builds on the concept of Indigenous food sovereignty by capturing Indigenous foods and practices in the form of recipes to reflect ancestral knowledge and guidance toward maintaining healthy food environments. One example of the challenges to recovering and reclaiming health, Mihesuah argues, is frybread, which historically has represented survival for many Indigenous communities, yet its identification as an authentic Indigenous food is controversial. Diane Tye's engaging volume *Baking as Biography: A Life Story in Recipes* takes a more personal approach, drawing on her mother's recipe collection both to explore her mother's life and identities and to "tell larger stories of how women of her generation balanced personal needs against the demands of family and community."[15] This rich volume intersperses recipes throughout recollections and discussions of shared foodways, everyday food encounters, and themes such as community and resistance.[16]

Our book is also influenced by Jessica Kuper's *The Anthropologists' Cookbook.* First published in 1977,[17] the book offers recipes from a range of anthropological field contexts, along with short discussions of the contexts and cultural meanings of specific dishes. Including written recipes raises questions about how this changes the culinary experience and intention behind these foods. Arjun Appadurai discusses the simplifications and classifications that can occur when oral recipes are translated into written cookbooks, and the ways cookbooks intersect with changes to food boundaries and consumption practices while also speaking to and reflecting pressures and expectations beyond the act of cooking a specific dish.[18] Kuper points out that some of the contributors to *The Anthropologists' Cookbook* raised concerns about losing context and aspects of the authenticity (including through ingredient substitutions) in translating recipes into a book for individual consumption, thus removing these living practices from their original social and cultural environments.[19] In the context of our volume, it is important to point out that the recipes that authors have included are based on the oral and hands-on knowledge exchanges that happen as a result of relationships built in ethnographic and community-based research and everyday encounters. Yet in converting these recipes and their associated interactions within social and food environments to a written format, we lose the feel, touch, and tastes of our experiential encounters.

Our volume contributes to these bodies of food-related academic research by highlighting the personal within research, while drawing on concepts of reflexivity, everyday practice, and relationship building. Although each chapter draws on different experiences, communities, and environments, there are overlapping themes that emerge: authenticity of food origins and ingredients; reclaiming and resistance through food; complexity of research relationships; and the central theme of reciprocity, whether small- and large-scale, everyday or policy-based, individual-to-individual, or Nation-to-Nation. For example, Adrianne Lickers Xavier and Kitty R. Lynn Lickers chronicle their kitchen-table conversations in the form of soup stories that integrate Haudenosaunee knowledge within their mother-daughter relationship. Monica Cyr shares her personal experiences of reconnecting with her family's Métis foodways along with her own identity through conversations with relatives and her local community. These forms of knowledge or Indigenous Knowledges have been defined as "practical common sense based on teachings and experiences passed on from generation to generation," or most simply "a way of life."[20] These ways of knowledge generation often combine the information and practices of two worlds or diverse knowledge systems in *Etuaptmumk*, or Two-Eyed Seeing.[21] The two worlds are not necessarily balanced in research or practice, as Indigenous people are often forced to integrate their epistemologies into Western paradigms. A CBPR methodology is based in the co-production of knowledge, which prioritizes the equalization of power dynamics between and among communities and researchers.[22]

Lauren Classen, Elizabeth Finnis, Karine Gagné, and Penny Van Esterik write in their chapters about the complex navigations of relationship building in the cultural settings of rural Malawi, Paraguay, India, and Thailand (respectively), involving not only specific social contexts but the evolving so-called postcolonial[23] food systems in these settings. Political and cultural shifts in the commodification and evolution of foods and their preparation are described from the international perspectives of Japan and Nepal by Satsuki Kawano and Tina Moffat, and within Indigenous communities by Hannah Tait Neufeld as well as by Breanna Phillipps and Kelly Skinner. Most of the authors in this volume share recipes from families and communities they do not identify as their own. In doing so, they add layers of complexity in relation to their positions of power within academic institutions, where knowledge is cultivated to be commodified. Reflexivity is an essential part of the process of developing knowledge in a reciprocal form to be shared more freely and nourished in the form of relationships to food and each other.

We encourage readers of this volume to think about the ways that food and acts of culinary practices and traditions can build, reinforce, or resist relationships, whether interpersonally or more broadly within national and international contexts, and also to consider the meaning of knowledge in this range of settings. How might the making of food be implicated in everyday or political acts of reciprocity, and how can this shape the experience of field-based and community-based research and our understandings of the evolving nature of culinary practices and foodways? How can acts of learning recipes, cooking with one another, and making and sharing food lead us to better understandings of other processes, concerns, or priorities for the communities with which we build these reciprocal relationships? How can these diverse forms of knowledge be framed in dynamic terms that allow for an exploration into the ways that food is often portrayed in academia as gendered, racialized, and colonized?

We leave readers with an invitation to reflect on how food, cooking, and recipes have shaped—or may shape—their own research and personal experiences, in both expected and unexpected ways. We also encourage readers to try the recipes that are included in most of these chapters, recognizing that these recipes, presented often as stories and shared orally and through practice, are shaped by the need to put something on paper that follows expectations for the ways knowledge in academia is presented. This gives the recipes in this volume the appearance of culinary stasis. Yet "ethnographers commonly report quite wide variation in modes of preparation of even standard dishes, and every cook adds a personal signature."[24] For Indigenous Peoples, food is "one of the most basic yet profound ways in which we express Indigeneity . . . as a deeply meaningful strategy for remembering our original instructions encoded within our kin-centric relationships to the land, water, people, plants and animals that provide us with our food."[25] We therefore remind readers to experiment with the recipe frameworks and narratives that we have collectively included here, while reflecting on how these preparations form the basis of knowledge that is shaped by available ingredients, the origins of these ingredients, taste preferences, cooking options, history, power, practicality, time, place, and space.

Notes

1 Madden, *Being Ethnographic*.

2 Ibid.

3 Ibid., 16.

4 LaVeaux and Christopher, "Contextualizing CBPR"; Kirkness and Barnhardt, "First Nations and Higher Education."

5 Douglas, Introduction to *The Anthropologists' Cookbook*, 1.

6 Mintz, "Food at Moderate Speeds."

7 Neufeld, Richmond, and Southwest Ontario Aboriginal Health Access Centre, "Exploring First Nation Elder Women's Relationships with Food."

8 Iacovetta, Korinek, and Epp, *Edible Histories*; and Bannerjee-Dube, *Cooking Cultures*.

9 Hayes-Conroy and Hayes-Conroy, *Doing Nutrition Differently*.

10 Wilk, *Fast Food/Slow Food*; Finnis, *Reimagining Marginalized Foods*; Srinivas and Ray, *Curried Cultures*; and Shukla and Settee, "Revitalizing the Past."

11 Koc, Sumner, and Winson, *Critical Perspectives in Food Studies*; and Mihesuah and Hoover, *Indigenous Food Sovereignty*.

12 Coleman, *Food*; and Counihan and Van Esterik, *Food and Culture*.

13 Tye, *Baking as Biography*.

14 King et al., *Messy Eating*.

15 Tye, *Baking as Biography*, 17.

16 Another approach to integrating recipes outside of cookery books while also drawing on the personal can be found in Sheikh's enchanting memoir, *Tea and Pomegranates: A Memoir of Food, Family, and Kashmir*. Sheikh takes readers through rich descriptions of Mughal food, each chapter centred on a recipe and embedded in stories of family, history, and childhood.

17 Kuper, *The Anthropologists' Cookbook*.

18 Appadurai, "How to Make a National Cuisine."

19 Kuper, Preface to the Second Edition, in *The Anthropologists' Cookbook*, x–xiii.

20 Cochran and Geller, "The Melting Ice Cellar," 1405.

21 Bartlett, Marshall, and Marshall, "Two-Eyed Seeing."

22 Smith, *Decolonizing Methodologies*.

23 As Smith discusses in *Decolonizing Methodologies,* naming the world as "post-colonial" from Indigenous perspectives is to name colonialism as finished business, meaning that the colonizers have left. Even where they have left formally, she argues, the institutions and legacies of colonialism remain, 101.

24 Kuper, Preface to the Second Edition, in *The Anthropologists' Cookbook*, xii.

25 Morrison, "Reflections and Realities," 21.

CHAPTER 1

Momo Parties: Crafting Dumplings, Knowledge, and Identity in the Field

Karine Gagné

In this chapter, I revisit fifteen years of relationships with people in three different communities of North India by focusing on "*momo* parties," or gatherings with friends that revolve around making Tibetan dumplings. My aim is to examine the production of knowledge in the field. By considering social gatherings that centre on the preparation of food, I ponder the role of convivial gatherings and friendship in generating ethnographic insights and on the shaping of researchers' identity and positionality in the field. In doing so, I also reflect on identity as it relates to food by considering different *momo* recipes and different values attached to the ingredients used in the preparation of the recipes.

Much has been said about how the ethnographer's positionality shapes her research subject and about the power of the ethnographic gaze in shaping ethnographic truths.[1] Another important insight from the reflexive turn in ethnography concerns how the researcher's positionality can shape the understanding of ethnographic elements. For instance, in their now-famous pieces, both Lila Abu-Lughod and Renato Rosaldo reflect on how their personal life experiences have led them to shift their understanding of ethnographic elements or situations from the field.[2] Far less has been written, however, on how the field itself shapes and transforms researchers. Reminiscing on how he had to accept ideas related to witchcraft, a central component of the Azande's belief system, in order to make social life practical and possible while in the field, Edward Evans-Pritchard wrote, "If one must act as though one believed, one ends in believing, or half-believing as one acts."[3] In this, the renowned anthropologist gives us a glimpse of the transformative potential of living in different cultural contexts and of encountering different systems of knowledge. But beyond anecdotal hints, we know little about the various transformative processes that anthropologists undergo in the field, whether these are momentary or enduring. We also know little about the trajectories that lead anthropologists to their field sites and their disciplines, information that is relevant if we are to take the exercise in reflexivity seriously.

While the reflexive turn has considerably inspired the work produced by anthropologists from the 1980s to the early 2000s, these discussions have since been largely obscured by the sometimes-heavy theoretical discussions that often dominate the material produced by our discipline. Overall, what happens behind the scenes in the production of ethnographic knowledge is something that occupies little space in published work. In this chapter, I propose to consider some of these elements of reflexivity by focusing on commensality—the practice of eating together—in the field, a productive vantage point from which to consider the shaping of ethnographic knowledge.[4]

One thing I discovered when I started teaching anthropology was the prevailing idea among students that there is a clear and well-delineated trajectory leading to this profession. Yet for me, as for many of my colleagues, this path was not clearly defined. Rather, life experiences, friendship, and the cultivation of related interests brought me to the discipline. I am an anthropologist conducting research on the interaction between humans and the environment in the Himalayas. My research also brings me to examine human-animal relationships and how people interact with the sacred geography that surrounds them. While my research interests have slowly developed over the years, their seeds were partly sown during *momo* parties, long before I set foot in Ladakh, my main fieldsite. Moreover,

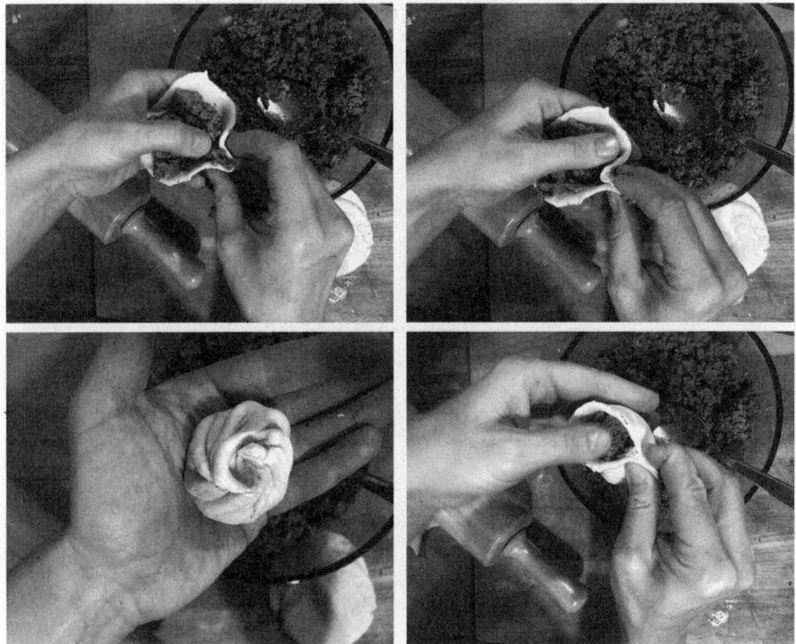

FIGURE 1.1. Assembling a momo. Clockwise from top left: (a) put a teaspoon of the filling in the dough circle; (b) pinch the edges strongly and by following the shape of the circle; (c) if the filling comes out, press it gently back inside; (d) close the momo by pressing the edges firmly, so that the filling does not leak during the cooking process.

I found *momo* parties significant because of the learning experiences they provided. Thus, although my own research does not examine questions related to commensality, it is a significant aspect of my research trajectory.

A *momo* is a small dumpling, steamed or sometimes boiled, and filled with meat or vegetables. In her book *Dumplings: A Global History*, Barbara Gallani explains that the dumpling has developed in an independent manner in different parts of the world. Travel and commercial exchanges, for instance along the Silk Road—to which Tibet and Ladakh, two regions discussed in this chapter, were connected—have contributed to the evolution of dumplings, through the transfer of different shapes and flavours.[5] In his *Food in Tibetan Life*, Rinjing Dorje describes the *momo* as a very special Tibetan treat and a meal of great importance; people learn to make *momo* in early childhood.[6] In spite of its seemingly banal and bland appearance, I also cherish this little ball of stuffed dough, as it recalls the many nights I spent with friends sharing stories, telling jokes, playing cards and board games, and singing songs. And more than anything, *momo*, or more precisely, their preparation during parties, are associated with transformative and rich learning experiences.

Momo Recipe

Dough

6 cups flour (all purpose or whole wheat)

1 teaspoon salt (or adjust as required)

Water as needed

Add water in parts and knead to a stiff dough. Roll out the dough and cut into circles.

Filling

Meat momo

Mix the following ingredients:

2 pounds ground meat (beef or mutton)

1/3 cup water

1 cup finely chopped celery leaf

Salt to taste

Vegetable momo

Mix the following ingredients (all chopped into very small pieces):

Fresh ginger (about 2 inches)

2 cloves garlic

1 large cabbage

6 to 8 carrots

A little bit of ghee

Salt to taste

Tomato chutney

Mix the following ingredients:

5 small tomatoes

Chopped green chili, to taste

Chopped coriander, to taste

3 small cloves garlic

Salt to taste

Coriander yogurt chutney

Mix the following ingredients:

Chopped coriander, to taste

Chopped garlic, to taste

Chopped green chili, to taste

Salt to taste

Dharamsala: The Beginning

I first set foot in India in the early 2000s, a few years before I embarked on my journey to do a PhD. My goal was clear: I would work for non-governmental organizations (NGOs) dedicated to the Tibetan cause. At that time, I had just completed my undergraduate studies and had happened upon the Canadian documentary *What Remains of Us*. Shot clandestinely, it covered the survival of the non-violent resistance movement in Tibet. This is what eventually brought me to McLeod Ganj, a neighbourhood in the upper part of Dharamsala, the North Indian town where the Dalai Lama and a large community of Tibetan refugees reside. What started as a planned stay of six months to work on the production of a documentary for a local NGO on the democratization of the Tibetan government-in-exile extended to many months over several stays, during which time I ended up doing research for different organizations. Over the years, my knowledge of Tibetan culture, Buddhism, history, and political issues grew incrementally. But what remained the most inspirational aspect of these experiences, and what influenced my research ideas when I decided to further my education and start graduate studies in anthropology, was the friendships I developed with Tibetans.

In particular, I grew very close with a group of friends who were all from Amdo, one of the three regions of Tibet. Many of our evenings revolved around what my friends referred to as *momo* parties, get-togethers during which we would prepare *momo*, indulge in drinking whiskey or rum, play board games, cards, share stories, jokes, and sayings. These young men had all been herders in Tibet before they came to India as refugees and, during these evenings, they would also inevitably start singing beautiful songs about Tibet, its landscape and its beauty. These songs were very descriptive and passionate. I was amazed at how notions of morality and references to animals and elements of the natural landscape were dominant in these elements of their oral tradition. This is how my interest in the affective dimensions that link humans to their environment started to develop and eventually became a key component of my research as an anthropologist.

The *momo* parties were always held at the same place. My friends were running a restaurant which was closed in the winter, the low tourist season. This was also their place of residence, and at night the cushioned benches transformed into beds for these five young men in their mid-twenties. Outside my working hours for NGOs, I spent a considerable amount of time there. The restaurant, on the top floor of a building, had a large balcony with an impressive view of the magnificent mountains of the Dauladhar range, which is a part of the lesser Himalayan chain of mountains. It was one of the most coveted places in town to watch the sun set. The building had been erected on a steep mountain slope; the slope was eroding a bit more each year from the monsoons. This construction seemed irrational, especially since the region is prone to seismic activity. In fact, McLeod Ganj and Dharamsala had been entirely destroyed in 1905 by an earthquake (known as the Kangra earthquake) that took the lives of close to 20,000 people, the traces of which are still visible in the landscape. We were all aware of this, but this was at a time in our lives when the few responsibilities we had made the benefits of hanging out in an amazing setting outweigh the possible risks.

The preparation for *momo* parties normally started in the afternoon, when we would shop for the necessary ingredients. In Tibet, the meat would have been beef, yak, or pork. But the meat *momo* we prepared were most often filled with mutton (Figure 1.2). Beef would have been by far the favoured option, but in a Hindu-majority country where the slaughter of cows is extremely controversial, this was nearly impossible. Occasionally, someone travelling from Delhi, where beef is more accessible than in Himachal Pradesh state, would smuggle beef in the overnight bus. But this was a rare event.

When we were not preparing meat *momo*, we would prepare what I have come to think of as the food of longing, *chu-tse momo*. *Chu-tse* is Asian chives, a species of onion native to China. In Dharamsala, people grow *chu-tse* in their gardens or even in flowerpots. *Chu-tse* is sometimes confused with garlic chives, but both have a distinct flavour. *Chu-tse* tastes strong, but the flavour is not that of garlic chives, which are usually used for seasoning. Its leaves are long and flat rather than tubular, and when *chu-tse* blossoms its flowers are white, not purple like garlic chives. *Chu-tse momo* are particularly prized by Tibetans from Amdo. To me *chu-tse* was an acquired taste. I found the taste rather pungent at first, so much so that I could not understand how my friends could be so excited when they found *chu-tse* to make *chu-tse momo*. As I came to understand, *chu-tse momo*, unlike mutton *momo*, were commonly eaten in Tibet. Like the songs and stories shared during these parties, eating

FIGURE 1.2. A man preparing the filling for mutton *momo*. Photo by Josianne Robichaud.

chu-tse momo allowed these young men to travel back to Tibet, through sensations and memories.[7]

In the restaurants of Dharamsala, one can find many different types of *momo*, and the vegetarian options creatively combine different ingredients, including cheese, potatoes, carrots, cabbage, green bell peppers, and spinach, in a variety of ways. These friends were not open to experimenting with *momo*, or with any other food. In general, Tibetan food is quite simple, using very few ingredients and often the same ones. One day, while eating at a restaurant with a Tibetan friend, I ordered a plate of jacket potatoes, something he had never seen. He looked at the dish for a moment and burst out laughing. He saw the attempt to "disguise" the potatoes, as he put it, as incredibly absurd. After all, a potato is just a plain, ugly vegetable, he explained, and does not deserve all this ornament. The same applied to *momo*, which these friends thought should be kept simple. Any experimentation with the filling was considered "Indian style" and rejected as not being "our food," a reflection that reminds us of the structuring capacity of culture and which echoes Mary Douglas's argument that food systems are intricately linked to social systems and can be central to the identification of group boundaries.[8]

Momo are often accompanied by a soup, and the version prepared here was quite bland in flavour. It was made from the water used to steam the *momo*, into which had dripped the fat from some of the *momo* that inevitably ended up breaking. *Momo* are eaten with a variety of sauces, but for this group of friends, only three things were deemed worthy: light Chinese soya sauce, Chinese dark vinegar, and a very spicy sauce made from packaged dry crushed red chilis. These products, often brought from Delhi, were available in the makeshift shops in the streets of Dharamsala and sold by Tibetans. While these young men came to India as refugees and had rather bitter feelings for the People's Republic of China, their taste buds did not always abide by their political convictions. As one of them once put it, "I am observing a complete ban on products coming from China, but the only thing I cannot give up is their vinegar."

Making *momo* takes time, and we would produce them at a leisurely pace while chatting. Everyone had their role in the production. One person would be in charge of finely chopping the filling ingredients, whether meat or *chu-tse*, and then mixing them in a large stainless-steel bowl with oil and seasoning.

Another person would prepare the large steamer, filling the bottom part with water, and spreading oil on the inner pot to keep the *momo* from sticking. Someone else would prepare the dough, using refined flour, and then roll it out. The dough was divided into small balls that would be flattened into perfect circles with a small rolling pin. The edges would be rolled to become thinner, while the centre was kept thicker. This would ensure that the edges of the dough could be easily pinched together to close the *momo*, while the centre would remain strong enough to keep the stuffing from bursting out. My role, together with four to five other people, was to assemble the *momo*.

There are plenty of tutorials on YouTube explaining how to make *momo*, but what they fail to capture is how difficult it is to properly shape them. It took some time to learn the skill of making *momo*, and my friends were always quite patient with me. The shape adopted by Amdowa (people from Amdo) looks like a rose, known in Dharamsala as the "Amdo *momo*." A friend also tried to teach me other methods of closing *momo*, such as what this group of Amdowa referred to as the "Lhasa *momo*," which looks like a crescent moon. But I always failed miserably. Using the right amount of filling is also a skill. The less you use, the easier it is to close the *momo*, but this compromises the flavour. Conversely, using too much filling makes it difficult to properly close the *momo*, which means it might end up breaking in the steaming process.

Once the dumplings were sealed, they would be steamed for a few minutes in a nested aluminum steamer. In the past, when steamers were not available, *momo* would be boiled directly in a pot of water. Once the *momo* were ready, we would eat them while they were still fresh and hot, and another steamer would be immediately filled with more *momo*. We always made plenty, and we would eat the leftovers the following morning by frying them in a pan. Once the *momo* production was finished, the night would unfold. Songs and stories would open up a whole new world, and I was fortunate to be able to travel through poetry to the pastures of Tibet, immersing myself in a way of understanding the world that is predicated on an emotional connection with the environment. Little did I know then that my research imagination was developing at the same time.

In Ladakh: Friendship in the Field

In the region of Ladakh in North India, the lengthy preparation of *momo* is in many families reserved for special occasions, for instance Losar, the New Year. I first had *momo* in Ladakh when the son of my host family in Leh, the capital of the region, along with his friends, decided to organize something special for me on Christmas Day, knowing how much I loved the dumpling. This group of young adults, men in their mid- to late twenties, was quite amazed to see that I could craft a reasonably good *momo*. In fact, I was as good at the task as some of them. I felt very proud, because by then I had not made *momo* for a number of years. But what surprised them even more was that I was making what they referred to as "Tibetan *momo*." As I came to understand, what I had known as the "Amdo *momo*" is a design not generally made around Leh (Figure 1.3). Yet my skills were praised and from then onward, on a number of occasions, I was introduced by these friends as someone who "knows how to make a *momo* like a local."

Something else also surprised me that evening. The *momo* party did not lead to the much-anticipated songs and stories I had come to love in Dharamsala. Instead, music in English and Hindi blared from the small speaker of a friend's phone. At that point, still early in my fieldwork, I had only seen people singing during marriage ceremonies. This prompted me to inquire whether singing was something people did outside of ritual contexts. It appeared that this was becoming less and less frequent.

I was initially disappointed by the absence of singing, which I was keenly anticipating. Yet these parties were also, in their own way, a window onto the lives and experiences of a younger generation of Ladakhis. This was not something I was considering directly in my research work, which was more oriented toward elders. Unlike the group of Tibetans I had befriended in Dharamsala, these friends had never been herders. In Ladakh, as in Tibet, singing often accompanies the long days spent in the high pastures or even in farming work. But in providing employment opportunities, the restructured economy of Ladakh, a region that was reconfigured as a border area after the independence of India, had significant implications for the slow but steady waning of the local pastoralist economy. The challenges of living in a society that has experienced profound social changes with its transition from

FIGURE 1.3. The crescent-shaped *momo* is commonly made by Ladakhis, whereas the rose-shaped *momo* is sometimes referred to as the "Tibetan *momo*." Photo by Josianne Robichaud.

a subsistence agropastoralist economy to a cash economy are manifold. In Ladakh, this is compounded by the fact that work opportunities, although more abundant than in the past, leave a significant number of highly educated youth unemployed. The ensuing unfulfilled aspirations were often at the centre of my conversations with Ladakhis.

I rarely had meat *momo* in Ladakh, where meat is only consumed moderately or reserved for special occasions. When I did, the meat used for the filling was mutton. The more usual filling was a mixture of carrots and cabbage, to which cheese was sometimes added and a few pinches of turmeric-based seasoning. Indeed, unlike the kitchen of my Amdowa friends, food of Indian inspiration has largely made its way into Ladakhi households, where rice, lentils, and Indian spices are commonly consumed at least once a day. My neighbour in Leh was a young Nepali woman who had grown up in Ladakh and was an expert *momo* maker. When she was around, she would add to the filling her special ingredient, soya chunks, locally referred to as "nutri." This texturized plant protein is a little nugget of defatted soy flour, which is sometimes used in curries in India. Packaged food is another culinary influence that has made its way to Ladakhi kitchens. The soup we had with the *momo* was made using Knorr or Maggi brand instant dry soup mixes, products appreciated by some for their convenience and time-saving aspects. The *momo* were served with a spicy tomato chutney, which could not be prepared in winter, as the necessary fresh ingredients are not available then. The preparation of the *momo* was also slightly different than in Dharamsala. A large quantity of dough was rolled out and circles were cut out using a stainless-steel drinking glass (Figure 1.4). The edges of each circle were carefully flattened with the fingers before the filling was placed on them. My move from Dharamsala to Leh also allowed me to discover a new style of cooking *momo*. In Leh restaurants, as in Dharamsala, *momo* are sometimes deep-fried. But in Leh there is also a hybrid version, the *kothey momo*. This *momo* is first steamed and then fried in a pan for a few minutes, but only the base is fried.

In ethnographic fieldwork, friendship, especially when it develops with research participants, is often considered a potentially fraught thing.[9] If friendship was a defining feature of the time I spent in Dharamsala, this was equally true of my fieldwork in Ladakh. But in Ladakh, it was as an ethnographer that I participated in *momo* parties, which, as a learning experience, blurred the line between everyone's respective roles, namely mine as a friend and a researcher, and that of my friends as research participants. But commensality in the field is important for its potential for cultural learning and to form friendships.[10] Moreover, friendship and the events that revolve around it can also be learning opportunities for researchers, helping to develop their ethical compass. The first *momo* party I was a part of in Ladakh and the discussions that filled that evening made me realize the necessity of rejecting some of my Tibetan cultural referents in order to understand Ladakh. Culturally, Tibetans and Ladakhis share many affinities, including Tibetan Buddhism, culinary traditions, and ways to celebrate. But each community has its own history and culture, and one should be careful with comparisons and expectations.

In Zanskar: Fieldwork and Family

A researcher does not enter the field as a neutral research tool. The researcher's gender will impact participant observation, from what the researcher can access to how she is perceived by a community.[11] Tony Whitehead and Mary Conaway reflect on how gender attributes such as being a mother or being married have implications for researchers in the field and may even facilitate the research process.[12] The beginning of my fieldwork in 2016 in Zanskar, an isolated region of North India, sometimes described as a sub-region of Ladakh, also marked my transition to a woman doing fieldwork in North India. By then, I was a mother to a little girl who has been accompanying me to the Himalayas nearly every year, gracefully coping with all the challenges this entails.

Scholars have called for the recognition of how accompanied research, in particular with children and family members, has implications for methodological issues related to fieldwork, including questions of positionality, relationships developed in the field, and research outcomes.[13] As Julie Cupples and Sara Kindon remind us, the observer is also observed, and identities are also constructed for the research in the field, something that is impacted by who is accompanying us.[14] How we change as fieldworkers over the years and how this impacts how we are viewed in the field are questions that remain to

FIGURE 1.4. Everything required to prepare *momo*: a *momo* steamer, a rolling pin, a stainless-steel glass, a cutting board, the dough, and the filling.
Photo by Karine Gagné.

be discussed, but these reflections suggest that doing research with children in tow has methodological implications. While becoming a mother has transformed how I do fieldwork, sometimes in challenging ways, the new conditions of my presence in the field are such that I am no longer able to hang out as often and as late with young adults as I did during my years in Dharamsala and Ladakh. However, my new social status also facilitates my interactions with families in the field. While I do not bring my daughter with me when conducting interviews and meeting research participants, she is often by my side during ceremonies and rituals, and for all of the everyday activities that are not work related, such as shopping for food in the market or washing and hanging clothes outside. This often leads to interactions and exchanges with other children and mothers, shapes the social connections I develop in the field, and provides a new window on some dimensions of life in the Himalayas.

The *momo* parties I have thus far been a part of in Zanskar reflect this new identity, as they are quite familial in nature. One example of this is the get-togethers organized by my research assistant, Stanzin, and his wife, Ishey, at their home at the end of my research stays. The event usually starts in the late afternoon. While the children play outside, eventually going to the grazing area to bring back the cows, Stanzin and I turn our attention to matters that need to be finalized before I leave Zanskar. First, with my notebook open, I ask Stanzin some of my remaining research-related questions, and we go through things I want to clarify or validate. Stanzin answers each of my questions patiently while preparing the filling and the dough for the *momo*. Then we move to monetary matters. Stanzin always refuses any money from me until this last day, before we embark on the two-day journey to Leh. On that evening, I also update my records to balance the books: the number of days we worked together, the time Stanzin spent running errands for research purposes, the places we travelled to in his dilapidated car, which amazingly, as he often likes to remark, survives the rough roads of Zanskar. Once the sun sets, the kids gather inside. They start to play different games, and sometimes we join them. Then, later on, we prepare the *momo*. These evenings are always filled with much laughter. While the children sip on juice purchased for the occasion, otherwise considered a luxury in Zanskar, the adults drink *chang*, the local homemade barley beer, freshly made by Stanzin's wife. Sometimes, we drink a shot or two of *arak*, a strong, locally distilled spirit. But our consumption remains rather moderate, to the benefit of our aging bodies.

Like the *momo* I ate while in Leh, the *momo* filling I have in Zanskar is made with a blend of vegetables, generally only carrots and cabbage, to which cheese is sometimes added. The key aspect of *momo* that Stanzin and Ishey's family ties to its identity is the use of whole wheat flour. Refined flour is commonly used by restaurateurs in Ladakh and Zanskar, and is increasingly found in the households of Ladakh (Figure 1.5). This was the flour used for the *momo* I had in Leh. This flour is not a product of people's land but is purchased at the market. This is somewhat paradoxical, given that wheat is a dominant crop grown by farmers in the region. However, there is a certain status ascribed to refined flour. Many people in Ladakh and Zanskar would agree with Pierre Bourdieu's theory of cultural capital, which links the expression of taste to class.[15] In Leh, people explain their preference for refined flour by emphasizing the heavy feeling left by whole wheat flour, in addition to its being less gratifying to the palate. But others, like Stanzin, whose family identifies as farmers, see more in this rejection. In Ladakh, and to some extent in Zanskar, farming is increasingly looked down upon, particularly because unlike paid work it leaves many aspirations that are linked to material gain unfulfilled. Being a farmer today is sometimes seen as having failed to make it on the extremely competitive job market, and the use of old-fashioned whole wheat flour can be seen as an extension of this perceived failure.

But, for Stanzin, the use of whole wheat flour is indicative of properly caring for one's body and one's family. Care has been examined by anthropologists as an ethical framework, an affective disposition, an act of resistance, and a mode of engagement toward the self and others, whether humans or nonhumans.[16] This is the form of care that Stanzin has in mind when he describes whole wheat flour as having more nutrients and giving more strength and energy than refined flour. The origin and nature of this flour are also known, as it comes directly from the farmer's land. In a place like Zanskar, where organic farming dominates and where people have largely rejected the state's efforts to modernize farming with the introduction of

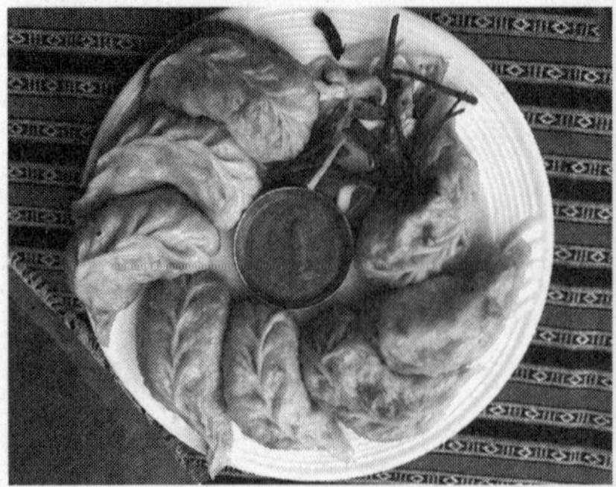

FIGURE 1.5. The image on the left shows a plate of *momo* served in a restaurant in Leh and made with refined flour. The image on the right shows a plate of *momo* made with whole wheat flour. The dough is thicker, and for someone not used to making *momo* regularly, a bit more difficult to manipulate. Photos by Karine Gagné.

hybrid seeds and pesticides, this is important. This form of care has resonance with feminist scholarship that links care to practices that bind material, mind, body, and self.[17] These same dispositions can be read in the yogurt and coriander chutney prepared by Ishey. Served with the *momo*, it is made with fresh yogurt produced from the family's *dzo* (a hybrid between a yak and a cow) and consists of very few ingredients.

By now, after more than fifteen years on my Himalayan and *momo*-making journey, although I am not an expert, I am able to impress with my *momo*-making skills. I have not yet mastered any other style of *momo* than the rose-shaped *momo* of my early days in Dharamsala, and I still surprise people with this style. The *momo* parties organized by Stanzin also have a different meaning to me than those in Dharamsala and Leh. In one of the very few pieces of writing that ponders researchers' relationships with and recognition of their research assistants and main guides in the field, Bhoju Ram Gujar and Ann Gold repeat the reflection made by Joseph Casagrande in 1960 that "significant relationships with individuals who have been our close associates for many months are as a rule memorialized in a mere footnote or a few brief prefatory sentences."[18] Writing thirty years later, Gujar and Gold agree that Casagrande's reflection remains accurate, as it still does today, more than sixty years after it appeared. An interesting exception is found in the 2014 special issue of the journal *Ethnography*. Tackling this gap in the reflexive turn and noting the centrality of research assistants in the production of ethnographic knowledge, Townsend Middleton and Jason Cons ask, "Are research assistants simply 'employees' in the field, or are they constitutive of 'the field' itself?"[19]

Stanzin is not only my employee but also someone who plays a critical role in what Zanskar as a field is for me. He is also someone I consider a dear friend. When I am in Zanskar, I walk considerable distances to reach remote villages. When I can no longer find the strength to carry my daughter on my shoulders—now that she is older, this is becoming more frequent—Stanzin always enthusiastically insists on helping me (Figure 1.6). When one of us gets sick, or worse, injured, Stanzin is always there to help. When I reach Ladakh, he makes the twenty-hour or so drive on rough roads to pick us up in Leh and get us safely to Zanskar. At the end of my stay, he will do the same and return us safely to Leh. Whenever we take to the road, whether on the half-built new connections within the region or the rough road to Kargil, Stanzin spends considerable time finding the most reputable drivers. When I approach him with my research project ideas, which are often difficult to accomplish given the limited time I can spend in the field between teaching semesters, he does his best to make them happen. When I come to him with vague ideas, he always takes them seriously and helps me transform them into something more concrete. I am well aware that without him, I would not be able to do the research I do in Zanskar, with all the challenges it entails. And he probably knows this as well, but always remains gracious. I recognize that for Stanzin, organizing a *momo* party is a way to thank me for a work opportunity. But I also like to think of it as an occasion to celebrate the bond between our two families.

Anthropologists have reflected on the usage of the notion of "friend" to describe the relationship they have with companions, fixers, and research assistants in the field.[20] Certainly, the idea of friendship can easily become blurry when it is also mediated by an employer-employee relationship. A friend is a person one enjoys spending time with, a person one trusts and wants to help, all feelings that characterize my relationship with Stanzin. The time I spend with Stanzin and his family is not always transactional and

FIGURE 1.6. Stanzin carrying my daughter on the long and challenging trek to the isolated village of Relakung in Zanskar. Photo by Josianne Robichaud.

predicated on work. Our mutual trust has withstood the demands brought on by working under sometimes-challenging situations resulting from political turmoil, such as road blockades, and a sometimes-unforgiving environment where we have encountered avalanches, landslides, altitude sickness, and other injuries over the years. I regularly help Stanzin and his family by attending to their needs, even though it seems to me that no material goods match the value of his support. Because of the nature of our relationship, I cannot think of Stanzin as only an employee. Rather, I prefer to think of him as a loyal friend or, perhaps more accurately, a relative. In Tom Fricke's beautiful reflection on the man who guided him through his research in Nepal over many years, he writes, "When I think of Yhebe now, I still sometimes use words from my profession. But when I more truly imagine him, I lose these abstractions and see a man, a man with whom I am joined in a common story."[21] Fricke then reflects on the impasse in trying to name this type of relationship: "The language we anthropologists have not yet found is the language adequate to friendship and to love."[22] I cherish the *momo* parties in Stanzin's home, and in many ways, they epitomize what the language of my profession, anthropology, has failed to develop. The affective feelings of bonding with a family, the pleasure of meeting again after one year of absence and of seeing our children play together is something that remains difficult to situate in the terminology we anthropologists use to describe our relationships and interactions in the field.

Conclusion: Food, Reciprocity, and the Ethnographic Self

One of the most fundamental lessons that the study of culture and society has taught us is the variability in the meaning of things and events. The *momo* recipes adopted by the three different Himalayan communities I have been interacting with demonstrate how food is intricately linked to identity, whether one accepts or rejects the influence of the flavours from India and ingredients that are not from the land. Commensality, the practice of eating together, may also take on different meanings. For my Amdowa friends, *momo* parties were an occasion to travel back home, through the preparation and savouring of familiar food and by singing songs about Tibet and its landscape, as they would have in the past when herding their animals in the mountains. In Ladakh, for the young adults with whom I developed friendships, *momo* parties were moments of intimacy conducive to reflections about new aspirations in an eroding agrarian economy. In Zanskar, *momo* parties bring closure to seasons of fieldwork and have the ambiance of a family reunion.

Momo parties have been a defining feature of the time I spent in the Indian Himalayas over the years. Whether in Dharamsala or Ladakh, evenings that revolve around the preparation of *momo* have been unique opportunities to access a cultural universe that otherwise did not present itself in that form to me during my everyday interactions. When I think about the *momo* parties of Dharamsala, I also understand that they were for me the opportunity to cultivate my research imagination by better understanding how people relate to a place, something that still constitutes an important dimension of my research work. The *momo* parties of Ladakh enabled me to reconsider my cultural referents and to better understand a generation of Ladakhis on their own terms. The *momo* parties I have attended in Zanskar embody a transition in my fieldwork in North India, where my presence is defined by my identity as a mother, a status that enables me to cultivate different relationships in the field.

When we think about commensality and sharing food, the notion of reciprocity is often imagined in material terms. For instance, we practise reciprocity by inviting people home for dinner. In his famous analysis, Marcel Mauss tells us that through the notion of reciprocity, gift giving is a principle of domination, something never truly altruistic but fraught with deceit and coercion.[23] Typologies of reciprocity—generalized, balanced, and negative—have shed light on the complexity of repayment.[24] But these economic models of exchange leave little room for the intangible and immaterial in reciprocity.

In his introduction to *Food: Ethnographic Encounters*, Leo Coleman reminds us that the exchange of food is a form of ethnographic co-presence that is not only about nourishing the material but also always involves intangible aspects.[25] It is also an experience that takes place between subjects, with all the implications that these experiences may entail. Commensality here provides a window onto the potential of these elements of co-presence in shaping our own identity. When I think about *momo* parties, I think about how my friends in the field have been amazing teachers. The friendships I forged in the Himalayas, whether as a researcher or someone working for NGOs in a community, had (and continue to have) significant implications in my life. Perhaps more importantly, I like to think that these relationships also transformed me (and continue to do so) as an individual as I learned from people's life stories, their world views, and their aspirations. The value of this learning experience certainly exceeds the narrow scope of a material outlook on reciprocity. Nor am I convinced that there is a way of reciprocating that would match the significance of these formative human experiences. Ultimately, these dimensions of the research process tell us that the shaping of ethnographic knowledge is never just about the methodological tools that we mobilize but also the various life experiences we go through and the connections we forge in the field, some of which are celebrated during social events like eating together.

Notes

1 Clifford and Marcus, *Writing Culture*; and Marcus and Fischer, *Anthropology as Cultural Critique*.

2 Abu-Lughod, "A Tale of Two Pregnancies"; and Rosaldo, "Grief and a Headhunter's Rage."

3 Evans-Pritchard, *Witchcraft, Oracles, and Magic*, 244.

4 Coleman, *Food*; Haines and Sammells, *Adventures in Eating*; and Sutton, "Food and the Senses."

5 Gallani, *Dumplings*, 30–31.

6 Dorje, *Food in Tibetan Life*, 82.

7 Holtzman, "Food and Memory."

8 Douglas, "Deciphering a Meal."

9 Van den Hoonaard, *Qualitative Research in Action,* 65–66.

10 Jordan, "In Search of the Elusive Heirloom Tomato."

11 DeWalt and DeWalt, *Participant Observation*, 83.

12 Whitehead and Conaway, *Self, Sex, and Gender*, 7.

13 Cornet and Blumenfield, *Doing Fieldwork in China*; Frohlick, "'You Brought Your Baby to Base Camp?'"; and Gibb, "Not Just Parenting in the Field."

14 Cupples and Kindon, "Far from Being 'Home Alone.'"

15 Bourdieu, *La Distinction*.

16 Mol, Moser, and Pols, *Care in Practice*; Ticktin, *Casualties of Care*; Martin, Myers, Viseu, "The Politics of Care in Technoscience."

17 Mol, *The Logic of Care*; Puig de la Bellacasa, *Matters of Care*.

18 Casagrande, *In the Company of Man*, xii, quoted in Gujar and Gold, "From the Research Assistant's Point of View," 73.

19 Middleton and Cons, "Coming to Terms," 280.

20 Crick, "Ali and Me"; Grindal and Salamone, *Bridges to Humanity*; Jenkins, "Assistants, Guides, Collaborators, Friends"; and Kumar, *Friends, Brothers and Informants*.

21 Fricke, "Imagining Yhebe," 199.

22 Ibid.

23 Mauss, "Essai sur le don."

24 Sahlins, *Stone Age Economics*.

25 Coleman, *Food*, 31.

CHAPTER 2

Poppycock and Puffed Rice: Recipe Knowledge in Thai Buddhist Communities

Penny Van Esterik

I do not remember tasting Poppycock until I married into the Van Esterik family. My husband's parents would stuff a large tin of the popcorn-based sweet into their children's Christmas stockings, even when they were adults. The children recall receiving animal-shaped popcorn treats and giant canisters of popcorn when they were growing up. Sometime after we married, I received my own tin of Poppycock at Christmas and really felt included, like a daughter, a part of the family. But I gave nothing comparable back to my in-laws. I had no popcorn memories from my own childhood. Marriage, of course, changes food traditions, as individuals adopt new practices and adapt old ones.

The taste of Poppycock is not unlike a dish I had in villages in central Thailand many decades ago. It was called *krayasat*, or heavenly rice (*khaw thip*), and was a very sweet confection made from peanuts, palm sugar, rice, sesame seeds, and coconut combined into a sticky paste, often held together with a milk-based product like sweetened condensed milk or coconut milk. It was very rich and yummy, and reminded me of Poppycock. I first ate it—mountains of it—in Crocodile Village, Suphanburi Province, central Thailand, in 1972, where my husband John and I spent several months in the early '70s, carrying out fieldwork. We watched as households in the village

FIGURE 2.1. "Heavenly rice" in New Rice village. Image Credit: Penny Van Esterik.

made vats of it in giant pans under their houses, where food was prepared. Women householders carried plates of the sweet to offer to the monks in the village temple. Later, I watched families bringing some to their relatives, neighbours, and to us. The next day, you could see offerings of the sweet dessert at house shrines (*san chaw phum*), crossroads, and in rice fields.

Making *Krayasat*

When asked how *krayasat* was made, women spoke casually about dry roasting ingredients and mixing them together in large pans. The dry ingredients included peanuts, glutinous rice, popped new rice, coconut, and sesame seeds. After mixing them together, they added either a can of sweetened condensed milk or a mixture of palm sugar and coconut milk until the ingredients stuck together. The proportions varied, depending on the available ingredients in the household.

Krayasat Recipe

To make krayasat *in a North American kitchen, try the following recipe:*

Dry roast the following ingredients and place in a large mixing bowl:

1 cup glutinous rice, lightly ground

1 cup skinned peanuts

1 cup sesame seeds

1 cup sunflower seeds

1 cup pumpkin seeds

1 cup shredded coconut

Add 4 cups Rice Krispies or puffed rice. Heat 2 cups of palm sugar until bubbling; add 1 cup coconut cream and mix well. Pour over dry ingredients and mix until they are coated and sticky. Shape into mounds or press into a greased pan and cut into squares.

I also recalled tasting a similar sweet in New Rice Village, Ayuttaya Province. My husband and I were accompanying a group of urban Thai students learning how to do village ethnography. We watched as young girls dressed in white and wearing crowns "mixed the heavenly rice" in large pans filled with a mixture of rice grains, sugar, and milk, assisted by older village women in the open hall on the temple grounds. The Bangkok students snickered at the young age of the village girls dressed in white, hinting that they would have to be about ten years old in order to participate as virgins. When we asked what they were doing, the villagers explained that they were making a sweet to commemorate Sujata, offering the Buddha a dish of sweet milk rice called *khaw thip* (heavenly rice). Again, the Bangkok students disparaged the villagers as not being real Buddhists but rather carrying out superstitious animistic rituals. Village participants described the event as a Brahman ritual, with the village ritual specialist dressed in white as if he were a Brahman priest. Students ignored this interpretation, explaining to us that the man just liked to dress up.

The few faded photographs I found some forty years later show a group of female relatives in Crocodile Village winding rice noodles into packets and stirring a huge vat of *krayasat* under the house, and a very posed, serious photograph of an unsmiling woman in her best clothes carrying plates of *krayasat* to the temple. From New Rice Village, my camera gravitated to the white-and-gold-attired old man and the nervous-looking young women in white stirring vats of the rice mixture. Other shots show older women helping to stir the heavy confectionery, with men and boys in the background.

Looking back, I shudder at the arrogance of thinking we could do an ethnography of a Thai village or help Bangkok Thai students do ethnographies of their rural compatriots. We, as well as the students, came to the events noted above loaded with baggage. We were concerned with being accepted in Crocodile Village, eager to please or at least not to offend, and trained to expect holism, every act connected to everything else. Our village informants were glad to comply, answering all our questions with "it is a Thai custom." Our Bangkok students came to New Rice Village with urban assumptions, including nostalgia for a romanticized rural past and disdain for rural ignorance and backwardness compared to sophisticated Bangkok Buddhist practices.

In this chapter, I begin to unpack the layers of what I have learned since these two fieldwork encounters and then reconsider these events in hindsight. Looking back over old fieldnotes and photographs decades after these events took place, I am struck by what I did not admit to myself about doing research and the questions I did not ask myself or my research participants.

Being in the Field

I was never a natural-born fieldworker; while I wanted to experience everything I could while I was in Thailand, I was most comfortable observing pre-framed events like rituals, where I could bring my "attentive observation"[1] to activities that others were also watching—events where I knew where the edges were in time and space. These events made it easier to be an outside observer in a rural Thai village. But that meant that I often neglected to consider the context of ritual events or had no opportunity to observe the backstage preparations.

Crocodile Village is a large rice-growing village in west-central Thailand. My husband, John, and I spent several months there in the early 1970s, planning and carrying out fieldwork, and made subsequent return visits. There were two possible roles for a foreigner/outsider in a Thai village in the '70s—missionary or communist. Either identity might well result in a beating or death, not a happy thought for a couple of graduate students with rudimentary Thai language skills. Fortunately, we were not aware of the seriousness of our situation and only learned much later that we were protected by villagers who trusted that we did not fit into either category. In that case, how could we explain what we were doing there? "Why did you come to Crocodile Village?" they asked. We said we were Canadian students who wanted to learn about Thai Buddhism and life in a rice-growing community. We had particular interests in lay meditation and Brahman rituals. They assumed that our *kam* (karma) in former lives had brought us to their village in particular. "Why would you want to do research?" they repeated. "So that we could get a university degree," we explained. "Why?" "So that we could get a job and make money in the future." Now that (as well as our karma) made sense to them. We were tolerated, not accepted, except by those who became friends and took it upon themselves to let us know when we made serious mistakes. Only in hindsight can I admit how difficult I found the experience. My mind has selected and recalled all the wonderful field moments while repressing the problems. These challenges include the difficulty of learning the rules of reciprocity, particularly around food; labelling and oversimplifying religious beliefs and practices; integrating texts with observation; and accounting for the biases of time and memory.

In sum, interpreting food events draws attention to the difficulty in finding the balance between over- and under-interpretation in field research.

Reciprocity

The recipe for *krayasat* reminds me about field dilemmas around reciprocity and the complexity of food exchanges in Thai and Lao Buddhist traditions. How could we practise reciprocity in a place where we did not know the rules of reciprocity? And even if we had known the rules, we had nothing valuable to exchange. But we sensed a quid pro quo was always there, sometimes obvious, sometimes not. We had no facilities to prepare and share meals. We were ignorant foreigners, always needing guidance from others. But there was a possibility that we might have politically useful Bangkok connections, and we could read and translate English labels and signs (often inaccurately). As graduate students on a small research grant, we had very little money, although we were often asked for cash, which we provided primarily for ritual events.

Reciprocity was at the heart of many of the fieldwork challenges we experienced. Thai meals provide occasions for generalized reciprocity, but we could barely reciprocate with meals, as we did not have a functioning kitchen and had no cooking skills. We only ate *krayasat* on the occasion of a ritual called *Sat Thai*, held in September. *Krayasat* was exchanged in a form of balanced reciprocity. But we had nothing to give in return for the plates of the sweet we received; we did not have the knowledge or access to ingredients to make it. *Krayasat* became a painful reminder of unbalanced reciprocity. During ritual events, we really were strangers, socially distant from our Thai neighbours. It felt like we were thus the target of a great deal of generosity, which the distribution of *krayasat* made more obvious.

At the same time, we needed to figure out how the dynamics of sharing operated in a complex hierarchical system that appeared on the surface to be visibly egalitarian. For example, our closest neighbours offered to let us use their outdoor latrine, explaining that "Thais share." But when they realized that we intended to take them up on their generosity, it became clear that we were not meant to accept their offer. Whenever we used the latrine, there would be a grumpy family member waiting impatiently outside looking daggers at us. We soon realized we would need to build our own latrine. As we learned more about the kinship system, we realized that the rhetoric of egalitarian relations between neighbours masked subtle ranking of families based on wealth, allowing exploitative patron-client relations to flourish, even among relatives. We were expecting the hierarchical ranking of monks as superior to laypersons, but not the exploitation of poor cousins. Thais share, yes, but there was a constant tension between hierarchy and reciprocity in the village. Often hierarchy trumps reciprocity; yet while ritual events stress the hierarchy of renouncing monks over laity, they also downplay hierarchy among families and stress the reciprocity expected between community members.

I recall sitting in the weekly chanting service in the village temple and realizing that I had forgotten to bring money to make a donation to the temple, as was our practice. I was contemplating going back to the house for some money, when women began to pass me coins. I was embarrassed and shook my head to decline their offers and tried to explain I would contribute next week. I felt like I was the focus of critical stares and comments after the service. Much later I learned that passing money to others before it is offered to the temple increases the merit made, as each person touching the coins makes merit, and the original giver benefits more by "rejoicing in the giving of others" (Pali, *pattidana*).

Food Exchanges

Reciprocity around food sharing was also difficult to understand. The negotiations around who pays for casual meals in markets and restaurants are complex and fraught with visible and hidden patron-client relations. As meals are shared, both reciprocity and hierarchy determine who pays for the meal, and the rules are intricate and difficult for an outsider to learn. There were no opportunities to "split the bill" among a group of colleagues eating lunch together. Knowing when one should pay for the table was a skill acquired slowly, if ever. In both rural and urban Thailand, food exchanges are unique and carry more complex meanings than other kinds of exchanges.[2] At one level, foods such as puffed rice carry widely shared symbolic meanings: puffed rice without sugar is sprinkled on the ground before funerals as an offering to dangerous spirits.

But at another level, it is the relations created through food exchanges that are more significant. Food exchanges are basic to creating and maintaining social relations in village communities and elsewhere. You do not pay off the debt acquired through eating and feeding others, because you would be cutting off a relationship. Food as a medium of exchange is an important way of showing nurture and care. This theme is encapsulated in the Thai/Lao term *liang*, meaning to nurture, foster, or support someone or something by feeding and caring for them or it. *Liang* also has connotations of hospitality and hosting a party. One must *liang* rice, orchids, monks, and children (and politicians, but that would take us in another direction). In rice-growing villages, the relation between growing rice and nurturing children was obvious—they both need to be nurtured; connections to fertility are pervasive in the community. But *liang* is not a gendered concept and rather stresses nurturing power. However, there is ambiguity attached to eating and feeding and an alternative reading is possible, as the acts can be both nurturing and devouring—eating as exploitation.[3] Spirits who have not been fed can be vengeful and dangerous, particularly those who are loosed from hell during *Sat Thai*.

In the events described above, I was most concerned with the question of why exactly the same food is exchanged among households, as plates of *krayasat* made from the identical recipe using the same ingredients moved around the village, and they all tasted exactly the same. Other examples of this kind of food exchange occur in societies without the grain surpluses that are available in Thailand. For example, reciprocity among the Maisin of Papua New Guinea takes the form it does because foods like taro, sweet potato, squash, and fish can rot within a day or so of harvesting and preparing. Most households prepare the same meal every day for dinner. But following dinner, they send dishes of leftover food to their kin and neighbours who reciprocate, sending the same food back to them. In a gift economy, people remember details about food gifts.[4] While the Maisin exchange food on a regular basis, Thai households generally prepare and consume meals using their own stores of food. As it does for the Maisin, reciprocity provides the moral orientation for life, although ritual exchanges of foods like *krayasat* are quite distinct from everyday meals. These ritual exchanges are not about redistribution of surpluses, addressing hunger, or the inequitable distribution of food in the community. They are about strengthening relationships and alliances across the village community. As a young fieldworker, I saw the dessert being shared with others and accepted the exchanges as neighbourliness in a friendly community. At the same time, I knew in other, non-food-related situations, fierce self-interest dominated village interactions. We received and consumed many plates of *krayasat* and had no opportunity to reciprocate and participate in the exchanges. How I wish I could go back and make a batch of the rich treat for my Thai neighbours. But we lacked the facilities, the knowledge, and access to the raw ingredients.

Feeding Spirits

The ritual of *Sat Thai* (Pali, *sarada*, autumn), where the deceased are invited back to the communities, is always held in September, on the full moon of the tenth month, during Buddhist lent (*phansa*, three-months' rains retreat). Rice is at a critical stage during this time, at the height of the growing season following the monsoon rains but before the harvest. However, the explanation for the timing of the ritual works well only when there is one crop of rice a year.[5] New rice varieties allow for shorter growing seasons, throwing the agricultural calendar out of sync with the ritual calendar. In Lao People's Democratic Republic (PDR), this event is celebrated as *boun khao padap din*, festival of rice packets decorating the earth, and *boun khao salak*, the day of the ancestors, where baskets drawn by lots are presented to the monks. Similar celebrations, or ghost festivals, as they are referred to there, are held in Cambodia.

In these rituals, the dead are recalled and invited back to the community, where they are honoured communally, fed with special foods like *krayasat*, and in Lao PDR, given gifts that are ritually transferred to the deceased but used by monks.[6] Monks become the intermediaries for transferring the merit made by living relatives to their deceased relatives. This is accomplished by the ritual of *kruat nam* (or *yat nam*), where the merit made by giving offerings to monks, including *krayasat* in Thailand, is transferred to deceased relatives. As the residents of Crocodile Village explained, "If you do not offer *krayasat* to monks, then your dead relatives will have nothing to eat and will have no gratitude to their benefactors and will come back as hungry ghosts to cause you trouble." Villagers say that they cannot enjoy the new crops and desserts like *krayasat* until the "first fruits" are given to the monks and to the ancestors. Without these food gifts, deceased relatives might come back to earth as hungry ghosts with mouths so tiny that they can only consume thin noodles called *kanom chin*, served around the same time. *Krayasat* is also given to deceased ancestors within the house, at household and village spirit houses (*san chaw phum*), and at crossroads for wandering spirits whose relatives did not feed them. In Lao PDR, the offerings are made directly to the spirits to help them ease the transition from the suffering hells to their rebirth as humans.[7]

The ritual food exchanges of *krayasat* blur the boundary between the living and the dead, humans and spirits, youth and elder, patron and client, secular and sacred, lay householder and monastic renouncer, excess and asceticism. The sensuous excess of *krayasat* forms a striking contrast to the asceticism of monks, who are supposed to eat before noon and only as necessary, and not consume "superior foods" like *krayasat*. The Lao in particular encourage the generosity that leads to excess food offerings, driven by compassion for the ghosts from hells who come to earth hungry and thirsty.[8] The ritual exchanges also hint of the relation between growing rice and deceased relatives, as *krayasat* is placed in rice fields so deceased relatives could protect the growing rice. Rice rituals evoke ancient fertility rituals that are important to nurture the young rice plants and celebrate a successful harvest.[9] There are both royal and village versions of these rituals, performed differently by different members of society.

Royal Style

Texts about ritual matters apply to royalty, not to rural villagers. But many aspects of the event that I recall seeing in Ayuttaya conformed to what I called royal style ritual, defined as a manner of performing certain acts that express a relation between commoner and royalty.[10] I suggested that "royal style in village ritual provides a symbolic pattern for visualizing and manipulating the relation between royalty and commoner."[11] This was clearer in the Ayuttaya event, where the ritual practitioner was dressed up like a court Brahman. But some rice farmers in Crocodile Village attributed their successful farming to royal rituals: "An old man commented on the dependable quality of his rice crops over the decades. Asked if this was due to his great store of merit and his actions as a lay leader in the community, he replied, no, that his success was due to the regularity with which the king performed the first ploughing rite (*raek na*). We informed him that the ritual had not been performed from 1932 to 1960. He scorned our obvious misinformation: since his rice was plentiful, the ritual must have been done."[12] Others have explained the relation between royal and village guardian spirits: "The King . . . addresses higher beings in the hierarchy of gods and angels. With word passed down from on high, the many local guardians are prepared to assist in every valley and backwater."[13] Thinking back over these events, I recall that both Crocodile and New Rice Villages were located near former royal centres, Uthong and Ayuttaya. Would these food exchanges only have taken place in former royal centres, where royal Brahmans were employed as ritual specialists and the recipe for *krayasat* was passed down over the centuries? At the time, I never explored that question.

Texts and Practice

What does the exchange of *krayasat* mean? I would ask neighbours. "It means nothing; it is just a Thai custom"—better translated as "don't bug me." At the time I participated in these events, I knew very little about the Pali canon (Theravada Buddhist scriptures preserved in the Pali language), and other Thai religious texts. I assumed that few Thai villagers other than men who were former monks would know the canonical texts or even use them as a point of reference. I was repeatedly told that only monks and men who had been ordained for even a few weeks or a single lenten season (*phansa*,) knew anything about texts. But that does not mean that texts have not informed stories told and rituals performed at some level by both men and women. I have argued that Thai women's knowledge of Buddhism is expressed through food offerings: women's use of food demonstrates their practical knowledge of the complexities of textual Buddhism and their devotion to Buddhist practice.[14]

Sanskrit and Pali texts make reference to first fruits and harvest rituals and rituals that honour deceased relatives. For example, the *Satapatha Brahmana* refer to Vedic rituals that include boiled grains and milk. The Indian Vedic texts have not been translated into Thai, and Sanskrit texts that do exist in Thailand are incorporated into Buddhist chants and sermons.[15] The Siamese royal harvest ritual was probably derived from a Cambodian state ritual, modified by Siamese into the Ceremony of Conveying Home the Padi (harvested rice), performed as a royal ceremony as well as a village harvest festival celebrated in September. According to Horace Quaritch Wales, the royal ceremony has "long since ceased to exist," although he writes that "a revival of the royal ceremony might be beneficial" for the government.[16] State rituals were added or dropped from the seasonal calendar for political purposes. I never explored whether Conveying Home the Padi still exists as a royal ritual or whether it was ever reintroduced, much like other royal rituals that appeal to tourists. For example, the royal First Ploughing ritual was reintroduced in the 1960s and developed as a tourist event. Tourists could pay for privileged access if they behaved appropriately, but the ancient ritual was not altered for their benefit. First Ploughing rituals were also known in neighbouring Cambodia and Burma.[17]

A related ritual known as *Bidhi Sarada*, Saivic in origin and later an occasion for Buddhist merit making, was revived in 1928 by King Rama VII as a private royal ceremony. The event began as Brahmanic, featuring special foods offered to the gods, and later became an occasion where special foods were presented to Buddhist monks. During the Ayuttaya and Bangkok periods, a special confectionery was prepared in the palace and royal monasteries, accompanied by prayers for seasonal rains to insure the welfare of rice. Young girls would then "mix the heavenly rice" in large pans filled with a mixture of rice and grains, fruit juices, sugar, and milk, to commemorate Sujata offering the Buddha a dish of sweet milk rice. *Khaw thip*, or heavenly rice, was then presented to the king (in the royal ritual), to the monks, to the ancestors, and to the spirits of the dead. Often these offerings were left at crossroads for wandering spirits.

A wide variety of texts describe first fruit rituals, harvest rituals, and rituals that honour deceased ancestors. Certain elements from texts have been appropriated into local practices. Many elements, particularly those involving sweets, appear to be of Indian origin and linked in some way to Brahmanic rituals, which have been grafted on to indigenous Thai fertility rituals, all reinterpreted as Buddhist.

Syncretic Religion

Thailand is a Buddhist polity, regardless of the religious practices and beliefs of individual households. Residents of both Crocodile and New Rice Villages would consider themselves Theravada Buddhists who support their monks in their local temples. Their concern with feeding local spirits and their deceased ancestors is an active part of their Buddhist lifestyle, as natural as feeding monks every morning on their alms rounds. And when their ritual practitioners celebrate events like building a new house, they are behaving like Brahmans in the royal palaces. Yet both guardian spirits and Brahmans are incorporated in a single Buddhist cosmological order. Events where special confectioneries like *krayasat* are prepared and offered to a wide range of recipients reinforce the syncretic nature of the Thai religious landscape. Spirits, too, depend on human care and feeding. They reside in localities as guardian spirits and offer assistance when petitioned. There are complex and contested explanations around these reciprocal relationships. Locality spirits probably predate the arrival of Buddhism in Southeast Asia, and today they all have places in the Buddhist cosmological system.[18]

Brahmans and Brahman substitutes have special roles in Buddhist countries. The few Brahmans in Thailand (fifteen individuals as of 2012) claim descent from Tamil Brahman families from Nakorn Sri Thammarat in southern Thailand who were brought to Bangkok to serve the Thai royal family centuries ago. Brahmans served in the royal court in Ayuttaya in the seventeenth century.[19] Most of the current Brahmans were formerly ordained as Buddhist monks or novices. Brahmans are a part of Thai Buddhism, not Hinduism, a religion almost absent in Thailand.[20] They conduct public ceremonies associated with royalty and consecrate protective deities. Monks and

Brahmans move easily in the same ritual space, reading astrological charts, blessing amulets, and consecrating new buildings and businesses as well as spirit houses (*san chaw phum*). Brahmans engage with household rituals of no concern to monks in a ritual division of labour of great antiquity. The ritual specialists in rural communities who act like Brahmans preside at rites of passages like births, tonsures (top-knot cutting), and weddings, as well as at special events that emulate royal rituals.

Time, Modernity, and Writing

As this case reminds me, often we write before we have unpacked enough (or unpacked too much that we wish we could take back). How easy it is to over- or under-interpret events. But once our initial impressions are out there in the form of preliminary publications, we seldom have the opportunity of going back, correcting, restudying, rethinking, revising. Once published, the publications remain forever; everything is retrievable online. Years later, decades later, I can unpack more layers of meaning and context that I missed initially. This is a reminder to myself (and to my readers) that we often write and publish before we know enough. Those particular ritual events are gone forever, unlike the publications, which remain in libraries and online forever, warts and all. What has disappeared are the original observations on which the publications are based, unless they are preserved in ethnographic archives of very thick-skinned ethnographers.

I always thought I could go back to Crocodile and New Rice Villages and restudy events as I remembered them, to correct past errors and test out new hypotheses. But they remain events captured at a moment in time, ethnographic snippets that have stayed in my memory. They are so out of sync with modern Thailand that when I asked a few Thai colleagues to help me understand *krayasat*, they did not respond and have not been in touch since, as if my questions did not make sense to them. They probably did not. Were it not for this volume, I would have let *krayasat* lie unreflected upon, a recipe for how not to do fieldwork. In the '70s, the ritual cycle in which *krayasat* played a part probably fit with the agricultural cycle. But now that households can plant a variety of crops, and more than one crop of rice per year, the ritual cycle makes no sense. Change the cropping patterns, and you change the time when there are demands for labour and when there is likely to be cash in the household; what is fixed is the time when men can enter and leave the monkhood for the period of the rains retreat. But that time may no longer fit with men's labour opportunities. What used to fit seamlessly no longer fits at all.

While many special Thai desserts have moved from sacred to secular foods and been made available in urban supermarkets, *krayasat* does not seem to have made that transition. However, several different versions of the recipe are available on the internet, including some where the *krayasat* is shaped like cones and wrapped in banana leaves, with no mention of its appeal to spirits. Some versions are gift-packaged for sale, probably destined for prepackaged plastic buckets packed with offerings for monks on sale near temples.[21]

Other Village People

Food studies raise unique field problems. We are that which we study. Contemplating *krayasat* speaks to an orientalism—an attraction to the exotic other—I thought I had outgrown. But the recipe held an important place in ritual settings, even if I did not know what the food item meant at the time. As a result of the COVID-19 pandemic (April 2020), I am writing this chapter while sitting isolated in Guelph in a seniors community with a comparable number of households as in Crocodile Village. My mind is constantly on food—how to get it safely, how to use it to reduce boredom and increase health (or build healthy immune systems). I crave *krayasat* for both its rich candy-dessert taste and its implications of social inclusion.

Universally, food exchanges form the basis of social relations. Western models of prepared food exchange include the potluck model, where what you bring is basically left to chance, with strategies to avoid having too much of the same thing (some bring first course; others, second course or appetizers). Occasionally, offerings get out of balance with too many chocolate desserts and no savouries, or too many salads and no desserts. But this is relatively rare, in my experience. Dinner parties are another way to share meals. They are a form of generalized reciprocity but can get competitive.

But the potluck model is a far cry from the exchange of *krayasat* among Thai villagers, where the identical food is exchanged.

My neighbour has just brought over herbs and stuffed them in my mailbox. I've returned the favour by putting a bag of homegrown bean sprouts in his mailbox. In the village we live in today, seniors without family close by "look after each other." The day after we moved in, an elderly neighbour brought us two fresh muffins. When my husband was sick, we received cookies and occasionally cooked meals (an extra plate prepared from that evening's dinner, fresh or frozen). The downside was that at the time, we had no opportunity to return invitations and could only "pay it forward" to other senior households. Memories of Crocodile Village!

Certain households make honey or shortbread cookies, others grow herbs or tomatoes, others, homemade wine, but we are hardly a subsistence economy. When gifts are exchanged between households, the honey household gives honey to some friends and may receive cookies or wine in return. But the idea that all households would exchange the same cookies or wine would be preposterous. While wine might be brought by all visitors to a house party, the givers would not return with wine or any other counter-gift. When households are unable to reciprocate right away (in our community, often for health reasons), debts accumulate, at least in people's minds.

One household in our seniors village was faced with two health crises at the same time. Instead of leaving the food gifts to chance, villagers organized around the Meal Train app, where people who want to help sign up to bring a particular dish on a specific day. The giver can see what others are planning, to make sure they are not bringing the same dish. In this way, the household receives a variety of meals and can even specify preferences and limitations such as food allergies or sensitivities. The advantage is that nothing is left to chance and there is less waste. The recipients had never been supplied with meals before and were surprised and overwhelmed by the generosity of their neighbours. The household came to rely on the meals and enjoyed the experience of having a variety of different meals every day for the month that they were unable to look after themselves—the month that they both felt like "turtles stuck on their backs." They tried to reciprocate but could not with so many people in the "train." Their solution was to put a notice in the village newsletter after their recovery, thanking everyone for their generosity. Meal Train institutionalizes the neighbourliness that was once expected and is an adaptation to new conditions, including mobile populations, concerns about food surplus and waste, global pandemics, and digital resources.

The logic underlying our seniors village food exchanges is mostly grounded in a general internalized Judaeo-Christian morality ("it was the right thing to do") and reflects cooking as an expression of love and religious duty of women.[22] The exchanges have nothing to do with hunger and the need to redistribute food from the "haves" to the "have nots." Even in Crocodile Village, the distribution of *krayasat* had little to do with redistributing food resources. Bellyaches from overeating the sweet were probably evenly distributed across the village. Nevertheless, some acts of food charity in our seniors village include those by volunteers who are motivated by personal memories of hunger and feel the necessity to respond to a need in others. This differs from the logic guiding Thai/Lao Buddhist food exchanges, where reciprocity was more explicit and the gift exchanges included a wider range of recipients—guardian spirits, monks, and deceased relatives. In fact, the merit accrued from feeding others is extended to all sentient beings in a protective verse called *Samannanumodana Gatha*. In this time of stress, we could all use an extra blessing, so here is an opportunity to let the universe know that you have nurtured self and others: "May all evils vanish, may all diseases disappear, may danger not come to you."

To refresh my mind about Poppycock I googled the term and learned that it meant "soft poop" (*pappekak*) or "as fine as powdered doll's excrement" in a Dutch dialect, unlikely referents even in a family of Dutch ancestry. It also is a polite way to say nonsense. The snack called Poppycock, composed of clusters of popcorn, almonds, and pecans in a caramelized candy glaze, was invented in Detroit in the 1950s and developed as a gourmet snack in the '60s.

I recently asked my ninety-seven-year-old mother-in-law about the Poppycock gift, seeking a meaningful memory about including me in the family. She thought back and had to be reminded that she had given her children cans of Poppycock at Christmas; then she speculated that her husband had had an opportunity to buy caseloads of Poppycock from a wholesale grocery outlet. And I recalled my Thai neighbours responding to my questions about exchanging *krayasat*: "It is a Thai custom." Sometimes it is easier to just remember the taste of Poppycock and *krayasat* and treasure the memories and merit that come from the ritual of feeding others.

Notes

1 Ingold, *Making*, 4.

2 See Grieshop, "The Envios of San Pablo."

3 High, *Fields of Desire*, 42.

4 Barker, *Ancestral Lines*, 48.

5 See Tambiah, *Buddhism and the Spirit Cults*, writing about the northeast part of the country.

6 Ladwig, "Can Things Reach the Dead?"

7 Ladwig, "Feeding the Dead," 121.

8 Ibid., 126.

9 See O'Connor, "From Fertility to Order."

10 Van Esterik, "Royal Style in Village Context," 104.

11 Ibid., 103.

12 Ibid., 105.

13 Hanks, *Rice and Man*, 78.

14 See Van Esterik, "Feeding Their Faith."

15 McDaniel, "This Hindu Holy Man," 191.

16 Quaritch Wales, *Siamese State Ceremonies*, 230–31.

17 McDaniel, "This Hindu Holy Man Is a Thai Buddhist."

18 See also Van Esterik, "Interpreting a Cosmology."

19 Wyatt, *Thailand*, 129.

20 McDaniel, "This Hindu Holy Man Is a Thai Buddhist."

21 See also Ladwig, "Can Things Reach the Dead?"

22 See Rouse and Hoskins, "Purity, Soul Food and Sunni Islam."

CHAPTER 3

Drinking Tea in Nepal

Tina Moffat

In his review of food and the senses, David Sutton calls on anthropologists to engage with "gustemology," a consideration of cultural issues through taste and other sensory aspects of food.[1] What Sutton does not address, however, is the anthropologist's more reflexive project to consider their own gustatory experiences during fieldwork, experiences that they may share—or not—with research participants. During fieldwork an anthropologist's senses are alive and being bombarded with novel experiences. Taste and smell, in particular, invoke strong sensations that can be recalled many years afterwards. Part of ethnography and fieldwork is a process of embodiment of "the field" that is literally ingested through smells, tastes, and food. A reflection on those sensory experiences may lead to some insight about the culture worlds we are studying and our own role in this shared project. Ethnography is, after all, a relational process of storytelling.[2]

Food is a material object, and by focusing our attention on it we can "situate the individual embodied experience of food within the broader context of social relations, cultural practice, and political economic dynamics."[3] This has been exemplified by Sidney Mintz's exploration of sugar in his book *Sweetness and Power* and his essay "Time, Sugar and Sweetness."[4] He uses sugar as a stepping-off point to examine the colonial and capitalist apparati that produced, exported, and consumed sugar through the exploitation of bodies and labour to accumulate wealth for both individuals and nations. Specifically, he implicates sugar as a catalyst for the forced migration of Africans to sugarcane-producing countries controlled by European colonialists. Mintz further explores the pleasurable and addictive properties of sugar as part of its transformation in regulating human labour with sweetened coffee or tea breaks in the rise of industrial capitalism and as a major ingredient in the modern food system. Black tea and coffee containing caffeine are like sugar, in the category of what Mintz calls "drug" foods—highly coveted by people throughout the world and consumed by many on a daily basis.[5]

In this chapter I discuss the role of tea and tea culture as an embodied symbol of both my position and feelings of acceptance and of being an "other," separate from the Nepali people with whom I did fieldwork in the 1990s. This also connects to my reflections on the privileged position I occupied as an anthropologist from the Global North doing research in the Global South. I argue that an in-depth investigation into some of the foods we eat or drink while doing fieldwork helps us to situate these gustatory experiences within a deeper culture-history associated with the food. Like anthropology and anthropologists,[6] tea is also imbricated in the colonial history of the British in South Asia. Tea and tea drinking are significant parts of food culture for Nepalis. They consider tea to be their national beverage, and it is consumed daily by almost all Nepalis. And yet as I shared many cups of tea with study participants, research assistants, and Nepali friends, I never reflected until now on either the importance of this ritual or the way tea as a material object connected us through our linked heritage and histories. I discuss the role of tea both in understanding my position as an anthropologist doing fieldwork in Nepal and as a material object that has affected Nepali political economy and social relations. At the end of the chapter, I briefly reflect on the more recent introduction of coffee and coffee culture in Nepal, with thoughts on changing tastes connected to globalization.

Drinking Tea in Nepal

During my fieldwork in Nepal (1995–96, and again in 1998), one of my most regular gustatory experiences came from drinking tea (*chiya*) in two forms: one was sweet, milky tea, fragrant with spices such as cardamom and ginger (also known as *chai* in India), and the other a salty, buttery tea, known as Tibetan butter tea, or *nun chiya* (translated literally as salt tea). All Nepalis drink *chiya*, but *nun chiya* is more common in the hill and mountain regions of Nepal, as it originated in Tibet and is drunk by the people in Nepal of Tibetan ancestry. *Nun chiya* is made with yak butter, produced only in the hill and mountain regions.

Chiya

1 cup water
3 cups milk
2 teaspoons sugar (adjust per taste)
2 tablespoons black tea
1 small piece ginger, grated (optional)
4 green cardamom pods, crushed
4 black peppercorns, crushed

The three necessary ingredients are water, tea, and milk, and while cardamom and pepper seem to be common ingredients in many recipes I could find online, other added spices vary by individual and family preference. The tea is prepared by mixing all the ingredients in a pot and boiling them at a high temperature for several minutes. The mixture is then transferred to a large teapot or thermos for serving.

Nun Chiya (Salt Tea)/Tibetan Tea/Butter Tea

Water
Black tea
Salt
Yak butter
Milk
Butter and salt are mixed in a churn and then added to a pot of boiling water, tea leaves, and milk. The tea is then transferred to a large thermos for serving.

These are of course not recipes anyone learns from cookbooks, though they can be found in modern Nepali cookery books and in YouTube videos. The butter churn step in making Tibetan butter tea is impressive and something I witnessed women doing often in their homes as a daily chore.[7]

I drank a lot of tea during my fieldwork while investigating the health and nutrition of children under five years of age who were born in Kathmandu or who had come with their families to the city to work in the Tibeto-Nepali carpet-making industry. I lived and worked in an area just outside of Kathmandu called Boudhanath, or Boudha for short. This is the location of the Boudha Stupa, a UNESCO World Heritage site that is a sacred monument for Buddhist Nepalis and a tourist hotspot. My fieldwork consisted of visiting carpet factories, health centres, and family homes, where I conducted anthropometric, health, and infant and young child feeding surveys.[8] Each time I visited a clinic, carpet factory, health centre, or home, I was offered *chiya*, as is typical of Nepali hospitality. *Chiya khayo?* (Have you drunk tea?) was a familiar refrain if visiting someone's home mid-morning, but *chiya* is offered at any time of the day up until the evening.

As a Canadian woman and the daughter of immigrant parents from Britain, I was familiar with tea drinking. Indeed, there was no problem in our home that my mother could not solve with a cup of tea, and I began drinking milky tea from a young age. I am not sure if it was because I was the youngest in the family and nobody remembered to add sugar to my tea, or if I just do not have the proverbial "sweet tooth," but I only ever drank my Orange Pekoe tea with milk, no sugar. Drinking tea in Nepal was familiar but also different, as *chiya* is typically served in a small glass, not a china cup or mug, and is sweet and fragrant because of the added sugar and spices. Quite honestly, I disliked this tea, as it was for me a sickly-sweet taste, and I always drank it for the sake of not offending my hosts.

The taste and smell of tea became even more jarring and exotic when I did fieldwork in the hill region in 1998, again studying child health and nutrition of infants and young children, this time in a small village in the district of Sindhupalchok, just northeast of Kathmandu and nestled in the Himalayan mountain range.[9] Similar to when I was in Kathmandu, every time I visited a home, I was offered *nun chiya*; when making multiple visits in one day this would amount to copious mugs or small bowls of tea. Though there is tea in *nun chiya*, I never actually tasted it, as it is overpowered by the sour flavour of fermented butter and salt. As a way to drink this concoction, I told myself it was soup broth, not tea, and I began to appreciate it as a warming beverage that soothed my throat in the dry and chilly high-altitude climate.

Accepting offers of food or beverage at the homes of the people we work with in the field is an important part of creating social bonds with people. Though we do not often discuss the food we eat and share with people in the field, as Karine Gagné illustrates in her chapter on *momo* parties in North India (this volume), this commensality and reciprocity is an integral part of fieldwork and of the formation of our identity as anthropologists. Though I sometimes did not want to drink tea, I rarely refused it; indeed, it was also what I deemed as a safe offering, since I was frequently ill in Nepal from intestinal parasites and pathogens transmitted through contaminated drinking water and food. I figured that since tea was boiled, it was my safest bet in terms of accepting hospitality. By sharing tea, I set myself apart from the other foreigners who often eschewed any food or beverage from Nepali hosts for fear of contamination. As I drank my host's tea, we shared the common need for sustenance and the pleasure from the warmth and stimulation of the caffeine. At the same time as I was sharing the experience of drinking tea, however, my gustatory experiences (both sweet and salty varieties) were constant sensory reminders of my embodied differences from my fieldwork companions and study participants. These included language, gender norms, customs, and access to wealth and mobility arising from our locations in the Global South and North. These divisions are mirrored in the story of tea and global tea culture, to which I now turn.

Tea and Tea Culture

Tea and tea culture are global phenomena with rich histories in ancient civilizations and empires. As described by Helen Saberi in *Tea Culture*, the tea plant (*Camellia sinensis*) and its varieties were first cultivated in China.[10] Legend attributes the discovery to the Emperor Shen Nong (2737–2697 BCE), but more probably by the first century BCE people in Sichuan were drinking tea brewed with water for medicinal purposes. Tea is usually grown between 300 and 2,000 metres above sea level, and those plants grown at higher altitude have better flavour. The way the tea leaves are processed creates the many different types of tea; black tea is completely fermented, which turns the leaves a dark colour.[11]

By the end of the fifth century CE, tea was traded with Turkish and Mongolian merchants and exported all over East Asia and along the Silk Road to Central Asia. The Dutch first brought tea to Amsterdam in 1610, and by the late seventeenth century it was a popular though expensive drink. The Dutch then marketed tea to other countries in Europe, and it caught on especially in England.[12] Tea ended up surpassing coffee as the beverage of choice in England, and once the love affair with tea started for the English, they could not get enough of it. Between 1699 and 1721, tea imports increased almost a hundredfold; tea was consumed by all classes and at all times of day, and especially at the afternoon "tea time" ritual. By the early 1800s, Britain had a tea-based trade deficit with China , which was partially resolved by selling opium produced in India to China, but opium profits were not enough to offset the trade imbalance.[13] When Britain lost its tea monopoly with China in the 1830s, it began investigating its tropical colonies for cultivating tea. Through trial and error, the British began growing tea in India from cultivars that were secretly absconded from China by a Scottish spy named Robert Fortune and a wild variety of tea indigenous to the Assam region in the Himalayan foothills of northern India. Tea was also grown on plantations in the Nilgiri mountains that stretch across Tamil Nadu, Karnataka, and Kerala in South India. South Asia is still the second largest tea producer with some of the most famous and well-known types of tea, such as Darjeeling and Ceylon (now known as Sri Lanka).[14]

Once the tea industry in India was running smoothly in the 1870s, British expatriates there began drinking tea in earnest. It became an important part of their lifestyle in India, replete with servants bringing them tea in bed in the morning and tea parties. In the 1900s the British realized they were missing a big market among Indians, and so they set up the Indian Tea Association, which marketed tea through tea stalls in coal mines, cotton factories, and the Indian railways. It was not until the 1950s, though, that tea, or *chai*, as it is known in India, became a beverage of the masses.[15]

There are many anthropological and historical examples of global foods that are adopted, shared, or rejected by both the colonized and colonizers.[16] Tea is just another one of these dishes that was circulated and modified. The British adopted tea from the Chinese and then passed it on to the Indians. Unlike the Americans, who rejected tea during their war of independence from Britain, Indians did not reject tea when their country gained its freedom from Britain in 1947. According to Andrea Wiley, Indians had been drinking boiled milk with spices and sugar for millennia, so rather than preparing tea the way the British instructed, the *chai wallahs* (tea sellers) basically adapted Indian boiled milk by throwing in tea leaves.[17] *Chai* is prepared, as described above in the Nepali *chiya* recipe, with milk, sugar, and spices, setting it apart from the British style of tea. Perhaps it is because *chai* is uniquely Indian that it is therefore not considered a product of the British Raj. Wiley explains, moreover, that in the early twentieth century tea marketers promoted it as an indigenous product to energize the Indian populace and build their nation.[18] *Chai* is still consumed all over India, though coffee is the drink of choice among the middle class in South India where coffee is grown.[19]

Unlike India, Nepal was never colonized by the British. The British to be sure kept their hold over Nepal by propping up the exploitative and imperialist Rana family that ruled Nepal from 1846 to 1950. The Ranas kept the country impoverished to support their own self-serving, luxurious way of life, which included British royalty joining them for holidays that featured hunting for tigers and rhinos, and of course drinking tea. The British also regularly employed the Nepali Gurkha soldiers, who had a fearsome reputation and fought alongside the British to quell uprisings and maintain control over British India.[20] *Chai* came to Nepal as *chiya* through cultural diffusion from India. Nepal shares its southern border with India and was settled historically by Indo-Aryans. Prior to 2008, when the Nepali monarchy was abolished, Nepal was officially a Hindu state, with a caste system and culture similar to India's. The hill and mountain regions were populated by Tibeto-Burmese people who came ancestrally from Tibet. Butter tea, or *nun chiya,* was brought to Nepal from Tibet, and thus two different types of tea from different origins are now commonly consumed in Nepal.

The addition of salt to tea instead of sugar marks the important place of the salt trade in Tibet. Tibetan rock salt mined from the Himalayan plateau has been an essential commodity in trans-Himalayan trade.[21] While modern populations take salt for granted, and indeed worry about its ubiquity in processed food, it is essential for human physiology and was a precious commodity in earlier times.[22] In the Himalayas, salt was added liberally to food and beverages, in part aiding in electrolyte loss resulting from the arid, high-altitude climate, and that tradition continues today in the mountain regions of Nepal, though many younger generations prefer the sweet tea. Yak butter packs a good wallop of energy and fat into tea, which aids people living at high altitude withstand the energy loss from thermoregulation to the cold as well as maintain body mass with high levels of physical activity.[23]

Like salt, the additional ingredients of sugar and milk in *chiya* are also significant food materials. Unlike the milk that the English add separately to their teacups, with some preferring it black with lemon, Indian *chai* and Nepali *chiya* are prepared with a substantial amount of milk, as described above; since the tea is prepared in one pot with milk, it is never served without milk. As Wiley describes in her book *Cultures of Milk*, milk is an important food commodity in India, with fluid milk consumed most commonly in tea.[24] Milk holds symbolic significance for Hindus as a product of the sacred cow. As already noted, *chiya* in Nepal is a drink that starts the day, is drunk throughout the day, and is offered to any valued and respected person entering the home or place of work. As in many countries around the world, in Nepal tea sweetened with sugar serves as an energy boost and is part of the rituals of industrial working life.[25] *Chiya* is consumed regularly in Nepal by labourers as well as by those working in offices, where it marks a short break from work. In government offices, lowly workers known as peons perform a variety of menial tasks, but the main one is to prepare and serve *chiya* several times a day to the higher-level bureaucrats.

The Political Economy of Tea in Nepal

Shortly after tea plantations were established in Darjeeling, India, in the 1850s, hybrids of tea bushes were used to establish Nepal's first tea plantations, Ilam and Jhapa Tea Estates, in the high-altitude regions of Ilam and Jhapa Districts. At that point these tea estates served as a supplier to the Darjeeling factories as the Nepalese industry was still fledgling, even failing to provide enough tea for the country's own domestic consumption. This was mostly due to the lack of governance and backward policies under the Rana dynasty.[26] In the 1950s, Nepal developed a new constitution and unified under a quasi-democratic system under the reign of King Tribhuvan. The country opened to the rest of the world for the first time in history, ushering in new economic liberalization and tourism. New, private capital flowed into the Nepali tea industry, and in 1966 the government set up the Nepal Tea Development Corporation (NTDC) to aid its development. In the late 1970s, two new factories were set up in Ilam and Jhapa Districts for processing tea leaves, and in subsequent decades the NTDC attempted to help small producers market tea as a cash crop. Nepal's tea production accounts for only 0.4 percent of the total world tea output.[27] The tea sector in Nepal is estimated to contribute about 0.0105 percent to the National Gross Domestic Product and 0.0347 percent to the Agricultural Gross Domestic Product.[28] This is small compared to other major tea producers in the world such as India, but still an important part of the agricultural sector in the eastern region of Nepal.[29]

There are six major districts in eastern Nepal where tea is cultivated: Ilam, Panchthar, Dhankuta, Terhathum, Sindhulpalchok, and Kaski. The tea grown in Nepal is similar to the tea produced in Darjeeling, West Bengal, India.[30] Since 2017, however, Nepali tea has gained ground as a cheaper version of Darjeeling. This began in 2017, when worker protests in Darjeeling shut down production for several months. But Nepali tea has continued to gain ground and is now successfully competing with Darjeeling teas from India.[31] Because of free trade agreements between India and Nepal, India cannot block Nepali tea from export to India, one of its biggest markets, though Nepal also exports tea to other countries in Europe and North America.[32] Over 60 percent of the workers in the Nepali tea industry are women.[33] Unfortunately, as is the case for many agricultural labourers around the world, tea plantation workers in Nepal are exploited and not paid fair wages, earning half of the minimum wage set for the nation. Though workers are provided with housing on the plantations, conditions are often substandard, without running water or electricity. Generations of people work and die on these plantations, while the owners become rich.[34]

Changing Tastes: Coffee in Kathmandu

In the summer of 2019, I visited Kathmandu with my family. I had not been there since 1998, and I was eager to see Nepal again and reacquaint myself with friends I had not met in person for over twenty years. Much had happened in Nepal in those intervening years: the Maoist conflict, also known as the Nepalese Civil War (1996–2006); the Nepalese Royal Massacre (2001) by Crown Prince Dipendra, killing King Birendra, Queen Aishwarya, and seven other members of the royal family; the abolishment of the Kingdom (2008) and the creation of the Federal Democratic Republic of Nepal; and in April 2015, a terrible earthquake that took 9,000 lives and substantially damaged buildings in Kathmandu and homes in rural areas. In the years since my last visit, Kathmandu had modernized and expanded, engulfing the peri-urban greenspace that had previously circumscribed the city. One of the communities where I did fieldwork in 1998,[35] a squatter settlement just outside of Kathmandu, was no longer there. The premium real estate on which the settlement was located had been bought by middle-class Nepalis, and those who used but not owned the land for almost thirty years had been evicted.

During my trip to Nepal in 2019, I did not have a chance to drink *chiya* again. In the hotel where I stayed, I was able to drink my morning beverage of choice, coffee, and it was too hot to drink tea in the afternoons. My visits to friends' homes all took place in the late afternoon or evening, where in the warm weather soft drinks were served, not tea. Unlike many of my favourite foods that I looked forward to, like *momo*s and *dal bhat* (rice and lentils), Nepali *chiya* was not something I had any desire to drink. During my fieldwork in 1995–96 and 1998, I missed coffee terribly. Though there were a few tourist cafés adjacent to the Boudha Stupa where I could buy instant Nescafé coffee, the only coffee served in Nepal at the time and mostly to tourists, it really was not the kind of coffee I liked and I had to drink many cups to get the caffeine hit I desired. Early in my fieldwork sojourn, I convinced my mother to send me a few care packages containing coffee beans. My partner and I crushed them with a mortar and pestle, and we managed to rig up a drip coffee system with a funnel and a pot. Later we located a store catering to expats that sold a somewhat drinkable coffee bean grown in Nepal, but not of very good quality.

On my return visit in 2019, however, I serendipitously discovered some delicious coffee in Kathmandu on my way to visit the Narayanhiti Royal Palace Museum, located in the heart of downtown Kathmandu. The palace is an imposing modernist structure that was built in 1963 for the royal family, with a huge gate that was always closed to Nepalis and tourists alike until 2010. After the monarchy was abolished in 2008 the palace was turned into a museum with decor set in the 1970s, the heyday of the royal family. As well, in the museum there is a display of the family room where the family was murdered by the prince with a submachine gun, replete with signs pointing out the bullet holes in the wall. I, like many Nepalis who visit the museum regularly, was excited to see such a mysterious palace laid bare to the public, with all its opulence and ugliness. We arrived early in the morning, too early in fact, because the palace museum did not open for another hour. So we wandered down the road seeking refuge from the heat and came across a café.

This café was not like any I had experienced in Kathmandu previously. It was indeed a full European-style café with espresso and cappuccino machines, serving café lattes and the like. I was delighted that morning to drink a café latte and indulge in a pastry. As I looked around the café, I noticed many tourists like us but also many young, urban Nepalis who were enjoying a cup of java in the morning. Clearly, coffee culture had arrived in Kathmandu, just like so many other things in the last twenty years, such as more electrification, newer models of cars, and much more traffic. The arrival of coffee drinking and coffee culture is an indication of the deepening globalization of urban Nepal that began after the opening of Nepal in the 1950s with the advent of tourism and the promise of a new era. Since tourism has been a major part of Nepal's economy since the 1950s, it is not just the demand for coffee by tourists that created this new arrival of coffee and coffee culture. Rather, it is also a growing urban elite and class of Nepalis who are travelling more to other countries and adopting new food consumption habits that are being recreated and consumed in Kathmandu.

Catherine Tucker writes in her book *Coffee Culture* that although coffee shops have been around for 500 years, they have exploded globally in the past few decades and are part of a transforming global food culture.[36] And this culture change is accompanied by economic clout: coffee is the second most valuable commodity traded in world markets. Coffee houses and cafés have historically been a location of intellectual and political debate.[37] More recently they have attracted customers by offering free Wi-Fi access. This is what I witnessed in Kathmandu in 2019, and no doubt coffee culture will grow, though I am quite sure that *chiya* will continue to be the beverage of choice in Nepal for years to come.

As they are for tea, the Himalayan high-altitude areas are ideal for growing coffee. Coffee production in the last few decades has increased in Nepal with the introduction of the Himalayan arabica coffee, and coffee production, particularly of organic coffee, a niche market for Nepal, is a significant opportunity for impoverished farmers in hill communities.[38]

Conclusion: Fieldwork and Food Culture

The gustatory experiences of drinking tea (both sweet and salty forms) signalled a certain tension and uncomfortableness for me of being in a land that was not my own. As an anthropologist, I was a guest, a consumer of knowledge to take home to my own land and spin into academic writing that would further my career without necessarily improving the lives of those in Nepal. These uneasy tensions we experience as anthropologists from the Global North doing fieldwork in settings in the Global South are encapsulated in this uncomfortable sensory experience of drinking tea that I have described. Tea too has a conflicted culture-history, because it is mired in a legacy of colonialism, empire building, and exploitation. But tea has been transformed and rendered into a food that Nepalis have made their own—a favourite beverage. Like Nepal and the Nepali people, tea has evolved and is resilient.

FIGURE 3.1. Coffee shop next to Boudra Stupa in Kathmandu, Nepal, 1995. Photo by Tina Moffat.

While I never thought tea would hold such a strong place in my experience of doing fieldwork in Nepal, upon reflection I realize that since it is so important to Nepalis' everyday lives, it had to be part of my fieldwork experience. Drinking tea is still memorable for me after all these years. Accepting and drinking tea with Nepali hosts was important in creating and sustaining social relations during daily visits. It represented for my interlocutors and me a familiar foodstuff, something we could all recognize and share. Tea, moreover, is a symbol of global interconnections: representing both shared and conflicted histories of colonizers and the colonized, as well as common food heritage with some variations. As a Canadian of British ancestry living in a country that was colonized by Britain, I drink the tea that was developed by the British and extracted through the labour of colonial subjects. In turn it was sold back to the colonized, who made it their own national drink. Despite the contentious history of that unbalanced reciprocal relationship, sharing tea enabled me and my Nepali hosts to connect as fellow human beings in a global world, even if our versions of tea were variations on a theme. As the discipline of anthropology and the profile of anthropologists diversify, with more anthropologists originating from the Global South and more anthropologists working "at home," I believe there is still something to be gained by the experience of encountering and connecting across global divides of North and South during fieldwork. There is no better way to do this than through the sharing of food and drink.

Notes

1 Sutton, "Food and the Senses."

2 O'Neill, *The Heart of Helambu*; and Stoller, "Ethnography/Memoir/Imagination/Story."

3 Abbots, "Introducing a Special Issue on Food Stuffs."

4 Mintz, *Sweetness and Power*; and Mintz,"Time, Sugar and Sweetness."

5 Mintz, "Time, Sugar and Sweetness."

6 Said, "Representing the Colonized."

7 For a demonstration on how to make *nun chiya*, see Wild Films in India, *Making Butter Tea*.

8 Moffat, "Urbanization and Child Growth in Nepal"; Moffat, "Parents' Estimation of Their Children's Body Size"; Moffat, "A Biocultural Investigation of the 'Weanling's Dilemma'"; Moffat, "Breastfeeding, Wage Labor and Insufficient Milk"; Moffat, "Diarrhea, Respiratory Infections, Protozoan Gastrointestinal Parasites."

9 See Moffat and Finnis, "Dietary Diversity, Dietary Transitions, and Childhood Nutrition."

10 Saberi, *Tea: A Global History*.

11 Ibid.

12 Ibid.

13 Bryson, *At Home*.

14 Saberi, *Tea: A Global History*.

15 Ibid.

16 Bickham, "Eating the Empire"; Dietler, "Culinary Encounters"; and Heldke, "Let's Cook That."

17 Wiley, *Cultures of Milk*.

18 Ibid.

19 Venkatachalapathy, "In Those Days There Was No Coffee."

20 Whelpton, "Rana Nepal."

21 Ross, "Adaptation to a Changing Salt Trade."

22 Bryson, *At Home*.

23 Bera, "Food and Nutrition of the Tibetan Women in India."

24 Wiley, *Cultures of Milk*.

25 Mintz, "Time, Sugar and Sweetness."

26 Mishra et al., "Status of Tea Industry in South Asia."

27 Thapa, "Concept Paper on Study of Nepalese Tea Industry."

28 Tiwari, Adhikari, and Dhungana, "Economics of Orthodox Tea Production."

29 Mishra et al., "Status of Tea Industry in South Asia."

30 Ibid.

31 Bolton, "Nepal's Tea Fortunes."

32 Ghosal, "Souring Relationship between India and Nepal."

33 Thapa, "Concept Paper on Study of Nepalese Tea Industry."

34 Devkota, "Exploitation in the Hills."

35 Moffat and Finnis, "Considering Social and Material Resources."

36 Tucker, *Coffee Culture.*

37 Ibid.

38 Himalayan Coffee Trading, "Nepal Shows Best Potential."

CHAPTER 4

Bannock: Using a Contested Bread to Understand Indigenous and Settler Relations and Ways Forward within Canada

Breanna Phillipps and Kelly Skinner

As food is a basic need and a product of the lands on which we harvest it, food culture is deeply tied to our collective and individual histories and the societies in which we live. The goals of this chapter are to better understand food as a powerful tool used in the settler-colonial state of Canada, and to connect bannock (in all its variations) to relations between settlers (including ourselves) and Indigenous Peoples within Canada, both historically and contemporarily. We discuss research projects, historical works, and media in which bannock has often been considered a traditional food. These sources allow us to highlight Indigenous voices speaking on the duality and complexities of bannock, and on sharing Indigenous cultures and food as a form of reciprocity among Indigenous and non-Indigenous people. Indigenous activists and research on this topic demonstrate pride in the self-defined traditional foods of Indigenous Peoples, whose diets have changed post-contact as a result of colonial oppression. Indigenous chefs whose work we cite have built spaces through their cuisine to feed their people but also extend the invitation for settlers to learn about their cultures and enact reciprocity by supporting these food businesses. For settlers in Canada, bannock can help to frame our understanding of place and our responsibilities within the settler-colonial state, including how our ancestors, governments, and we have failed and continue to fail Indigenous Peoples.

I, Breanna, first tasted bannock at a powwow hosted by the Waterloo Indigenous Student Centre, and soon bannock became central to my experiences of relationship building, by frequently consuming it or speaking about its importance with Indigenous people when exploring common interests of food and social justice. I come to this work as an early-career researcher and Canadian-born white settler woman of Scottish, German, Norwegian, English, and French ancestry. I have spent most of my life living on the unceded territories of the Algonquin Nation in Ottawa. As such, I have also spent most of my life unaware of the violent processes of settler colonialism within the nation I lived and the lived experiences of Indigenous people across Turtle Island. A defining moment in my career trajectory was the day I read Thomas King's *The Inconvenient Indian: A Curious Account of Native People in North America* (2012). Many of my conceptions about Canada and what it meant to be a white settler Canadian were shattered. In short, I started to develop a critical perspective of Canadian history, which I learned to apply in my studies of both health and social sciences. I had the opportunity to complete my graduate work in public health by contributing to projects relating to Indigenous Peoples' food security and food sovereignty, and the impacts of various policies on both. I interviewed Indigenous women who lived in urban centres on the Territories of the Anishinaabe People of Lac Seul First Nation in Sioux Lookout, and the Ojibway of Fort William First Nation in Thunder Bay. These women graciously shared their stories about accessing Indigenous foods, which illuminated the connection between lands, food, and the well-being of their families and communities. These shared experiences underlined the implications of government policies on the history of their communities and their own lives today.

FIGURE 4.1. Bannock for attendees at a cross-cultural on-the-land camp, Sahtú region, Northwest Territories, 2016. Image Credit: Mylène Ratelle.

I, Kelly, had my first encounter with bannock in my early teens when I found a recipe in a children's cottage activity book and decided to make it for my family. While I don't know where the author obtained this recipe, as an adult I have reflected on its inclusion in a cottage activity book as an inappropriate choice. I am a mid-career researcher and white settler of French Canadian and Scandinavian ancestry and grew up in the Territory of Fort William First Nation. I have been collaborating with Indigenous individuals, communities, and organizations, primarily in the Northwest Territories with Dene communities, and in northern Ontario on the Territories of Lac Seul and Fort William First Nations and the Territory of Mushkegowuk Aski, on Indigenous and northern food systems research for more than fifteen years. Throughout my years of food research and fieldwork with Indigenous people, a wide variety of types of bannock have been shared with me, from the first time a baked bannock recipe was shared by a friend who is Cree (a version that I have baked many times since) to the diverse assortment of bannock recipes that were exchanged by participants of the Aboriginal Nutrition Network gathering in 2014.[1]

Given our identities as settlers and the diversity of perspectives from Indigenous people of various identities covered in this work, we have chosen to use this space to explore our fieldwork experiences, including instances where bannock recipes were shared with us by community members. We do so to display the power of sharing space and food as part of the reciprocal relationships we hold with the Indigenous people with whom we work. We do not intend to position ourselves as experts on the history of bannock and the practice of preparing it, but rather have used the writing of this chapter as an opportunity to collect and present a wide range of Indigenous perspectives on this somewhat controversial Indigenous food while reflecting on our own relationships and research.

Bannock and Its Importance in Mainstream and Pan-Indigenous Culture

In North American society, bannock (or [Indian] frybread) is recognized as one of the most well-known and beloved symbols of Indigenous Peoples' food and culture.[2] In what is now called Canada, bannock's European origins and use of post-contact ingredients are intertwined with the often untold and unaccepted history of genocide and settler colonialism as part of the relations among Indigenous Peoples and settlers. Bannock is a type of flat, quick grain bread that is made without yeast. It is a versatile food staple in many Indigenous communities across Turtle Island. Different Nations make their own versions of the bread, including with unique ingredients and cooking methods, and the presence of the word "bannock" in many Indigenous languages demonstrates the multiplicity of this culturally valued type of bread across vast territories.[3] With a few basic ingredients, the baker has endless possibilities to make the dish unique by adding harvested foods such as blueberries or currants, to sweeten with sugar, or to form the base of a mixed dish such as the beloved "Indian taco" made with frybread. These breads are easy to make and a versatile complement to many types of meals.[4]

While there is no consistent consensus on how bannock and frybread differ from each other, a discussion on The Arctic Kitchen: Recipes of the North Facebook group in September 2020 suggests some common perspectives among posters. The original poster made the statement: "If you put it in the oven, it's not bannock, it's bread. Change my mind."[5] The responder comments (n=43) centred on three main themes: cooking method (e.g., "When you fry it, it is called frybread. When you bake it, it's bannock," and "It's 'bannock' from the oven . . . from over stove is 'fry bread'"); ingredients ("Bread needs yeast. Bannock needs baking powder"); or preferred terminology ("Where I'm from we have baked bannock and fried bannock"). From this example, it is clear that the terms bannock and frybread mean different things to different people. In this chapter, we will use the terms bannock and frybread according to which word was used in the literature cited or according to the name specific to the Indigenous group about which we speak. In the literature, sometimes "bannock" and "frybread" are used interchangeably, and sometimes the term used is associated with the cooking method: bannock for baked, frybread for fried.

Tina Brewer, on The New Brunswick Community College Indigenous Student Support Services' page,[6] highlights examples of various names and characteristics of bannock made in local territories and across Canada, as presented in Table 4.1.

This unique food is also a widespread symbol of identity and can foster a broad sense of pan-Indigenous unity and belonging.[7] The visible presence of bannock in Indigenous media, art, and fashion is likely due to its being the most well-known Indigenous dish in the settler-colonial society of Canada and its strong cultural symbolism. Bannock is mentioned in movies such as *Smoke Signals* and *Powwow Highway*, and in the celebratory song titled "Frybread," by Indigenous singer Keith Secola. This song shares a message of resisting oppression, making something positive out of nothing, and sharing love through food.[8] People even wear shirts with catchy slogans such as "frybread power forever" or "frybread inspector" that are clear expressions of Indigeneity.[9]

The word "bannock" comes from northern Scots English dialects, and from the Gaelic word *bannuch*, *bannach*, or *bannuc*, which means "morsel."[10] Most contemporary forms of this bread originate from the Scottish bannocks or breads, which are characteristically heavy and made with unleavened barley or oatmeal and were traditionally cooked on griddles of sandstone. These

NAME	INDIGENOUS COMMUNITY/PLACE/ NATION	UNIQUE CHARACTERISTICS
Sapl'il (pre-contact)	Across Turtle Island	Made from the starch, flour, paste, or meal from substances gathered from the forest such as corn, nuts (e.g., acorns), lichen, moss, cattails, stems of ferns, plant bulbs, or other plants and roots. Cooking methods include rolled in sand and pit-cooked, on rocks, baked in clay or rock ovens, or over an open fire (e.g., wrapped around a stick and held over the fire). Sometimes sweetened with a sweet syrup made from tree sap.
Bannock or frybread (post-contact)		Made from flour, lard (or other fat), salt, water (or milk). Some use baking powder and some add sugar, along with added ingredients (e.g., berries) and modern cooking methods (e.g., baked or fried).
THE FOLLOWING TYPES OF BANNOCK AND FRYBREAD ARE MADE WITH THE TYPICAL BASE INGREDIENTS OF FLOUR, FAT (E.G., LARD), SALT, WATER, AND BAKING POWDER; SOME HAVE UNIQUE CHARACTERISTICS OF ADDED INGREDIENTS OR SPECIFIC COOKING METHODS		
Pahkwesikan	Cree	Baked or fried
Ba'wezhiganag	Anishinaabe	Baked or fried
Luskinikn (or lusknikn)	Mi'kmaq	Baked
Four Cents	Mi'kmaq	Pan-fried version of luskinikn
Kcitqihikon	Passamaquoddy/ Wolastoqiyik	Cooked on coals
Tumahsis	Passamaquoddy	Fried
Lakalet, akalet	Wolastoqiyik	Fried
Palauga or muqpauyug	Inuit	Made over a qulliq (seal-oil lamp)
Bannock	Nehiyawak (Plains Cree)	Has currants and/or raisins, or other berries
Sapli̧'l	Coast Salish(Beecher Bay)	Made with ground camas bulbs instead of flour
Epangishimog Pakwejigan	Shuswap	Made with blueberries
La galette, galette de Michif, or les baigne	Métis	Generally round in shape

TABLE 4.1. Examples of names and characteristics of bannock according to different Indigenous groups in Canada. Only a small number of Indigenous groups within Canada are represented in this table, and even within these groups different terms might be used. This table illustrates just some of the diversity.

types of bannock were introduced to Indigenous Peoples living on Turtle Island by European traders during the late eighteenth century.[11] However, the unleavened breads made from cama bulbs, lichen, moss, cattails, corns, acorns, and other plants or roots cooked pre-contact in open fires, on rocks, in sandpits, and vessels were sometimes called *sapl'il* and were also considered bannock historically.[12] With the arrival of European settlers also came the introduction of the paradoxically named "five white gifts" (sugar, flour, salt, milk, and lard) to Indigenous diets.[13] These ingredients have also been labelled the "five white sins" because of their association with land dispossession and assimilation to settler society. Their use in bannock presents a beginning point for discussing the value, meaning, and tension of these breads as a traditional Indigenous food.

Colonization and Food Relief Policy in Canada: A Historical Context for Bannock

As white settlers coming to this work, we believe that framing our reflections on colonial history through a greater understanding of the use of food policy during Canada's settlement is key to understanding our roles in this space. The past and ongoing destruction of Indigenous food sovereignty is a function of colonialism in Canada, where assimilatory policies have legislated away food cultures through the destruction of languages, self-governance structures, sovereignty over lands, and hunting rights.[14] Active resistance by Indigenous Peoples continues to rebuild food security and sovereignty, despite what has been lost. Thus, we believe that a path toward reciprocal relations among settlers and Indigenous Peoples within Canada requires the acknowledgement of a more accurate history of our shared past.

Despite signed treaties recognizing the Dominion of Canada's responsibility to provide food aid to many First Nations in times of famine, a purposefully inadequate food aid system was constructed by the government as "Indian policy."[15] By administering food aid sparingly, the government transformed food into a tool of control that forced Indigenous Peoples into moving to reserve lands in order to secure the promise of supplemented food from the Canadian government. Accordingly, harvesting of traditional foods was diminished through federal control over lands and the 1885 implementation of the Pass System that barred Indigenous people from leaving established reserves without permission from Indian agents. This system had no legal basis but was intentionally implemented to restrain Indigenous people's mobility, impacting their lives in tremendous ways, including hindering freedom of movement for sustenance activities.[16] Food quality was continually questionable and choice was limited, while the ingredients used to make bannock, mainly flour and lard, were staples in the rations.[17] During the Second World War, after some Indigenous groups had become dependent on government rations, the federal government directed ongoing cuts to ration sizes, as there was a "delicate balance between its policy of starving holdouts into submission and onto reserves and the risk of scandal from widespread death from hunger."[18] The government systems, planned with malicious intent, carried out colonial power via policies of development, and by denying adequate food relief the government rejected its legal and moral responsibilities toward Indigenous Peoples. Limited mobility and economic options partnered with deplorable living conditions on reserves continued into the residential school era, entrenching poor health, including food-related issues such as diabetes, as a result. These structural and ecological factors are ongoing.[19] Reserve systems created an apartheid with slum-like conditions, and residential school diets promoted Western food and forbade traditional foods.[20] To this day, particularly in remote regions, access to market and traditional foods is integral to management of reserves and continues to be hindered by forced reserve settlement.

Despite having little control over their current systems and food choices, given the broader socio-political and natural environments, Indigenous individuals are often framed as responsible for circumstances of household food insecurity.[21] Hugh Shewell discusses how Indigenous Peoples within Canada can move toward emancipation from the domination of Canadian culture that is enacted through economics, language, law, and behaviour.[22] Non-Indigenous society currently holds the power to transform the governments and institutions of Canada in order to prioritize Indigenous Peoples' collective rights and individual human rights, and reinstate sovereignty for Indigenous populations.[23] As settlers, we have the responsibility to take daily steps to produce this transformative action. A food such as bannock can be an illustration of Indigenous people claiming control over their foods, collective identities, and histories while building relationships with settlers through the acknowledged significance and collective love for the food.

This historical lens can illuminate how consuming a food such as bannock may be an expression of identity for Indigenous people in the settler-colonial nation of Canada. As mentioned, colonial advances, historical dislocation, and assimilatory policies have disrupted family, community, and Nation-specific food knowledge and access to Indigenous foods while bringing in the "five white gifts" to take their place.[24] Some residential schools banned bannock because it was perceived by settlers to be a part of Indigenous cultures that needed erasure; as a result, bannock became both established as a symbol of home and associated with often-painful memories.[25] Colonial systems have created environments where Indigenous people disproportionately live in poverty and may rely on low-cost foods such as bannock, whose ingredients can be tied to government food rations. Increasing control over lives of Indigenous people changed the meaning of bannock to a necessary tool, superior to bread, to survive in times of government-induced dispossession, famine, food insecurity, and continual systemic food challenges.[26] Creating dependence on rations was how control of many of the foodways of Indigenous Peoples in the Americas was transferred to colonial powers that chose to alter diets toward highly processed, heavily preserved foods with lower nutrient density—a sharp contrast to the healthful traditional diets that have supported Indigenous Peoples since time immemorial. Thus, commodity foods such as powdered eggs, canned meats, powdered milk, commodity cheese, and frybread or bannock (a food prepared with commodity ingredients) conjure duality in their meaning.[27]

Exploring the Duality of Bannock: "The Great Frybread Debate"

The central question that tends to locate individuals in the bannock debate—whether it counts as a traditional food or not—is their view on culture as dynamic (changing over time) or static. Those who see culture and traditions as dynamic may be more likely to accept bannock as an Indigenous food that has been integrated and developed meaning within existing food cultures. However, what constitutes "traditional" varies by person and is tied to their unique level of connection to their tribal affiliation or Nation and the collective history of that Indigenous group—precisely how the individual has experienced colonialism, and how their group has been forced to change to serve the present generation in the current socio-political context. Thus, the question remains: Does tradition equate to familiarity, personal importance, or foods that were consumed by ancestors?[28] We want to note that the discussion on what constitutes "Indigenous," "traditional," "wild," or "country" foods is complex and must centre on definitions created by Indigenous people themselves. Typical definitions indicate that traditional food is what is harvested from the local natural environment, including through hunting, trapping, fishing, gathering, or agriculture. Some describe the traditional food category as broader and more flexible, extending to hybrid, fusion, or neo-traditional foods, which may integrate post-contact ingredients and market foods but still have strong cultural value.[29]

In a feminist and postcolonial analysis of cookbooks from the Northwest Territories released in the 1960s, Julia Christensen points out that integration of imported ingredients into local diets was commonplace, and recipes combining Indigenous ingredients and market ingredients had just as much cultural significance to Indigenous people in the region as did traditional foods such as caribou or Arctic char.[30] Qualitative research done in recent years has asked Indigenous people to define their views of traditional foods. A study with urban and rural Métis participants in Winnipeg and southern Manitoba found that neo-traditional recipes that included purchased ingredients such as dried peas, macaroni, rice, processed meats, and cheeses became go-to recipes for Métis families and part of their food culture passed down through generations. These foods continued to be made because of their inexpensive ingredients, desired taste, and convenience, and have now reached "traditional" status for many people.[31] Lise Luppens and Elaine Power designed a study to explore which foods Indigenous people living near Terrace, BC, considered to be their traditional foods, pointing to the fact that often Indigenous people are left out of the dialogue on what is traditional to their own cultures.[32] Although there was no consensus on which foods were considered traditional, participants shared many fusion dishes that they defined as traditional, including chow mein and meals incorporating bologna, potatoes, and rice. Potatoes and rice became traditional staples because they have been adopted by families in recent generations who experienced poverty as a result of colonial disruption. In relation to bannock, an immense variety was common among recipes as many were orally transmitted and not built around exact measurements.[33] Thus, boundaries surrounding traditional foods are not clear or settled upon within communities or across Nations.

This chapter was partly inspired by Kelly's experience at the second national gathering of the former Aboriginal Nutrition Network (ANN) of Dietitians of Canada in 2014 in Fort William First Nation Territory in northern Ontario, where she and the other organizers encouraged participants to submit one or more favourite recipes. These recipes were initially used for entering participants' names in a draw to win one of various cookbooks that had been donated to the gathering. Following the gathering, a working group of ANN members saw the value in sharing these recipes more widely in a format that was accessible, benefitting from recipe testing and inclusion of the unique stories behind the recipes. A recipe resource called a "Collection of Indigenous Recipes" was developed from twelve of the recipes submitted during the gathering and disseminated widely to various Indigenous groups within Canada.[34] Interestingly, of the approximately forty recipes submitted to the draw, eight were for different types of bannock. It is unclear whether the fact that such a large proportion bannock recipes meant that participants saw it as important and inherent to their culture, or simply that it was easier to recall the recipe for bannock in the moment. However, because the request was for "Indigenous" or "traditional" recipes, bannock appeared to be considered an Indigenous food by those participants.

One submission included an added note after the recipe: "This is my mom's family recipe. I only make this on special occasions because it brings memories of when my mom used to make *lusknikn* for us." Our working group decided that based on the high number of bannock recipes submitted, it would be meaningful for the participants and the audience for the recipe collection that we include at least one bannock recipe. We chose this submission because the participant chose to add the note expressing why the *lusknikn* recipe was important to her. What was common across these bannock recipes was that they all used post-contact ingredients, including flour, baking powder, and salt. Where the recipes differed were in the ways the bannock was cooked (pan fried, baked in the oven, cooked outside over a fire or on a stick) and what was added to the recipe (raisins, berries, or grated cheese). Several submissions also included options to make their bannock recipe "healthier," including switching out white flour for whole wheat flour, and baking in the oven instead of frying. The ANN working group chose to include a bannock recipe in the collection, and we have chosen to include a bannock recipe in this chapter. This version is meaningful to Kelly as it was shared with her by her friend Ruby when Kelly was doing research for her master's thesis in 2003 with Ruby's community. The first time they made this bannock together, with half of the pan plain and the other half with raisins, they shared it with Ruby's extended family. Kelly has made this bannock many times since and reflects on her time collaborating on research projects with this community during her graduate school studies.

Ruby's Bannock Recipe

5 cups flour
½ tsp salt
2 tbsp sugar
3 tbsp baking powder
2 cups water
½ cup vegetable oil
1 egg

1. Mix dry ingredients together. Add raisins if desired.
2. Mix wet ingredients together.
3. Add wet to dry ingredients. Knead and add flour until not too sticky.
4. Place in half of a 9x13 pan. Make a second batch for the other half of the pan.

5. Bake at 400 degrees for 35 to 40 minutes until golden brown on top.
6. After removing from oven spread margarine all over the top. Let cool and serve warm.

Decolonizing Diets?

In opposition to the view that bannock is a traditional food, some Indigenous people define traditional diets within the confines of ingredients that were used before contact with European settlers (i.e., foods indigenous to the land). This view of food culture can be seen in the decolonizing diet movement, which uses diet as an act of resistance to colonization and a way of unlearning colonized ways through food practices.[35] In these spaces, bannock is removed from consideration as a traditional food because of its history as a survival food throughout colonization and, more specifically, its association as a commodity food with the loss of traditional foodways.[36] Central to this movement is the idea that maintaining the integrity of Indigenous foodways that were developed over thousands of years is crucial to Indigenous well-being. Outside of strictly human health, motivations surrounding decolonizing diets are framed as requirements for the sake of biodiversity and stewardship of natural resources.[37]

Devon Mihesuah has attempted to debunk the common narrative around the timeline of frybread and its value as a food central to Indigenous identity in an American context.[38] Specifically, this work claims that the belief that frybread was created by Navajo people in their confinement at Bosque Redondo is not supported in government reports or by testimonies from Navajo people. This brings into question the common story that frybread was not made historically to save Indigenous Peoples from starvation, but was introduced after 1870 through trading posts on Navajo lands and did not increase in popularity until the 1930s; from the 1940s through the '60s, the health implications of the Westernized "trading post diet" became apparent. This false story of frybread's inception was spread to rationalize the mass consumption of a food with such poor nutritional qualities because of the enthusiasm for its cultural importance, which remains today. In addition,

Mihesuah's work indicates that many tribes created non–wheat flour breads that were boiled or baked, rarely fried. However, she mentions that in Canada and the northwest United States, bannock (as differentiated from frybread) may have been made earlier by Indigenous Peoples who were interacting with European fur traders and adopted this method.[39]

We want to reiterate that caution must be used if dichotomizing traditional and non-traditional foods, as this line of thinking risks discounting the vibrant and resilient Indigenous cultures that continue to adapt to changing environments.[40] The demonstrated ability to adjust to changing circumstances by incorporating new foods, such as modern forms of bannock, and indigenize them is a sign of cultural dynamism and strength. This conception of "fusion" foods is presented within a reality that exists beyond a strict traditional versus non-traditional classification of foods, a reality in which Indigenous cultures are flexible as opposed to the static stereotypes through which they are often portrayed.[41] The exact ways in which bannock became integrated into diverse and unique Indigenous communities and individual lives are not fully agreed upon, documented, or shared widely. Nevertheless, it is undisputable that ingredients used in modern bannock are not indigenous to Turtle Island; accordingly, at a certain point, settlers did play a part in introducing ingredients to be used in making this food.

Bannock and Health

Those who object to the consumption of bannock often cite the food as part of a lower quality diet of processed foods, which according to many researchers has sustained the epidemic of type 2 diabetes among Indigenous Peoples in North America.[42] Health professionals are known to discourage people at risk for or managing type 2 diabetes from including bannock in their diets because of its high caloric and macronutrient density (fat and carbohydrates) and lower micronutrient diversity.[43] These professionals may be defining health from a Western biomedical perspective that does not include a broader understanding of food as part of cultural identity and overall well-being. Consumption of bannock is often noted as contributing to the food-related health concerns in many Indigenous communities, while simultaneously sustaining the control and assimilatory power of governments today via the continued consumption of non-nutritious Western foods. However, the impact of bannock on diet-related chronic diseases can also be overemphasized and used as a scapegoat for the broader systemic colonial actions and policies described earlier, which continue to significantly impact the health and well-being of Indigenous people.[44] Kelly encountered this reaction when she was presenting findings from the Phase 3 First Nations Regional Health Survey.[45] Kelly chose to include the findings on bannock/frybread consumption in the list of traditional foods, as that was how the survey was designed. Following the presentation, an audience member stood up and stated that bannock/frybread was not a traditional food but a colonial food that did not deserve any place among traditional foods in the findings. Kelly evaded the question by responding that she had not been involved in the development of the survey and thus was only following the categorization that had already been decided on. Kelly recounted this exchange to her Anishinaabe co-author, who reiterated that for some people, bannock or frybread holds special comfort and meaning as part of their traditional practices and contributes greatly to their holistic well-being, while for others, it is a reminder of the devastating colonial impacts to their people. She expressed to Kelly that it is important that we acknowledge and respect all perspectives.

In an infamous article published in 2005 in *Indian Country Today*, Suzan Shown Harjo, a Muscogee and Cheyenne Indigenous rights activist, called on Indigenous people to stop consuming frybread and ranking it so highly in their individual and collective identities because of its devastating health impacts. Harjo attacks the healthfulness of frybread by citing its ingredients and the fact that many Indigenous people are in fact glucose and lactose intolerant. Bluntly, she writes: "If frybread were a movie, it would be hard-core porn. No redeeming qualities. Zero nutrition."[46] Framing frybread as a deadly cultural icon and the food of tragedy, Harjo connects it directly to obesity, hypertension, diabetes, dialysis, blindness, amputations, and death as a result of Western civilization disrupting access to healthy foods such as wild game and local plants.[47] Harjo calls on people to opt instead for breads that can be made simply by combining a fresh or dried base (e.g., corn, pumpkin, walnuts, beans, berries, sweet potato), water, and an Indigenous thickener (e.g., maple sap) to make a bread that will be culturally satiating and will contribute to health and well-being rather than taking away from it.[48]

Restaurants and the Rise of Interest in Indigenous Cuisines: A Path toward Improved Relations?

Despite Canada's constant claims to multiculturalism, systemic issues of assimilation and genocide have created a situation where Indigenous cuisine—the most inherently local cuisine—is poorly represented in the culinary scene in comparison to other ethnic cuisines. Only 1 percent of restaurants that specialize in Indigenous foods.[49] Nevertheless, Canada has seen a boom in restaurants serving Indigenous cuisines and in Indigenous chefs highlighting their traditional and contemporary takes on Indigenous foods through cookbooks or media. This space holds opposing views similar to those discussed above on what constitutes an Indigenous food, most significantly how the inclusion of post-contact ingredients affects the authenticity of a dish. Many of these restaurants focus on bannock, frybread, or mixed dishes made with these foods (e.g., Indian tacos, bannock burgers) that are enjoyed by both Indigenous and non-Indigenous people. Bannock is central to the rise in interest and support for Indigenous foods and fusion cuisines in Canada that have come about through the local food movement along with increased cultural awareness of Indigenous Peoples.[50] While there are Indigenous chefs who call for the strict use of only pre-contact ingredients, a large majority include bannock and its many variations in their cuisine.[51] Below, we present a few perspectives on bannock and the place of Indigenous foods in contemporary North American culture from successful Indigenous chefs.

Although not living within Canada, Sean Sherman, the creator of the Sioux Chef's Indigenous Kitchen and Owamni Restaurant in Minneapolis, Minnesota[52] has undoubtedly influenced the revival of Indigenous cuisines across Turtle Island.[53] Born in Pine Ridge, South Dakota, he focuses on providing modern, regional, pre-contact foods of the Oglala-Lakota, Dakota, and Ojibwe tribes as part of a mission to get people re-acquainted with holistically healthy and local Indigenous food systems.[54] Sherman frames his "nose to tail" cooking style, which does not include any use of European staples such as wheat flour, dairy, sugar, and domestic pork or beef, as revolutionary within the broader socio-political context of Indigenous food systems.[55] Frybread is clearly off the menu, and Sherman has been open about the negative associations of the food with traumatic histories of colonization. Rather, he chooses to experiment with pre-colonization diets and ingredients and works to expand all peoples' understanding of Indigenous food systems as consisting of more than just bison and frybread.[56] Through his work, he is sharing knowledge of traditional food systems before colonization while simultaneously presenting ways that people can return to Indigenous foods and thrive in current day without needing to rely on the "five white gifts." Sherman's Indigenous Food Lab is a training centre on the traditional Territory of the Dakota and Anishinaabeg, covering all aspects of Indigenous food service. The Indigenous Food Lab enables Sherman and his team to use their "shared heritage to build bridges and build power within and between Native communities and our allies."[57]

Other successful Indigenous chefs are less strict in their use of pre-contact foods, and some have introduced contemporary dishes that centre on bannock itself. Bill Alexander, the chef at the Grey Eagle Resort and Casino in Calgary, Alberta, owned by Tsuut'ina Nation, actively supports strategies to increase Indigenous culinary tourism in Canada.[58] He speaks of a common misconception that Indigenous cuisine is a fad centred on bannock and frybread; rather, it has been around for thousands of years, and today's trendy high-protein, low-carb, and good-fat diets are similar to traditional Indigenous diets. Alexander is excited to be able to share Indigenous cultures with non-Indigenous people in a positive manner through food and the tourism market.[59] He says, "Food is our conduit to share our culture with you so that we can all grow together and understand each other. I want to create experiences whereby people can experience Indigenous cuisine while simultaneously learning about culture. This is where we will turn moments into memories and build long-lasting relationships."[60]

Murray McDonald, executive chef at the Spirit Ridge Resort in Osoyoos, British Columbia, speaks of the renaissance of Indigenous cuisines as superfoods and fad diets rise. While his dishes primarily focus on pre-contact ingredients and highlight foraged foods, he also offers a variety of bannocks. McDonald continues to serve bannock while acknowledging its history in Indigenous-settler relations and its mixed associations for Indigenous Peoples.[61] He strongly believes in increasing awareness of Indigenous culinary traditions through collaboration with the Indigenous Tourism Association of Canada.[62]

Christa Bruneau-Guenther, member of Peguis First Nation and owner and chef of the restaurant Feast in Winnipeg, dedicated fifteen years to developing hundreds of recipes with Indigenous plants and animals from Manitoba. Without any formal chef training, she felt the responsibility to share the Indigenous food knowledge she possessed, prioritizing community and financial accessibility of local food "rooted in Indigenous tradition." When asked about her culinary style, she responded: "I don't like the term Indigenous-fusion because it's just what's reality for me being a family person. It's like, how do I cook my traditional foods mixed with everyday foods and still connect that to my culture?"[63] Her restaurant is one that highlights bannock as central to many dishes. Creative menu items include bannock tacos, bannock donuts, sandwiches, burgers, pizzas, and breakfasts (including eggs "banny," and BOB—breakfast on bannock).[64] Thus, contemporary Indigenous cuisine as it is emerging in the restaurant and tourism scene in Canada cannot be narrowly defined. In general, Indigenous chefs and restaurant owners describe a broad, positive cultural shift, and how food has begun to facilitate discussions of collective Canadian history and colonialism.[65] Bannock, although acknowledged as having settler roots, is clearly a significant part of the resurgence of Indigenous cooking and newly celebrated Indigenous cuisine in restaurants across the country.

Food can contribute to the process of preservation and strengthening of Indigenous languages and cultures. Further, it can be used as a tool for building cross-cultural connection and reciprocity in an era when reconciliation is increasingly on the radar and in the common discourse of non-Indigenous people within Canada.[66] Bannock is a perfect food for this task, thanks to its cultural significance, palatable taste, convenience, accessibility, and low cost. Bannock is already entrenched in Indigenous practices of community building and sharing. This "intensely personal food" is present in families and communities across Turtle Island, which have their own unique recipes and important stories attached to it that are passed down through generations.[67] The benefits of this food practice are that it serves people with strong Indigenous identity as well as those who are Indigenous but may have been separated from teachings and culture.[68]

Lauraleigh Paul Yuxweluptun'aat, owner of the Bigheart Bannock café in Vancouver, British Columbia, says that spiritual practices surround the preparation of bannock. Her view is that bannock as a traditional food can be part of the process of Indigenous people connecting or reconnecting to their spiritual practices surrounding food and harvesting for sustenance, encompassed within their rights as urban Indigenous people. Bannock provides an accessible option for culturally significant food, particularly for urban populations where wild fish and game may be inaccessible, or for any Indigenous person who may have been displaced and dispossessed from their territories.[69] This staple food is made in large quantities to be shared with others and can be associated with positive memories of preparation and eating with family and/or community at cultural events and community gatherings including powwows, ceremonies, and feasts.[70] Frybread is central to contemporary powwows, which are crucial for community building as they are a form of resistance to government policies that banned intertribal gatherings in the past.[71] The process of making, eating, and sharing bannock together has been described as medicine; through this food practice and through sharing recipes within and between families, communities, and Nations, people can connect to their culture and to each other.[72]

Food is a tool to express culture, and therefore sharing a piece of bannock, frybread, or a mixed dish such as an Indian taco is physically reclaiming and dispersing a resurgent culture among Indigenous Peoples and with settlers. This presents an avenue for improved relationships through mutual appreciation of food, which can contribute to the complex process of acknowledging history and working toward justice for Indigenous Peoples within Canada.

Connection through Traditional Foods and Bannock: Acknowledging and Understanding Its Colonial History

In some ways bannock may be a reminder of colonialism and of the governmental systems' intentions to eliminate Indigenous Peoples from Turtle Island.[73] Commodity foods, including bannock, are in fact "super-tribal identity symbols" (in the United States) and often directly associated with Indigenous foods, yet discourse surrounding them is ironic because they became widely popular through governmental dietary assimilation efforts. Thus, such foods can evoke both pain and pan-Indigenous unity and pride.[74] As explored in this chapter, some view bannock's centrality to Indigenous culture as detrimental because the food is not inherently indigenous to traditional lands but has developed as a traditional food from shared experiences of colonization, such as residential schools and reserve life, that are often unacknowledged or misunderstood in broader culture, Canadian history, and everyday interactions.

Indigenous cuisines within Canada have blossomed according to the vastly different environments from which ingredients are harvested. However, bannock is once again seen as the common element, despite the known genocide that preceded unwelcome culinary influence leading to changes in Indigenous food systems.[75] Dana Vantrease notes similarities between the frybread debate and the soul food debate of African Americans, citing common histories involving displacement, dispossession, and colonization that impacted food sources in reserves and through enslavement.[76] Bannock and other cultural food items are symbols of Indigenous life, just as crawfish represent uniqueness and unity in Cajun culture. Some believe that humour about commodity food in pan-Indigenous community spaces contributes to a shared sense of belonging while also engaging discussion surrounding identity, health, and self-determination within settler states.[77] The symbolism of bannock can be powerful. It is evidence of the perseverance and resilience of peoples despite their colonization. Historically, making bannock was an active form of resistance to colonial control through using existing resources to provide a tasty dish that gave sustenance for the family and community. Indigenous chefs are pioneering the resurgence of their cuisines among

Indigenous Peoples and bringing their dishes and cultures to mainstream settler Canadian society. Accordingly, continuing to acknowledge bannock as traditional food can be a way to honour ancestors; it is a symbol of sustenance and connection to Indigenous Peoples' rights to practise their cultures, including food practices.[78]

As white settler researchers, we must continually ask how we can facilitate the ongoing fight for food security, Indigenous sovereignty, and well-being when our privilege is deeply engrained in the structure of society, the field of academia, and the institutions within which we work. In our work, we seek to advocate for and hold ourselves accountable to research processes that centre relationships, reciprocity, and Indigenous self-determination.[79] Understanding the complexities of bannock within the colonial state is a way for both Indigenous people and settlers to recognize each other's personal and group histories, and can be leveraged as a step on the journey of restoration of overall health and well-being for Indigenous people within Canada.[80] In the field, some of the most ground-breaking conversations occur over a meal. It is in these moments that perceived and actual differences can be put aside as we all satisfy our hunger. We show up to our work as learners and collaborators, not experts. While sitting face to face with our Indigenous partners and participants, relationships can begin to grow and exchanges of knowledge, understanding, and ideas take place. Crucially, authentic reciprocal interactions can only begin when we acknowledge the past and current implications of colonialism and Indigenous genocide, and the continuing acts of resistance by Indigenous people. Bannock may be an ideal medium to share across Indigenous and settler cultures as we take on the responsibility to push for necessary societal change now and in the future.

Notes

1 Skinner et al., "Sharing Indigenous Foods."

2 Tennant, "Does Bannock Have a Place in Indigenous Cuisine?"

3 Ibid.

4 Cyr and Slater, "Got Bannock?"

5 Snow, "If You Put It in the Oven It's Not Bannock."

6 Brewer, "Breaking Bread: A Brief History of Bannock."

7 Ibid.; Snow, "If You Put It in the Oven It's Not Bannock"; Miller, "Frybread."

8 Miller, "Frybread."

9 Wagner, "Icon or Hazard?"

10 Stewart, *Pocket Field Guide.*

11 Tennant, "Does Bannock Have a Place in Indigenous Cuisine?"

12 Wastasecoot, "Bannock."

13 Tennant, "Does Bannock Have a Place in Indigenous Cuisine?"

14 Mintz, "The History of Food in Canada."

15 Daschuk, *Clearing the Plains.*

16 Barron, "The Indian Pass System."

17 Daschuk, *Clearing the Plains.*

18 Ibid., 130.

19 Daschuk, *Clearing the Plains.*

20 Burnett, Hay, and Chambers, "Settler Colonialism, Indigenous Peoples, and Food."

21 Martin, "Nutrition Transition."

22 Shewell, *"Enough to Keep Them Alive."*

23 Ibid.

24 Sagan, "Canada's Indigenous Restaurants."

25 Cyr and Slater, "Got Bannock?"

26 Ibid.

27 Vantrease, "Commod Bods and Frybread Power." In the United States, commodity foods are specific foods distributed by the American government free of charge on Indian reservations. Some of these foods can have distinct packaging and not be widely available outside of reservations.

28 Mihesuah, "Indigenous Health Initiatives."

29 Luppens and Power, "'Aboriginal Isn't Just about What Was Before.'"

30 Christensen, "Eskimo Ice Cream and Kraft Dinner Goulash."

31 Cyr and Slater, "Honouring the Grandmothers."

32 Luppens and Power, "'Aboriginal Isn't Just about What Was Before.'"

33 Ibid.

34 See "Baked Walleye," https://www.dietitians.ca/DietitiansOfCanada/media/Documents/Resources/Aboriginal-Nutrition-Network-ANN-Indigenous-recipe-collection-2016.pdf; and Skinner et al., "Sharing Indigenous Foods."

35 Mihesuah, "Indigenous Health Initiatives."

36 Tennant, "Does Bannock Have a Place in Indigenous Cuisine?"

37 Vantrease, "Commod Bods and Frybread Power."

38 Mihesuah, "Indigenous Health Initiatives."

39 Ibid.

40 Luppens and Power, "'Aboriginal Isn't Just about What Was Before.'"

41 Ibid.

42 Wagner, "Icon or Hazard?"

43 Cyr and Slater, "Honouring the Grandmothers."

44 Miller, "Frybread."

45 FNIGC, *First Nations Regional Health Survey*. Specifically, Kelly Skinner presented findings from the Nutrition and Food Security Chapter at the National Data Release conference in March 2018.

46 Harjo, "My New Year's Resolution."

47 Draper, "Native Dilemma."

48 Harjo, "My New Year's Resolution."

49 Mintz, "Where Are Canada's Indigenous Restaurants?"

50 Sagan, "Canada's Indigenous Restaurants."

51 Rosendaal, "How a New Guard of Indigenous Chefs."

52 Sherman, *The Sioux Chef.com*.

53 Sherman, *The Sioux Chef's Indigenous Kitchen*.

54 Sherman, *The Sioux Chef.com*; Ralat, "The Sioux Chef."

55 Treuer, "The Sioux Chef Spreading the Gospel."

56 Graslie, "The 'Sioux Chef' Is Putting Pre-Colonization Food Back on the Menu."

57 NATIFS, "Frequently Asked Questions."

58 Davidson, "Exploring Indigenous Cuisine."

59 Davis, "'Everyone Is Your Community.'"

60 Davidson, "Exploring Indigenous Cuisine."

61 Sasvari, "Redefining Indigenous Cuisine."

62 Brijbassi, "How a Newfoundlander Became a Champion for Indigenous Food."

63 Wasney, "A Veritable Feast."

64 Breakfast Menu, Feast Cafe Bistro.

65 Rosendaal, "How a New Guard of Indigenous Chefs."

66 Ibid.

67 Napoleon, "#Next150 Challenge: 'Bannock Challenge.'"

68 Giroux, "Bannock as Medicine."

69 Cyr and Slater, "Got Bannock?"

70 Ibid.

71 Miller, "Frybread."

72 Giroux, "Bannock as Medicine."

73 Cyr and Slater, "Got Bannock?"

74 Vantrease, "Commod Bods and Frybread Power."

75 Mintz, "The History of Food in Canada."

76 Vantrease, "Commod Bods and Frybread Power."

77 Ibid.

78 Gilpin, "At 'Bigheart Bannock.'"

79 Luongo et al., "The Retail Food Environment, Store Foods, Diet and Health."

80 Giroux, "Bannock as Medicine."

CHAPTER 5

Evolution and Revolution: Haudenosaunee Histories and Stories of Sustenance and Survival

Hannah Tait Neufeld

I was first introduced to the Three Sisters in the summer of 1994. I was born near Buffalo, New York, and grew up in Haudenosaunee Territory along the Haldimand Tract,[1] in the city now known as Kitchener, Ontario. Growing up, I knew very little about the history of the land and its Indigenous Peoples. After completing my undergraduate degree in nutrition at the University of Guelph and spending a year in northeastern Brazil, I returned to Waterloo Region and began a summer position at the Steckle Heritage Farm. The remaining ten acres of the original 1820s farm became a site for education that summer, teaching youth in the wider urban community about "respect for the land and each other."[2] One of the demonstration gardens we planted that first year was a Three Sisters garden. The farm's sole occupant, Dr. Jean Steckle, had worked for many years with Medical Services Branch of Health Canada, a federal agency, as a nutrition consultant. In her role, she documented the food practices of many Indigenous communities in northern and southern regions.[3] As staff and volunteers, we all learned a great deal from her, working in the gardens and with visitors to the farm that first summer. The knowledge Dr. Steckle conveyed at that time, I believe, started me on a path to study Indigenous foods and eventually brought me back to the Territory I set out from.

Fifteen years later, after close to a decade at graduate school in Manitoba and a brief stint as an international civil servant in Switzerland, I returned with my family in tow to re-establish roots and begin my postdoctoral work investigating the intergenerational knowledge transfer of Indigenous food knowledge among urban and reserve-based communities within southwestern Ontario. The main objectives for the project were to explore current knowledge surrounding access, availability, and Indigenous food practices, along with describing the historical context of present-day food environments. In this chapter I present some of the stories I encountered and knowledge shared, often as intimately as food is shared, in the context of those reciprocal relationships forged from conversations detailing Elders' lived experiences with foods nurtured from the land.

Communities and Context

The Indigenous women I have worked with over the last twenty years are from Anishinaabe and Haudenosaunee communities within Manitoba and Ontario.[4] This chapter incorporates the histories and stories of Haudenosaunee women from the present-day region of southwestern Ontario. Haudenosaunee means "People of the Longhouse." Haudenosaunee Peoples are also referred to as Iroquois or the Six Nations, comprising Mohawk, Cayuga, Oneida, Seneca, Onondaga, and Tuscarora Nations. These six Haudenosaunee Nations make up the Haudenosaunee Confederacy.[5] Haudenosaunee Territories straddle the current border between the United States and Canada, extending from northeastern New York State in the west into Quebec in the east.

For the purposes of this chapter, I focus on the communities of Oneida of the Thames and Six Nations of the Grand River. Six Nations is the largest First Nations community within Canada and is currently home to approximately 13,000 members living on reserve.[6] The reserve spans over 46,500 acres, which represents only 5 percent of the original 950,000 acres of land granted by the 1784 Haldimand Treaty. The community of Oneida Nation of the Thames uniquely purchased their current land base on the banks of the Thames River. In 1840, 240 members migrated from New York State to the reserve location, which now has a population of 2,029 residents.[7]

As part of my postdoctoral work,[8] beginning in the spring of 2014, I began to engage with the communities of Oneida and Chippewa of the Thames First Nations through programming organized through the Southwest Ontario Aboriginal Health Access Centre (SOAHAC). The SOAHAC Food Choice Study began in 2008 as a community-based participatory project designed in collaboration with Western University to examine circumstances of food security and Indigenous food use among First Nations families within southwestern Ontario. During the first, qualitative phase of the study, interviews were conducted with First Nations mothers (n=29). Women talked about access to knowledge and contact with Elders as integral determinants of health and well-being.[9] Subsequently, I conducted life history interviews with female Elders, focusing on mechanisms impacting the intergenerational transfer of food knowledge.[10] Part of this work included getting involved with the community and attending kitchen- and land-based workshops with Elders and other knowledge holders that SOAHAC organized for members of the wider Indigenous community to learn more about traditional lifestyles and foodways.

One of the first events I attended was a two-day corn soup workshop. Many of the interviews with mothers had described the complex process of preparing this revered Haudenosaunee staple, but I was unprepared for the level of instruction and time required. The recipe below was shared and the process led by a member of Six Nations of the Grand River, and included the preparation of the Haudenosaunee dried white corn, which needed to be boiled for several hours with hardwood ashes to soften the husk of the kernels. In the kitchen at the Chippewa of the Thames SOAHAC site, we all watched in amazement as the white seeds turned a glowing orange colour after being submerged in the black broth (Figure 5.1).[11]

A similar process was followed during a corn bread workshop I attended a few weeks later that was held by an Elder from Oneida Nation of the Thames.

FIGURE 5.1. Lyeing white corn. Photo by H.T. Neufeld.

Ash baskets were used to help rinse off the wood ashes and remove the outer husk of the corn (Figure 5.2) to prepare the corn to be ground, mixed with beans, and formed into beautiful bread wheels (Figure 5.3). These acts of resurgence, dedication, and wisdom provided an extended introduction to and metaphor for those Three Sisters I had helped to plant and tend all those years ago.

Corn Soup

4 quarts Haudenosaunee white corn
1 (900 g) bag red kidney beans
3 (250 g) packages salt pork
1 pinch hardwood ashes

Have enough water in the pot to cover the corn, bring to a boil, then add the ashes. The corn will turn yellow.

Bring to a boil and simmer for approximately 2 hours, or until the skin and hulls start slipping off. Test the corn frequently by using your fingers and thumb to see if the corn is ready to drain. Drain corn with cold water until clean (skin/hull is off corn).

Cut salt pork into small pieces. Put pork and kidney beans into a medium-sized pot to boil for 3 hours, until kidney beans are done.

After kidney beans and salt pork are cooked, add all 3 ingredients together.

Simmer all ingredients together for another 30 minutes, or until ready to serve.

Food Evolution

Corn has been described as a "cultural centre of Haudenosaunee way of life."[12] Corn planted with beans and squash (the Three Sisters, or Tey'o'nhekwen) as part of the agricultural system of the Haudenosaunee enabled communities to establish roots in their Territories, literally and figuratively. Providing food energy, these plants and seeds are referred to collectively as "our sustenance."[13] Growth of the Three Sisters from the body of Sky Woman's daughter illustrates the growth of one body into plants that become an interdependent unit of sustenance. There are agricultural, physiological, and cultural reasons why these foods were grown together. As a cropping system, or polyculture, for example, each plant serves a unique function. Corn is planted first in raised mounds to provide a structure for the beans to climb. Beans provide nitrogen to fertilize the soil, and the prickly squash vines cover the base of the mound, helping to retain soil moisture and deter pests.[14] This form of mound agriculture takes into account the complementary growth of each plant and provides the best possible conditions for the seeds to thrive. Dried, these foods were easily stored for long periods of time and provided a complement of nutrients; they also taught cultural concepts of sustainability and relational interdependence.[15]

FIGURE 5.2. Ash corn basket. Photo by H.T. Neufeld.

FIGURE 5.3. Freshly boiled corn bread wheels. Photo by H.T. Neufeld.

Indigenous Knowledge refers to traditions and values that continue to uphold these teachings and practices that have allowed generations to practise healthful relationships with their natural and social environments.[16] Many of these sustaining foods, such as the Three Sisters, are often referred to as "traditional" foods and are central to the health and well-being of Indigenous Peoples.[17] Practices associated with their harvesting, preparation, and consumption are integral for the preservation of Indigenous Knowledge, as these foods are situated within traditional or Indigenous food systems that include the socio-cultural meanings, acquisition, processing, and planting techniques associated with their interdependency and nutrient composition.

The term "nutritional colonialism" refers to the values and practices of the dominant food system.[18] It is characterized by cultural suppression and the removal of control over resources, along with increased rates of chronic disease conditions associated with sedentary lifestyles and dependence on wage economies. The introduction of foods often referred to collectively as the "five white sins: flour, salt, sugar, alcohol and lard,"[19] for example, has a long history in Indigenous communities. These ingredients have become the basis of certain so-called traditional foods such as frybread and bannock, yet these foods underscore processes of dispossession and forced assimilation that have had lasting impacts on Indigenous Knowledge associated with preparing pre-contact Haudenosaunee foods such as corn bread and soups using lyed white corn, beans, and squash. These "five white sins" have also been labelled ironically as the "five white gifts," as also noted in this volume by Phillipps and Skinner, perhaps given the non-reciprocal nature of their colonial exchange.

Agricultural traditions and the sharing of cultivated foods in Haudenosaunee culture have also been interrupted through processes of social disruption and dispossession. Elders I interviewed shared stories, for example, of the intergenerational effects of residential schools, particularly on the social structures of families and communities.[20] Dislocation from the land and through a greater reliance on waged economies shifted families and communities away from agriculture, hunting, fishing, preparation, and preserving practices. Households became more reliant on inexpensive staples that could feed large families. One of the Elders from Oneida, a

FIGURE 5.4. Bread before going into the oven. Photo by H.T. Neufeld.

seventy-year-old woman at the time of her interview, remembered living with her seven brothers and sisters through periods of food scarcity and told the story of her grandmother, who "used to just have water with milk and this flour . . . I don't know how she'd do it, but she'd mix it up in her hand. It would fall into [boiling water] and form a little, like an ear . . . curly stuff like that." Another woman from Oneida talked about her uncle making "slip and go down" cereal for her and her eight siblings. She described it as "just made out of, almost looked like little wee dumplings and kind of creamed and it was just made of flour and water and baking powder and salt."

These ingredients were the same ingredients that a variety of breads were made with as well, including frybread, oven bread, or *gunjin*. Another Elder from Oneida in her mid-seventies described the difference between frybread and oven bread: "the oven bread they usually use baking soda and sour milk or buttermilk . . . the fry bread you use baking powder." Her custom of preparing frybread was to "make little round ones and cut two slits and fry it up," but she also remembered her grandmother making oven bread by "making fire underground and she'd put the dough in there and cover it up in the ashes."

During another interview, an Elder in her fifties gave me the following recipe and made oven bread as we talked (see Figure 5.4). She described *gunjin*, or Indian bread, scone, or bannock as it is referred to "up north where their bread is flatter" and not as "puffy" as oven bread. She preferred oven bread, as it was "really filling . . . you never starve if you have a bag of flour."

Oven Bread

3 cups flour
4 teaspoons baking powder
1 teaspoon baking soda
3 cups buttermilk
pinch of salt
butter or margarine for top
Mix flour, baking powder, baking soda, and salt.
Add buttermilk to mixture. Mix all ingredients into a dough.
Sprinkle flour on counter and fold dough several times. Use knuckles to knead.
Cut into pieces and put into pan with small drops of butter or margarine on top.
Bake for about 20 minutes at about 350 degrees Fahrenheit.

Sharing Social Practice

Shifting from more localized and land-based food systems that included farming to waged economic pursuits changed the means of food provision. Losses associated with disruptions in knowledge transfer were frequently aligned with altered social interactions and relationships with parents, siblings, and extended family.[21] Instead of learning through observation and participating in daily activities associated with food procurement and preparation, the gradual individualization of lifestyles and marketed resources often resulted in limited opportunities to share food and knowledge. Reciprocal relationships or shared roles in the maintenance of foodways and agricultural practices, however, when strengthened to reinvigorate these social connections, can serve to foster connections with the land, food, and each other.

Land-based learning and healing properties of being out on the land have been at the forefront of Indigenous food sovereignty literature and practice as ways of fulfilling measures of food security such as access and availability.[22] In sharing her research with the community of Elsipogtog First Nation, Elisa Levi noted that when community members talked about the availability of foods in the past, they also talked about meeting their needs for survival in the local environment.[23] Historical practices for maintaining food security existed at individual, family, and community levels. Individual practices were linked to survival and skills such as fishing and hunting. Farming, gardening, and harvesting, along with recipes and the ability to cook, were viewed as more collective practices of preparing and sharing food.

Oneida Elders also spoke with a great deal of pride about the mutual responsibility of participating in the procurement and production of food. Many emphasized the importance of knowing where food comes from, its connection to the land and to those who helped to harvest and prepare it.[24] Several women illustrated these relationships through stories of social connections and warmth conveyed through food. One Elder talked about her butter bean soup as something her family would "fight for" every time she prepared it. She recalled with fondness the essential components that formed these memories, collected around seasonal ingredients she grew in her garden: "butter beans and you get the small new potatoes and throw some onions in there and put some butter in there and then that's it. It's a plain soup, but it was good!"

Indigenous food systems, communities, and families are bound in relationships.[25] Those with skills, knowledge, or involvement in any activities pertaining to local food production and preparation are expected to demonstrate the social values of sharing. These acts enable those knowledge holders to honour their reciprocal responsibilities to family and community. Along with sharing food, sharing knowledge through stories and practice are important components of Indigenous food systems. Oneida Elders illustrated these processes of sharing food and knowledge and taking care of each other through their stories; for example, bringing together locally harvested beans and adapting recipes as necessary to sustain each other. As one woman who shared her recipe for yellow eye bean soup elaborated: "The yellow eye beans you'd put some... cut up some salt pork and make dumplings... turn it down low and then put the lid on it. It'll cook like that in 10 minutes or so... or you could put it on top. Say you're just boiling potatoes, make a little wheel like this of the flour, cut two slits in it and then set it on top with a lid and then it'll cook like that and you can have that like a... I guess you call it a dumpling. They're something else to eat, you know?"

Food Revolution

The transition from local Indigenous food systems toward a greater reliance on pre-manufactured products is often discussed in the nutrition and public health literature as having significant health impacts associated with chronic disease conditions.[26] The introduction of processed foods with refined flours and sugars has been associated with higher rates of obesity and type 2 diabetes, health conditions that were rarely encountered prior to colonization. The Three Sisters, the ancestral foods of the Haudenosaunee Peoples, were nutrient powerhouses that grew in abundance. According to historical records from the sixteenth century, Haudenosaunee agricultural methods were reported as being immensely productive and were established in regions from the southern tip of North America to the shores of the St. Lawrence River in present-day Quebec.[27] Tuscarora scholar Jane Mt. Pleasant has studied extensively the agricultural productivity and sustainability practices of the Three Sisters, along with their unique nutritional characteristics.[28]

Intercropping corn, beans, and squash is more than a highly productive cropping system. Combining these foods not only provides sufficient calories or food energy—the Three Sisters together provide more protein than when any of these plants are grown, prepared, and consumed separately.[29] Beans and corn contribute to protein quality as complementary proteins, providing the appropriate mix of amino acids.[30] Squash or pumpkin flesh and seeds are also rich sources of vitamin A when harvested at maturity. The nutrient values of corn and beans also depend on when they are harvested and how they are prepared.[31] Green beans are made up primarily of water and cellulose, while dried beans have 100 times the energy and eight times the protein. Green or milk corn also consists mainly of water. Mature kernels have forty times the energy and three times the protein as sweet corn. Lyeing the corn (Figure 5.1) through the process of nixtamalization used in the corn soup recipe (above) exposes the dried corn to large quantities of calcium and potassium from the hardwood ashes, producing an alkaline solution.[32] This process allows the corn to cook more quickly by helping to remove the seed coat and contributes to changes in the kernels' nutrient composition. The bioavailability of calcium is increased to two to four times that of uncooked corn, along with several amino acids that collectively provide additional protein content as well as vitamin B3 (niacin) which otherwise would be deficient when consumed.

This nutrient narrative based in Indigenous foodways is unique in its reflection of Indigenous Knowledge, along with values of respectful relationships, reciprocity, and interdependency, which as Dawson argues can resist the more dominant biomedical narrative of food and nutritional health.[33] Constructing diverse Indigenous counter-narratives of food and well-being based in Indigenous foodways can put an end to the existing colonial narratives and bring Indigenous Knowledge to the forefront in the form of stories that share and celebrate Indigenous foods. Across a diversity of Indigenous Territories, methods, practices, and ethics of Indigenous food knowledge are being collectively shared. Indigenous community-based projects aimed at providing healthy food, protecting the environment, and reviving ancestral seeds, agricultural practices, and preparation methods have seen a resurgence across North America.[34] In their book *Indigenous Food Sovereignty in the United States*, Devon Mihesuah and Elizabeth Hoover examine local histories that have led to conditions of food injustice, but they also celebrate community members' actions in the present and highlight the potential for future growth. They caution, however, that in celebrating and revitalizing Indigenous foodways, we need to understand conditions of disruption and change specific to each place-based culture.

In 2014, the Haudenosaunee community of Six Nations of the Grand River began an initiative with an awareness campaign to share traditional food knowledge and practices associated with healthier lifestyles.[35] Healthy Roots was launched as a community challenge inspired by the Mohawk

FIGURE 5.5. Three Sisters garden. Photo by H.T. Neufeld.

(Entsisewata'kari:teke) and Cayuga (Esa;do:gwe) words meaning "you will become healthy again." The goal of the challenge was increasing access to pre-contact foods and activities, and promoting interconnectedness. Participants were encouraged to consume foods indigenous to the Territory and eliminate the "five white gifts" from their diets. At the same time, a number of gardening workshops and events were organized by Our Sustenance. At the time, Our Sustenance was an ongoing program that provided access to a greenhouse where fresh produce was available to community members, along with a community garden and farmers' market. In partnership with Healthy Roots, a series of gardening workshops and events was held to offer both cultural and practical skills on seed saving, planting, harvesting, and food preservation techniques (see Figure 5.5). The ongoing aim of the Healthy Roots partnership is to see continued growth in the community of Six Nations, in particular the growth of relationships on many levels: between individuals and their food, with each other, and among the larger community as a whole.[36] As expressed by Onondaga scholar Xavier, who has contributed a chapter to this volume, "The concept of having a garden and growing food represent[s] the central Haudenosaunee teaching of interdependence on all levels . . . the interdependence of food, culture, and community," beautifully illustrating the notion of reciprocity in practice.[37]

Forward Focus

Conversations around Indigenous foods and food practices are often situated in the past, yet the momentum of the food sovereignty movement, a revitalization of knowledge, and aspirations for change are being felt in Haudenosaunee communities and beyond. Sovereignty is about our long-standing relationship with food, along with our ability to feed and sustain ourselves.[38] Original foods such as the Three Sisters have been described as relatives with whom positive relationships continually need to be maintained. The relationships between human communities and other communities that make up Indigenous food systems place an emphasis on Indigenous philosophies of duality, equilibrium, and reciprocity to safeguard all relatives, including those with wings, fins, paws, and roots.[39] As Elizabeth Hoover maintains, this philosophy encapsulates the harmony that is established when these patterns of symbiosis are maintained through humans with their living relatives that contribute to food systems.[40]

As a result of the historical agricultural legacy of agriculture within Haudenosaunee communities, and adaptations of the land and those who continue to cultivate, seed stocks have evolved into a picture of cultural and environmental selection that continues to this day.[41] Mohawk seed keeper Rowan White reminds us that these corn, bean, and squash seeds are witnesses to the changes communities have gone through and a testament

FIGURE 5.6. Seed relatives. Photo by H.T. Neufeld.

to the Indigenous resilience of the seeds over the last many centuries of relocation, displacement, and war.[42] Seeds are "life capsules of memory," witnesses of the past and hope for the future.[43] Their beauty (see Figure 5.6) is connected to lands and communities of origin. The foods and recipes made from these seeds and the flesh they produce are intimately intertwined with well-being. The health of the people is intertwined with the health of the life-sustaining seeds, bound in a *reciprocal relationship* that extends back beyond living memory.[44]

Indigenous foods represent cultural, spiritual, emotional, social, physical, and mental nourishment.[45] Efforts towards Indigenous food sovereignty can only be accomplished by communities through the reclaiming of seeds, foods, and practices. There is the need to restore time-honoured relationships with plant and food relatives through the preparation and sharing of these foods for healing. These reciprocal relationships with food and seed plant relatives through sharing food and knowledge, as described earlier, make people who they are and give meaning and connection to all living things. Linkages with Indigenous ecological practices are integral to the well-being of the land and its new generation of caretakers, who also need to take care of each other. The care that goes into planting and nurturing gardens and the seeds that become plants to form relationships unto themselves, like the Three Sisters, is a metaphor for societal investments and the changing of the colonial relationship that has undermined these reciprocal practices among people and plants for generations.

Finally, it is important to listen to stories that symbolize these practices and agreements in order to continue to share in the knowledge of creation and stewardship into the future. The values of interdependency and sustainability are transferred through stories such as the Creation Story. The growth of the Three Sisters from the body of Sky Woman's daughter illustrates the growth of one body into plants.[46] Corn emerged from her breasts, beans from her hands, squash from her umbilicus, along with tobacco from her mind, strawberry from her heart, and sunflowers at her feet. An Elder from Six Nations demonstrated to me one summer the dedication and care she brought to the strawberry plants

FIGURE 5.7. Wild strawberry harvest. Photo by H.M. Neufeld.

she was growing in their community garden. She had transplanted several wild strawberry roots to a raised bed to provide the extra love and attention she felt was necessary to nourish these plants and give them an opportunity to flourish (Figure 5.7). These stories and ways of knowing not only provide social and spiritual guidance, they constitute a living guide to good health and well-being by connecting these levels or narratives of interdependence, incorporating the physiological (nutrition), the ecological, and the social by continuing to grow, harvest, and preserve these life-sustaining Indigenous foods.

Notes

1 The Haldimand Tract, land given to Six Nations of the Grand River and Mississaugas of the Credit First Nation in 1784, includes six miles on either side of the Grand River. Six Nations Lands and Resources, *Land Rights*.

2 Steckle, *Building Partnerships for Heritage and Environmental Education*.

3 Schaefer and Steckle, *Dietary Habits*.

4 I am grateful to all of the Indigenous women who guided this research, in particular Denise Bear, Summer Bressette, Freda Caribou, Winona Morrison, Miranda Paul, and Chantelle Richmond.

5 Xavier, "Longhouse to the Greenhouse."

6 Six Nations Lands and Resources, *Land Rights*.

7 Statistics Canada, "Community Profiles: Oneida Nation."

8 This project was funded through Canadian Institutes of Health Research (CIHR) Banting Postdoctoral Research Fellowship, along with funding from Western University's Office of Research.

9 Neufeld, Richmond, and SOAHAC, "Impacts of Place and Social Spaces on Traditional Food Systems."

10 Neufeld, Richmond, and SOAHAC, "Exploring First Nation Elder Women's Relationships with Food."

11 Lyeing corn through the process of nixtamalization involves making the cooking broth more alkaline, thereby altering bioavailability of certain nutrients like the amino acid tryptophan, making the lyed corn a complete protein and increasing the bioavailability of vitamin B3, or niacin.

12 Cornelius, *Iroquois Corn*, 91.

13 Cornelius, *Iroquois Corn*; and Xavier, "Longhouse to the Greenhouse."

14 Mt. Pleasant, "Food Yields and Nutrient Analyses."

15 Xavier, "Longhouse to the Greenhouse."

16 Cajete, *Native Science*.

17 Kuhnlein and Receveur, "Dietary Change and Traditional Food Systems."

18 Lindholm, "Alaska Native Perceptions about Food, Health, and Community Well-Being."

19 Elliott et al., "'We Are Not Being Heard.'"

20 Neufeld, Richmond, and SOAHAC, "Exploring First Nation Elder Women's Relationships with Food."

21 Neufeld, "Socio-Historical Influences and Impacts on Indigenous Food Systems."

22 King and Furgal, "Is Hunting Still Healthy?"; Wesche et al., "Land-Based Programs in the Northwest Territories."

23 Levi, "Indigenous Philosophies and Perspectives on Traditional Food Systems."

24 Neufeld, Richmond, and SOAHAC, "Exploring First Nation Elder Women's Relationships with Food."

25 Shukla and Settee, "Revitalizing the Past, Nourishing the Present and Feeding the Future."

26 Egeland et al., "Food Insecurity and Nutrition Transition."

27 Sauer, *Sixteenth Century North America*, 64, cited in Mt. Pleasant, "Food Yields and Nutrient Analyses," 87.

28 Mt. Pleasant, "The Paradox of Ploughs and Productivity"; and Mt. Pleasant, "Food Yields and Nutrient Analyses."

29 Mt. Pleasant, "Food Yields and Nutrient Analyses."

30 FAO, *Maize in Human Nutrition*.

31 Mt. Pleasant, "Food Yields and Nutrient Analyses."

32 Briggs, "The Hominy Foodways."

33 Dawson, "'Food Will Be What Brings People Together.'"

34 Hoover and Mihesuah, "Conclusion: Food for Thought."

35 Gordon, Xavier, and Neufeld, "Healthy Roots."

36 Ibid.

37 Xavier, "Longhouse to the Greenhouse," 11.

38 Hoover, "'You Can't Say You're Sovereign.'"

39 LaDuke, cited in ibid., 68.

40 Hoover, "'You Can't Say You're Sovereign If You Can't Feed Yourself.'"

41 White, "Planting Sacred Seeds in a Modern World."

42 Ibid.

43 Ibid., 186.

44 Ibid.

45 Hoover and Mihesuah, "Conclusion: Food for Thought."

46 Xavier, "Longhouse to the Greenhouse."

CHAPTER 6

Our Soup Tells Stories: Kitchen Table Conversations about the Connections, Creations, and Traditions of Soup Sharing

Adrianne Lickers Xavier and Kitty R. Lynn Lickers

Our soup tells stories, though my soup is actually her soup: my mom's, Kitty, or Muther as I sometimes call her. It is also our soup—the shared traditions I have learned and seen over the years becoming a recipe, a story about both of us. The conversation that follows is not so much a dialogue between us as it is a story shared by us with you, our readers. The conversation itself started in the usual way with us. I was asking questions. I was born curious, I think, and my mom has never disappointed when it comes to answering my questions. This particular time, I was asking my mom how she comes up with recipes. Not so much what they were, but the process of how she creates something, a food dish, and then figures out exactly how to share it. I realize now it was not exactly a lighthearted question. I was asking her to define her way of creating and sharing her food knowledge.

This chapter, and any recipe, is more than a recipe for food. The recipe we chose is one my mom has made a million times, it seems. Twisted Sister Soup is my mom's version of something much more traditional to our Six Nations community (see Figure 6.1). These staples are part of our culture and food system and integral to our community, in this case literally as soup.[1] The Three Sisters, Tionhnhéhkwen, the life-sustaining foods,[2] were not the idea that came to mind when I first wanted to tell the story of sharing recipes and soup. They are the ones that tell the best story because they are so integral to our culture and community. Corn, beans, and squash, known as the Three Sisters, are the foods that are referred to in the Haudenosaunee Thanksgiving Address.[3] This address is known as the words that come before all others, thanking all parts of creation and reminding us, as people, of our place in the world. Included in that acknowledegment are the Three Sisters as life-sustaining foods. The science behind the nutritional aspects of the Three Sisters is also documented.[4] Since we know that these three foods can sustain us, the recipe we chose was one that would make us thrive, not simply survive. This particular recipe is more of a testament to Indigenous foods in the modern world and our place in it. This is a recipe of personal observation, growth, and community.

Context for Soup Stories

The reason food, recipes, and knowledge sharing are an almost daily conversation for my mom and me is because we have been growing, sharing, and teaching about food in our community for years. The history and details of our personal journey will come later, but first we should explain how we have worked together before. In many roles and ways, we have worked within the Six Nations community. From 2011 to 2018 we volunteered, then worked at, and finally managed a market and garden program in our community that became known as Our Sustenance. It is no small coincidence that food and community are such a focus for us. Many of the things we will talk about, situations and experiences within our community, come from the perspective of community education and food security, something we have been focusing on specifically since 2011, at least professionally. The

FIGURE 6.1. Twisted Sister soup, prepared by Kitty R. Lynn Lickers for a community event in Ohsweken, Six Nations of the Grand River. Image Credit: Kitty R. Lynn Lickers.

program itself started as a farmers' market and community garden. I was the volunteer market vendor—the only one. My mom was the volunteer assistant. I didn't tell her that at first. I just brought home the market leftovers, and she canned and saved and froze them for us or for sale. I really should thank her more often!

The program grew over the years to include a large greenhouse where fresh produce was available to the community on a pick-your-own system. The greenhouse was also home to gardening classes. We added a community kitchen and outdoor gardens, food forest, and herbal apothecary; we had a kitchen herb garden and even some chickens for fresh eggs. The program was an example to the community of what sustainable food security could look like for the community and for individual families. We were able to partner over the years with many different programs in and outside of the community. The program made connections as well for people, organizations, and community to food, culture, and each other through the many types of programs we offered: cooking classes, gardening classes, food workshops, and the market. During that time, my mom and I also both went back to school. I finished my master's degree and started my doctoral research, and Kitty started her master's. Since then she has completed her degree and I have just recently done the same with my doctoral program.

The education part of this conversation is significant because my research for my master's degree was on food security and my doctoral research was on Our Sustenance. Kitty's work focused on the in-between space that Indigenous women experience, particularly around knowledge sharing and skills. Our combined academic and experiential work is part of the conversation that takes place here, with you. How do we share knowledge? Who shares it, and what does it become? I think it becomes a recipe. We invite you all to sit at our table, with my mother and me, and talk soup, share a cup of coffee or tea, and learn more about how recipes grow and build community. We will share with you the back and forth, the cause and effect of how something small—including soup—can mean so much to people.

Sitting around the fire, telling stories, eating soup, sitting around the lunchroom table talking about our plans for the weekend, I have seen my culture come to life. I have lived with my mom in the Six Nations of the Grand River Territory for more than thirty years. Haudenosaunee, at one time known as the Iroquois, we are the Six Nations: Onondaga, Tuscarora, Cayuga, Oneida, Seneca, and Mohawk. We are the People of the Longhouse. One of the most meaningful things to me about my community and culture is its connection to food and land. The Three Sisters, known as Tionhnhéhkwen (or Tyonhekwen) in Mohawk, are our sustainers. They are the foods that sustain us: corn, beans, and squash. They are not only the basis for this chapter but also for gardening practices of the Haudenosaunee. The Three Sisters grow together in a mound, and they also go together in a soup pot. When we started writing this, I asked my mom, Can we do your Twisted Sister Soup recipe, please!

Daughter: Where It Began

When I was a kid, I had no idea that food was going to be the focus of my life and work. I saw something that fed me, that I enjoyed, and that was part of my everyday life. I was lucky. My mom was a preschool teacher, a great cook, a great mom, and a great gardener. She has a green thumb that I swear reaches all the way to her toes. While my community is the Six Nations of the Grand River Territory, my childhood and connection to food is so much more than the sum of its parts. It is more than soup or a simple recipe. There are lifetimes of stories and families in a bowl of soup. "Stone Soup" is one of my earliest memories of both a book and a recipe. As a child, I was taught by my mom how to read and to cook. That book tells a story of need and of humanity. The story itself was about a traveller with a magic stone for making stone soup. The version I remember from childhood included a traveller with a stone and a soup pot. The story tells how the curious townspeople engaged with him, and eventually each one brought something to go along with his stone soup: a few veggies from a poor town becomes a full pot of hearty soup. A group with very little on their own can have a feast in a soup pot if they work together. As a young girl, the story was sweet and funny. I never realized how many things it was teaching me.

Years later, as a student and researcher, I asked my mom, What makes a recipe really work for someone? What does it make? When I sat down to write this story, to recount this recipe, I had an idea, and then I had another, and another. Before I knew it, I realized, I could have written a recipe book of all my favourite recipes that my mom makes. I will choose just one for the purposes of this particular chapter and truthfully, it is not even my favourite. Partly because I can't say I have just one.

What is my favourite thing is the process of soup. Soup is not just following my mom's recipe. This is the ultimate irony. If you want one of my mom's soup recipes, normally you have to ask for it, and she will either send it by text, or—her preference—grab a pen and paper and write it down. This is not because she has the recipe memorized, but because she will stop what she is doing, imagine in her head she is standing in front of her stove, and she will "make" the soup and measure it out in her mind. She will even then be able to modify it, based on the size of your family or if you prefer yellow corn to white, and include that in "her recipe." I have had soups that my mom has made hundreds of times, that have become famous in my community. Yet if I were to look at my mom's recipe books, what is in there are mostly things my grandma wrote. None of them soup! Most of them are hand-scratched versions of her most popular items, or more likely notes, newspaper articles, or recipes my Gram wrote out from something she saw somewhere. Muther's recipes are in her, and from her, not something referred to or captured in a book.

Kitty's (Muther's) Recipe

Twisted Sister Soup[5]

2 squash, any variety

3 cups cooked or canned beans (normally I use white or red kidney beans)

2 cups green beans

1 cup dried beans (navy beans, for example) *

3 cups lyed white corn **

3 cups various types of greens such as kale, Swiss chard, or spinach

* Beans can be canned or dried; the instructions below are for dried.

** Lyed corn is a process of taking white corn and boiling with hard wood ash or lye. This process is quite long and entails many rounds of boiling and rinsing to remove the hull and ash from the water and corn. Here in our community, there are people who make it and sell it already processed, or I will lye it myself and save it for future use in the freezer.

Begin by peeling the squash, cutting it up into bite-sized chunks and roasting it in the oven, drizzled with sunflower oil and sprinkled with salt. When it is browned on the edges, remove from the oven and divide it in half.

While the squash is roasting, take your dried beans and cover them in water and bring to a boil to soften.

Purée 1/2 of the squash and add it with 1 1/2 quarts of vegetable broth (even water will work) to a large pot. You can season now with sea salt and a bit of black pepper. I sometimes add a bit of thyme.

Bring to a boil, reduce to simmer, and add the green beans and previously boiled beans. Add the lyed corn and let simmer for approximately 45 minutes.

For the last 15 minutes, add the set-aside squash and the greens shredded into pieces. When the greens have completely wilted and before the chunks of squash have fallen apart, ladle the soup into bowls and enjoy!

Daughter: Back to My Initial Question—What Makes a Recipe? What Does a Recipe Make, Mom?

It makes a family, she said, a community. Soup day, on Wednesdays in our old market shed, the lawnmower beside the soup pot, and everyone we know stopping by. My mom is known for her soup. People ask for her soup recipes, and she has obliged many times, spur of the moment, pulling out a scrap of paper or a cellphone to quickly type a text to the person requesting her "famous" recipe. I have listened to the recipes over the years and never once have I written one down, unless requested to give to someone. What I have asked a million times, nearly every time, is, What goes next? Why do I have to wait, why do I have to keep stirring this constantly, Mom? When I think about recipes, and soup especially, what I think of is the stories that go along with them. It is never just soup. We used to have soup days on Wednesdays at Our Sustenance where my mom and I worked together for several years. It started one cold day, when everyone had been working outside. Co-workers and volunteers were taking a break out of the cold, and all of a sudden, my mom went out to the garden, dug in the fridge, and the next thing I knew, there was a big pot of soup on the stove. Years later, there are still people who miss soup day. What I realized later on was that soup was the glue. Food in general was the thing that stuck us together and was a recipe of a different kind. It is not just physical warmth on a cold winter day; soup also brings a sense of social and emotional warmth. At least that is how it felt. It is like being cared for, or taken care of to be fed or to feed others. You give and you receive in equal measure.

Muther: It's Just What I Do

We talk together all the time, my daughter and I, and it always surprises me the things that impact her the most. Well—at least the things that stick with her. I barely remember the first time I made the pot of soup at the program we worked at together, but she says it is so vivid for her. It is within me to feed people. I have been told it is a gift I have been given. I am not sure it is the gift of feeding people. I think it is more that the food is just the vehicle for connection. I have made my Twisted Sister Soup hundreds of times for many different people, but each time at a certain point everyone talks about similar topics. Twisted Sister Soup is a very good soup to draw out memories, thoughts of growing up, sometimes good and sometimes not so good. The important part for me is no matter the discussion around the table, everyone becomes connected. The importance of food and in this case a soup that is connected to the generations before us is more impactful than the ingredients. The ingredients are a key component because they connect us to the land where they were grown. That connection is what in turn connects us to our ancestors and invariably leads to conversation about how we need to connect or reconnect to how things were done before so we can and will still have those big pieces of who we are in place for the generations to come. Now I am not saying that heavy conversation happens over soup. It is more stories that come out of moms, aunties, and grandmas who have made soups or stews in people's lives, and having soup evokes those memories.

I think it is important to have a discussion at this point on how the imperialistic, patriarchal system the world has been forging needs to change.

Daughter: The System of Things

As usual, my mom is right. The discussion here needs to move toward the things that have caused soup and recipes to be disconnected from and connected to us. I don't think this is the end of the story, but the beginning of a new story. What are the ways we share? The very makeup of our communities used to lend itself to a closely knit, interconnected way of eating. Well, technically . . . living. We are known as the People of the Longhouse. We literally and figuratively have a culture that is founded on the creation of community space.[6] *The overriding impacts of colonization and the patriarchal world we are living in now is that we have learned through processes of cultural assimilation to be separate.*[7] *We now have to take classes in gardening and food preservation if we want to be connected and share this knowledge with one another. My own research shows how we are learning and doing what should be a natural act. What is now considered cultural history, sharing food and space in community, is a workshop or lesson that happens because we have become disconnected. This is the need for change my mom is talking about. We need more of those classes, more of that connection . . . more recipes maybe.*

I don't want to get caught in the cycle of sharing the reasons that we as Haudenosaunee people, and the larger Indigenous community we are part of, have been removed from our connections to food. It is important to understand the history behind it in this discussion. The legacy of hunger and food disconnection has been felt and is still something I struggle to fathom.[8] *What I want to point out is that the ability to reconnect to food, culture, and community were all things that the Our Sustenance program addressed.*

To address my mom's last comment, the world we live in is marching forward, with industrial agriculture, climate change, and a global pandemic the themes of the day. We cannot continue day after day living our lives as if we are separate from our food and land. There needs to be a shift in the way we do things, and this is what I think will prompt the changes that need to come. The truth of our culture and food system, our cultural recipe for change, was already present, slowly coming to the forefront. However, the reality of a global pandemic and politics of control have caused the world to take a pause, and for some, to re-evaluate things. Where does our food come from? What is the ideal combination necessary to make things better? This discussion, as strange as it may seem, actually brings me back to my original question to my mom: What makes a recipe? How is it that she causes a few ingredients to come together and make a cohesive flavour? That leads me to ask, What can we do to change the modern system based on capitalistic fervour? How do we combine the right ingredients to make a new and different food system? I think we may actually be on to something in that respect. Just ask my mom!

Muther: What Is the Secret Recipe (Or Is It a Secret Ingredient)?

There is no secret, I don't think. Just time, I think, patience, and the willingness to let things come together. Sometimes a recipe requires heat, or pressure, some pressing issue. For example, if you are starting a good soup, and you are brave and practised like me, you will turn the heat up high, add your oil, and drop in your onions. The high heat softens the onions quickly and opens up the flavour, to add your other ingredients into, salt and pepper; the slight crispness to the edges of the onion will be lost the minute the broth is added, but for the first few minutes, those things are what begins the magic. Just like in building relationships or sharing culture. Getting to know someone is sometimes intense, and being able to open up in that setting is part of what makes the opportunity for those first sharp edges, those initial fumbling attempts, to turn into a warm and welcoming place. Time and attention turn those separate ingredients, or people, into a cohesive flavour, a relationship. Could be that I just like to see the potential in the world.

Daughter: What Is Her Secret?

What do you think it takes to empower the change that people need? How does a recipe work for someone? I don't often think of recipes as a formula but more of a vision. I envision the end product and work back to the beginning, visualizing the ingredients and the method. How many times have you made your favourite dish? For me, it is not a specific dish or recipe I want to discuss, but the process of my mom's soup making. I swear my mom has made soup when there was "nothing in the house" as well as when the pantry was full. The soup is just as good, either way. The reality of her method is what gets me every time. I am not strictly talking about soup anymore, however.

When we ran Our Sustenance together, over the years we had classes, workshops, events, and so many gardens. The process of my mom making up a recipe was the same as the magic of seeing her with people. The connections that she talks about—her gifts are truly something that permeate this discussion. I prefer to think of it as magic; some part of me loves the process of seeing all the moving parts come together in a symphony of movements. When you make Twisted Sister Soup, you make connections, to flavours and textures. When you grow or build a food system, like my mom has done in our community, you do the same thing. The connections are visceral. The flavours are the personalities and the gifts people share, the textures are the approaches people take and the ways they do things.

I will give you a more concrete example. If you look back at our soup recipe, anyone could add together the ingredients. I have seen many new cooks over the years read an ingredient list and start adding things. I will confess I myself have many times (don't tell my mom) not read the directions and just cut and added vegetables. This is definitely a mistake. Not because it is wrong, but because there is an integration of ingredients and flavours that comes with following an order to things. It is also because a recipe takes into account the small details that not everyone knows or pays attention to. Green beans will cook fairly quickly, but if you notice the directions, the dried beans need to be previously boiled, as in they are actually boiling when the squash is roasting in the first stage of the recipe. If you add dried beans to this soup, you will have hard dried beans at the end of your hour of cooking. You will not have a cohesive flavour. They take time to soften and be ready. This is how community and connection work, too. Our culture is inherent in our language and our land, but if we aren't ready to hear it or see it, we will be just like the dried beans: unyielding and unwilling to take on the flavour of our soup—or culture in this case. This small description of previously boiled beans could change the entire soup. Now, if you have followed the recipe but did not notice this one key instruction, you could very easily leave the beans in and eat around them, or just keep cooking the soup till all your squash was cooked away to broth, or you could put it away for tomorrow and hope the beans soften overnight. Is that the soup you were hoping for?

The idea of this recipe being just about soup now seems almost too simplistic to me. I can see how our community as a whole is present in these twisted sisters. The corn, beans, squash, and greens are all vital pieces of this. What they also represent are the lessons and ideas that get shared. When my mom made soup, weekly for a few years, in fact, she was not just making soup. She was building sustainable community relationships. The soup was never just soup. It brought staff together on cold winter days, gave community members a friendly face, a warm meal, and a chance to be seen and heard. It also gave everyone the chance to pick a favourite or beg for their soup to be on the list for that month! Twisted Sister was usually on that list somewhere, and was often requested by people who would never eat random mixed greens any other time, but this soup made them popular.

Muther and Daughter: Soup Magic

Since our time together at Our Sustenance, we have seen other places where soup performed a similar feat. I, Adrianne, am working at McMaster University, and the Indigenous Studies space has a kitchen where students sign up weekly to make soup for anyone who stops by. They aren't required to make a specific kind of soup, only to make sure the ingredients and allergens are known. What is interesting to me is that I get to see the same thing happening as we saw at Our Sustenance. The joyful presence of hungry students and those seeking warmth from food, the building and their classmates all coming together on soup day. Conversations range from classes and instructor preferences to what the soup ingredients are, where they came from, and what the plans for the weekend will be. The culture being created is one of camaraderie and happiness. The same connections that people created at Our Sustenance are created here, with recipes and stories being shared, all over soup.

Mom smiles and shakes her head at me sometimes, because I am often interested in the strange details that are not quite part of the conversation. I love to see her in a crowd, with people leaning in, watching her animated face light up the world around her with ideas. These are the connections and stories being shared, the simple moments that are gone in a flash, but that mean so much to so many.

Daughter: Soup's Ready

Our soup tells stories. I have not forgotten where we started this conversation. I know in some part of me that I have shared with you things that my mom rarely takes note of in a real strict way. I mention them because time has moved on. We no longer work together at Our Sustenance. We each still do what we have always done, but not in the same way, or even in the same places exactly. I am now an assistant professor; she is now a community food animator.

We are both still doing things that mean something to us, and we are both still making soup!

Our community now also makes soup and shares knowledge. We continue to meet people and come across folks who remember when they met us all those years ago at the market or garden. Soup days and garden visits, greenhouse afternoons in the warm spring sun—these are the memories that come back to us time and again, through the eyes and mouths of friends and family who have learned to make and share their own soup.

I mentioned a lot of examples of recipes, ideas, and methods for sharing culture and community. In the end, the truth is that the relationships we build are the recipes we share. My favourite recipe will always be Stone Soup. Not because of the soup or the stone, but because the history of my community sharing food is what means the most to me. I share Twisted Sister Soup with people because it has the ingredients that are close to my heart, that live in my culture, and make me feel whole and full. The understanding that by sharing food we share our lives with each other, and by giving freely, we also open ourselves up to new possibilities. This all can sound very esoteric, but ultimately if I go back to my academic roots in anthropology, it is the truth of what I have observed and known and lived. The story itself is my recipe, much like my research tells the stories of the things I have found.

Conclusion

We see culture in artifacts, living history, activities, and images. Artwork, language, and ceremony are all factors that make up what a living culture is. This story and discussion does not create anything that doesn't already exist. What we are doing is giving a living example of the way in which knowledge is shared and transported through time and space. My mother's knowledge of plants, food, and growing comes from many places. When I say generational knowledge I do not simply mean her mother, who also gardened; I mean everyone she learned from over the years, including each book, every person, each walk through the bush to find wild herbs, berries, and spices. Every person who took the time to share with her in some small way took the time to share that with me, and now also with you. The way that culture and knowledge are shared is that magic that I see in my mom: time. Give your time to others, share your gifts. Not every person is a gifted cook or gardener. Speaking from experience as someone who struggles to get her jam to set and her jars to seal, I still count on Muther to make my favourite things. If I am honest, I am not sad about that, and I tease her that I hope she always will make them for me. The truth is, there will come a day when my nieces and nephew will want to cook and can food, and we have already started that. I will be there, guiding them along and learning with them in the hopes that one day, my jars of jam will also set. The careful time and attention paid to things like food, soup, and family are what create relationships.

These days my mom is making new recipes, still in the community garden, still sharing all her best tips and tricks. I am also making new recipes, but in the classroom. We are both still doing the same thing, opening up our communities to the reality around them and sharing what we know. I am the perpetual student and teacher, forever questioning things, and seeking knowledge and connection. My relationship to my culture has grown in the days since I left Our Sustenance, and for that I am grateful. Spending time learning in the Longhouse, I have come to realize that was not what connected me to culture. It was connecting to the lessons, the people, the values of my community. Protecting culture means protecting the knowledge, but it really means protecting the people who carry knowledge. The responsibility and reciprocity of sharing that knowledge belongs to everyone. What it requires is asking those who hold the knowledge to be willing to spend time with us. I won't say that this is a role for Elders only; however, the history of our community lives in them, as do the lessons, language, and culture. I hope to always remember that. I think next time I meet a new friend or visit an old one, I will take soup and ask for their story.

Notes

1 Cornelius, *Iroquois Corn*.

2 Delormier et al., "Reclaiming Food Security in the Mohawk Community."

3 Xavier, "Longhouse to the Greenhouse." You can see the full Thanksgiving Address here: https://earthtotables.org/essays/the-thanksgiving-address/.

4 Cornelius, *Iroquois Corn*. The combination of corn, beans, and squash provides sufficient and ideal protein, carbohydrate, and amino acids; enough to sustain us nutritionally. See also the chapter by Neufeld, this volume.

5 Twisted Sister Soup is Kitty's take on the much more well-known Three Sisters Soup made from corn, beans, and squash. The twist here is the inclusion of more than just those three things: the addition of the greens and more than a single type of bean and squash. If you are of the "right age" to know the rock band Twisted Sister from the 1980s, you will get the reference; Kitty refers to this soup as Twisted Sister because she says it is the rocker version of Three Sisters Soup.

6 Longhouses were single-structure homes that were added to time and again, to include everyone. See Gadacz, "Longhouse."

7 Neufeld, Richmond, and SOAHAC, "Exploring First Nation Elder Women's Relationships with Food"; Settee and Shukla, *Indigenous Food Systems*; Cornelius, *Iroquois Corn*.

8 Mosby and Galloway, "'Hunger Was Never Absent.'"

CHAPTER 7

Making and Eating *Chipa* and *Mbejú* in Rural Paraguay

Elizabeth Finnis

In this chapter, I focus on two Paraguayan breads, *chipa* and *mbejú*. Both are typical Paraguayan foods made with the same core ingredient: cassava flour (*almidón*). They can be eaten as snacks, meal accompaniments, or as meals themselves. In discussing *chipa* and *mbejú*, I reflect on the roles that preparing and consuming food can play in everyday research experiences, and what the processes of making, eating, and sharing *chipa* and *mbejú* meant for me as an anthropologist, living and working within a rural Paraguayan community. I explore how these two breads encompass both different and overlapping meanings in the fieldwork context of rural Paraguay, and examine rural-urban, local–not local, and individual-group dichotomies. In doing so, I share recipes as taught to me,[1] and consider the values and dichotomies that can be intertwined in these breads and the implications that food preparation has for fieldwork relationships and everyday reciprocities.

Anthropology has a long history of engagements with issues of food production and consumption, past and present. There are excellent broad overviews by Ellen Messer and by Sidney Mintz and Christine DuBois;[2] other reviews address a range of more focused topics, such as food and globalization,[3] food and memory,[4] food and the senses,[5] infant feeding,[6] genetically modified crops,[7] and feasting.[8] Specific recipes have been incorporated into anthropological writing in various ways, including as part of detailed ethnographic records,[9] and as a way to illustrate processes of change.[10] For example, Part 1 of Franz Boas and George Hunt's "Ethnology of the Kwakiutl"[11] includes preparations of a range of dishes, primarily based on various fish and sea life but also including ways to prepare, serve, and eat other foods, including mountain goat, crabapples, clover, and lily bulbs. Preparation information ranges from brief sketches to taste notes and accompaniment cautions. Instructions for some dishes highlight "the social procedures and personnel involved in the acquisition, preparation, serving and social meaning of food," as Helen Codere indicates in her analysis of the ways rank is incorporated into dish preparation.[12]

Jessica Kuper's edited volume *The Anthropologists' Cookbook*, originally published in 1977, provides a range of dishes with ingredient and preparation notes, as well as brief commentaries on the meanings of recipes from diverse cultural contexts. In her preface to the second edition, Kuper writes that contributors "have brought home—and domesticated—something of their experience of fieldwork."[13] Yet, the translation of recipes can mean losing the context, affecting perceptions of authenticity and obscuring the personal styles of individual cooks and households.[14] *The Anthropologists' Cookbook* offers a range of recipes or, in some cases, more general treatments of flavours and processes. Some recipes, such as Greek *galopita* (milk pie), have accessible ingredients and standardized measurements,[15] while others, such as the instructions for Faroese Roast Puffin,[16] do not. Dishes are sometimes placed within broader contexts, as demonstrated by Bakoly Ramiaramana's discussion of Malagasy cooking,[17] which includes consideration of the relative value of types of cooking, complete with a proverb that reinforces the status of cooking in a pot; or, as in Aurore Monad-Becquelin's account of food taboos and prohibitions in the cooking of the Trumai Indians.[18] The book also includes a list of possible ingredient substitutions, although as a result of the ongoing globalization of foods, tastes, and people, many ingredients that were considered hard to access when the volume was first published (e.g., lemongrass, coconut cream, galingale [galangal]) are now readily available in the Global North.

Processes of globalization as reflected in food preparations and preferences are not new, and this has been explored by Richard Wilk in the context of Belize.[19] Wilk uses recipes to illustrate food practices, food preferences, and how these can be shaped by processes of globalization and local tastes, intersecting with issues such as status, taste, national identity, and livelihoods. Each chapter of his book, shaped around different periods of Belize's history, offers a recipe that reflects critical issues of the time period. For example, in the chapter on nation making and food, Wilk includes a recipe called Winter Fruit Salad, which includes tinned pineapple and apricots along with fresh oranges and bananas. This recipe demonstrates the incorporation of fresh local foods (oranges, bananas) with imported, processed fruits.

In offering reflections on what it means to cook and eat *chipa* and *mbejú* in rural Paraguay, I discuss how the act of learning to make dishes can have implications for better understanding food contexts, while also building relationships that are shaped and reinforced in other ways during fieldwork. In doing so, I encourage others to think about these issues in both their past and future fieldwork. What can practices of everyday reciprocity through food preparation mean, both in terms of methodology and in terms of understanding broader research questions or contexts?

Community and Methodological Context

My chapter is situated in the context of cultural anthropological fieldwork, where participant observation, "living as well as viewing," is the central method.[20] Penny Van Esterik highlights the importance of grounding our understandings of food systems in "learning by doing."[21] Participating in cooking food can become an important part of knowing what goes into what our hosts eat and share with us. Much of my fieldwork time in Paraguay, India, and more recently in northern Ontario, has taken place in kitchens. This is particularly the case in Paraguay and India, where my research with smallholder farmers on agricultural and dietary transitions has included spending time talking with women about what they grow, cook, and eat. Participant observation in kitchens has been a key part of this research, and practically speaking, I have found that women are most likely to have time to speak with me when they are already seated next to a cookfire. Helping with cooking tasks such as peeling raw *mandioca* (cassava) tubers, cutting tomatoes, garlic and onions, grinding grains, stirring meals as they cook, and mixing and shaping local breads has become part and parcel of the time I spend with women in or just outside of kitchens. This can mean learning the steps to make specific dishes, representing both everyday and special foods.

From 2009 to 2013, I worked with households in Lindo Manantial,[22] a rural Paraguayan farming community located in Piribebuy District, about seventy-five kilometres outside of the national capital of Asunción.[23] As a *mandioca*- and citrus-growing region, with other crops such as peanuts, beans, and maize also cultivated, the community was experiencing ongoing local challenges, including a significant decrease in the livelihood viability of farming. This was related to changes in agricultural infrastructure, including the closure of the *mandioca* mills that had formed the major market for locally grown tubers. Farmers also highlighted poor infrastructure in general, especially roads, the out-migration of young people and subsequent agricultural labour shortages, and environmental unpredictability as contributing factors in the decline of agricultural livelihoods. My research collaborators at the Universidad Nacional de Asunción and I have addressed these themes in depth elsewhere.[24] Data were collected through semi-structured interviews, focus groups, and participant observation with community members over three field seasons and a follow-up community visit. The field seasons took place between May and August—winter in Paraguay—and the community visit took place in October.

The overall goal of our project was to track agricultural livelihood changes and the implications these had for dietary and culinary practices and for food sovereignty potentials. Part of this meant learning about favourite foods and changes to food access over time; while living in the community, I experienced which foods were ubiquitous and which were special treats. In this part of Paraguay, two agricultural products were readily available and plentiful during the fieldwork periods: *mandioca* tubers, which could be dug from households' fields, and citrus fruits, primarily oranges, which were so plentiful and lacking a consistent market that it was not unusual to see them rotting under the trees. There were often simply too many oranges for a household to eat or sell. Other fruits such as apples were rare. While I would get excited about the prospect of freshly picked oranges, my host family, especially the children, would be excited about the grocery store apples I would bring them when I arrived from Asunción.

For me, eating oranges became associated with sitting outside in the sun on a warmer day, chatting with household members or guests in the late afternoon. *Mandioca*, however, as a food and an agricultural product, was the focus of most of my research conversations in one way or another, chiefly with regards to growing it, its relative marketability, and the importance of both the tubers and *mandioca* flour (*almidón*) in everyday meals. *Almidón* is a critical ingredient for both *chipa* and *mbejú*. Learning to make these two dishes helped me build relationships and gave me insights into the conditions of cooking and sharing foods.

Mbejú

The first time I remember eating *mbejú* was at a farmers' market in central Asunción. The stands at this weekly market were typical farmers' market tables located under a large, roofed parking lot, surrounded by some enclosed shops along the periphery. One of these shops sold Paraguayan fast food. I noticed one person ordering a thick flatbread, and I thought it looked interesting. I ordered some. It was not at all what I expected.

Unlike flatbreads such as Indian naan and chapati, *mbejú* is made with cheese. With an approximate two-to-one ratio of *almidón* to cheese, *mbejú* is very cheesy. The traditional cheese, *queso Paraguayo*, can be made at home. *Queso Paraguayo* is crumbled and mixed with the *almidón*. Some people will add a bit of corn flour, but this is not necessary. The uncooked mixture is not a traditional smooth dough. Instead, it is a slightly moist, loose mixture that is patted flat onto a pan and cooked to make a mildly crumbly, thick flatbread. *Mbejú* is a deeply satisfying food, especially when freshly baked. Each bite squeaks slightly on your teeth as you chew, and the texture is wonderful. It is a filling food, and it is so good that, at least for me, it was hard not to want another piece as soon as the first one was finished.

Despite first trying *mbejú* in an urban setting, it does not, at least in my mind, signify a particularly convenient urban food. When cold, *mbejú* becomes stodgy and far less pleasant to eat. It does not lend itself to packing for a later meal, and its slightly crumbly nature means it is a bit messy to eat while walking around. Eating it fresh can mean eating it when it is almost too hot to carry comfortably. Other than a snack if I happened to be in Asunción for the weekly farmers' market, *mbejú* was something that I associated with rural mornings. It was something I ate—and helped make—over a wood-fuelled cookfire in an outdoor kitchen for breakfast. While not an everyday breakfast, it was part of the regular rotation in the household where my research assistant and I stayed, accompanied by *cocido*—sweet, hot, mate tea—and maybe some cold, leftover boiled *mandioca* tubers from the day before. Sometimes an egg was cracked over the *mbejú* to add to the meal.

How to Make *Mbejú*

Equal amounts (by weight) butter (or lard) and cheese

Almidón equal to twice the amount (by weight) of cheese

Salt to taste

Milk or whey

Crumble the butter or lard, *almidón*, and salt together. Add a small amount of milk or whey until you get slightly larger, stickier crumbs. It will look dry, but will stay together when you press it into the pan.

Add a large handful of the dough to a greased, hot pan. Pat flat with your hand or with a spatula. Cook for about 10 minutes, until the cheese has melted enough to make it easy to lift the edges with a spoon or another utensil (you can put a lid over the *mbejú* while it is cooking if you prefer). Flip over to cook on the other side for a few minutes. Eat while warm.

If you want to add an egg, crack it on top of the *mbejú* and cover with a lid. Cook for a few more minutes, until the egg is the consistency you desire. Serve immediately.

Mbejú was in many ways a relational transaction—cooking, eating, and sharing it was about starting the day in a home atmosphere. Since *mbejú* was cooked in small batches, my research assistant and I would often sit around the fire in the outdoor kitchen in the mornings and help our host cook while engaging in quiet morning conversation. I learned to crumble the ingredients together, even when, in the early days, I was not entirely sure what they all were. We would cook for the household and for each other. Sometimes we would send some *mbejú* to our host's mother, who lived nearby and did not always cook for herself in the mornings. After, we would clean the dishes in cold water, a sharp contrast to the warmth of sitting around the hearth, and then we would go about the next tasks of the day.

Making and Eating *Chipa*

Chipa is ubiquitous in Paraguay, even understood as a national symbol.[25] Made with *queso Paraguayo*, maize flour, *almidón*, eggs, and lard (or butter), the bread is easy to find in urban areas. In the mornings and afternoons, *chipa* sellers can be found at bus stands and on buses, selling warm, fresh *chipa* from cloth-covered baskets. These sellers typically wear a shirt indicating the bakery (*chipería*) that made the *chipa*. The *chipa* itself may be in various shapes, with the most common being narrow, oblong pieces and round, bagel-shaped pieces. Sometimes when I was on the Universidad Nacional de Asunción campus, sellers would come to sell *chipa* to faculty, staff, and students around lunchtime or in the afternoons.

Unlike *mbejú*, *chipa* is something I largely associate with economic transactions. I have purchased *chipa* at stores, on buses, at highway-side bakeries on the way to or from Lindo Manantial, and from a small, home-based bakery while working in the village. It is a portable, convenient, and filling food. Although we sometimes made it at my host's house, the process was more complicated and time consuming than that for making *mbejú*. There are more ingredients, processing some of these ingredients takes time, and the *chipa* oven has to be prepared.

One sunny and cool day in late May during my first fieldwork year, my host decided that we would make *chipa*. This was during my first stay in the community, although I had visited several times as part of the project preparation. We set up a heavy wooden table for the work. First, dried maize kernels were sorted to discard the undesirable pieces. Then, the kernels were hand ground into flour. Some villagers grew their own maize, and cobs were hung to dry (Figure 7.1). My host explained to me that as a result of rainfall changes, her household did not typically grow their own maize anymore. Instead, she had purchased some from a neighbour. Each batch of maize had to be ground several times to get it to the desired consistency. The ground maize was then sifted through a sieve, separating the coarser pieces from the fine flour. My host and I alternated these tasks—grinding the maize was hard work and sifting the flour required attention to detail.

Once the maize flour was sifted, we poured it into a large plastic bowl and mixed it with the purchased *almidón*, the cheese, and the rest of the ingredients. Because my host made her own *queso Paraguayo*, she used whey as part of the recipe. With the addition of the whey, the mixture went from

FIGURE 7.1. Drying maize in a Lindo Manantial household. Photo by Elizabeth Finnis.

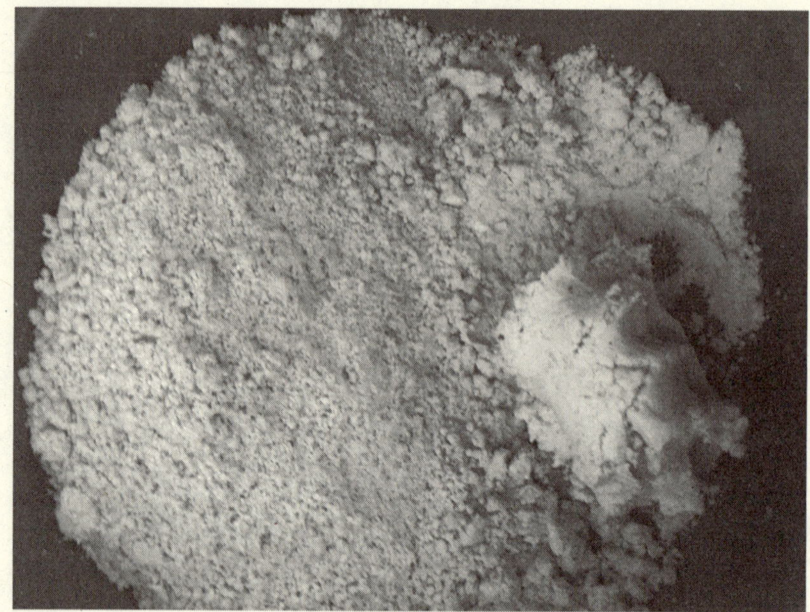

FIGURE 7.2. *Chipa* mixture, ready to shape. Photo by Elizabeth Finnis.

FIGURE 7.3. Different shapes of *chipa*. Photo by Elizabeth Finnis.

fine and crumbly (Figure 7.2) to wet enough to shape into individual pieces. We added a palmful of anise seed, and then we started the process of shaping the *chipa*. The children who had been hanging around came over to help. First, we shaped *chipa* into oblong pieces about five inches long, rolling each piece on the table to get the right shape and length. Each piece was placed on a banana-leaf-lined metal tray. Then, my host's mother showed me how to cut the pieces into the shape of birds (Figure 7.3). They looked delightful, but I was terrible at making the birds. We laughed about it, and I stuck with the basic oblong shape.

Then, the oven needed to be prepared. This was a wood-fired, brick structure, located under a simple but effective open-sided shelter. It did not look like the traditional half-circle *chipa* ovens, called *tatakúa*.[26] Instead, this was a large, rectangular brick oven. Trays of *chipa* were pushed into the oven and left to cook. I remember that there was a lot of anticipation while we waited for the finished product. The children were eager to eat the fresh treat, and I was excited to see how my first homemade *chipa* would turn out. It had taken us so long to prepare the bread—most of the afternoon—and we were all looking forward to the warmth of the *chipa* out of the oven. Even when it was cooked, we still needed to wait a few minutes for it to be cool enough to pick up. But the wait was worth it. Our *chipa* was warm and chewy, the flavour punctuated by the occasional taste of anise. It was delicious.

How to Make *Chipa*[27]

Approximately 500 grams *queso Paraguayo*[28]

Approximately 500 grams each *almidón* and maize flour

6 or 7 eggs, depending on size, beaten

Butter or lard, approximately 1 cup

Enough whey or milk to moisten dough enough to shape into dense pieces

Salt to taste

A palmful of anise seeds (optional)

Mix together the *almidón* and maize flour, and crumble in the cheese.

Add the butter or lard, crumbling it into the flour and cheese mix.

Add the beaten eggs and mix the dough by hand.

Add the whey or milk, a little at a time, until the consistency is enough to shape the dough. You may need slightly more or less than 1 cup.

Add some salt to taste.

Add anise seeds and mix into dough.

After the dough is thoroughly mixed, shape into equal-sized pieces, about 5 inches long. Alternatively, you can shape them into ovals.

Place on a baking tray and bake at approximately 400 Fahrenheit, about 30 minutes (this is an estimate and you may need to experiment!). You may need to check them after 20 minutes. This should make about 30 large pieces of *chipa* (but maybe more).

Mbejú, *Chipa*, Resources, and the Problem of *Almidón*

I only made *chipa* a handful of times. Although I often purchased it, in urban areas and sometimes in rural communities, homemade *chipa* was not a regular food during my fieldwork periods. There are plenty of reasons for this. One is the time it takes. The commitment to make *chipa* is significant and means setting aside other daily work, such as laundry, working in agricultural fields, and caring for animals. Grinding the maize down to flour takes time, and so does the cooking, requiring checks for doneness in an oven that does not have a consistent temperature. No one wanted the time and effort of making *chipa* to be wasted with a burnt batch! In her short article on *chipa* in Concepción District, Paraguay, Sanra Ritten points out that the effort it takes to make *chipa* means it makes sense to make many pieces in one sitting.[29] My host had a similar perspective. If you are going to take the time to hand grind and sift maize flour and get the oven fire going, you may as well cook many pieces that day. It is also true that all the *chipa* will get eaten. There will be no shortage of desire for multiple, fresh pieces, and unlike *mbejú*, *chipa* will keep and still be good (although not quite as good!) when it is cool, and into the next day. Large batches have another advantage: anyone who misses the fresh-out-of-the-oven *chipa*, perhaps because they are working or at school, will still be able get some later.

Chipa and *mbejú* also have some different resource signifiers, even though they are made from some overlapping core ingredients. With *chipa*, the need for maize flour and eggs, along with the larger amounts of the dish being made, adds financial cost to the bread. Cheese can be expensive to purchase, and being able to buy and look after the cows needed to make your own cheese is a considerable economic outlay. My host made her own cheese, selling some of it to other community members.[30] Her cows had been purchased with remittances sent by a son who worked in an urban centre. Having an oven also has resource implications, including the need to prepare enough wood for burning. In contrast, *mbejú* is less resource intensive, both in terms of supplies and time.

At the heart of both *chipa* and *mbejú* is an ingredient that raises questions and concerns: *almidón*. Neither can be made without this flour, which is also critical for other Paraguayan dishes. Community members talked about foods like *chipape* (small fried *chipa*), empanadas made with *almidón* dough, *chipa* with peanuts, and the use of *almidón* as a soup thickener as examples of the valued centrality of *almidón* in everyday cooking. Traditionally in the village, *almidón* was ground at local mills, using the *mandioca* that households grew in their own fields. These *mandioca* tubers would primarily be sold to mills as a source of income, but some of the flour would be reserved for household use. Daily life in this community is shaped around *mandioca* as food and *mandioca* as a crop. People would say, for example, that food was not food without *mandioca*, or that when there was no *mandioca* at a meal, it was missed. During my fieldwork seasons, we ate *mandioca* in some form (often whole tubers) with every meal. Children in the household would at times eat cold, leftover *mandioca* tubers as an after-school snack, sometimes dipped in honey. As my research partners and I have explored in detail elsewhere,[31] one of the realities of this is the tension between whole *mandioca* and *almidón*, and local and non-local foods.

With the closure of local mills, villagers had largely become reliant on purchased *almidón*. Aside from having to pay for it, the purchased *almidón* represented the unknown. Similar to Karine Gagné's discussion of local versus purchased flour in Zanskar, India (this volume), there are questions about the nature of purchased *almidón*. How was it produced? Under what conditions was it grown? What might it be contaminated with? How would this affect its quality? Concerns with the quality of Brazilian *almidón* were particularly salient. This product was described by community members as grittier and less tasty, which affected the quality of the cooking and the sensation of being full. People told me they knew that their *mandioca* had been grown without the use of pesticides. In contrast, they did not know how Brazilian *mandioca* was grown, or what this meant for the healthfulness of the *almidón* they bought. In this way, while foods like *chipa*, cooked in a wood-fired oven and made with the right ingredients, were still "authentic" Paraguayan food and much-loved, they were also a marker of concerns about quality, locality, and agricultural changes over time.

Thinking about Food and Reciprocity in Fieldwork Contexts

Food and relationship-building can emerge as central themes in our fieldwork notes and experiences, even if we are not necessarily studying issues around food production, livelihoods, or culinary practices (see Gagné, this volume, for example). And, as Penny Van Esterik (this volume) discusses, the eating and sharing of food can also highlight what we do not know or how we cannot reciprocate. In my case, I *was* in Paraguay to engage with issues around food production and consumption changes, and acts of cooking became both acts of reciprocity and important data collection and understanding events. Hands-on experiences with learning to prepare foods in the context of anthropological fieldwork can contribute to "culinary chats," kitchen-based conversations about food that can contribute to more than understandings of the cooking tasks at hand.[32] Understanding the processes behind food preparation or the reasons why certain tastes may be mobilized and served can allow researchers to understand broader issues or contexts.[33] For example, in their discussion of fieldwork in Niger, Paul Stoller and Cheryl Olkes demonstrate how the serving of bad sauces with unpleasant tastes can be a way for the cook to express social frustrations and power inequities.[34]

Learning to cook dishes like *chipa* and *mbejú* is also part of learning to recognize the "right" textures, tastes, and processes for recipes. These acts of learning can be understood as an aspect of an anthropology of the senses,[35] acts of participant observation that take into account the practical, everyday realties of food preparation and consumption. Michael Herzfeld has noted the difficulties of representing smells and tastes in anthropological work;[36] Stoller and Olkes have pointed to the importance of considering "tasteful fieldwork," where "the smells, tastes, and textures of the land, the people, and the food" are described and recorded alongside other, more traditional forms of data.[37] In the fieldwork context, *mbejú* represented to me a relatively quick breakfast with my host around a cookfire, and quiet companionship as we woke up and prepared for the work of the day amid the warmth of the fire and the smell of wood smoke; it represented one-on-one relationship building, tentative in the early days of the project and then reinforced in every fieldwork season. This was a more private, contained process, encompassed by the small space of the outdoor kitchen where we cooked and ate the dish. It is entirely possible that most community members did not come to know that I had learned how to help make *mbejú*, for others and myself.

Making *chipa* represented something different. In contrast to *mbejú*, I remember *chipa* as a cold process. We were working outside, and although some aspects of the work—like grinding corn kernels—were temporarily warming, standing outside and making piece after piece of *chipa* in the winter is chilly, if busy, work. More importantly, *chipa* was about effort and consistent busyness, excited children, and a palpable feeling of anticipation. It was a group activity, with different people wandering in and out of our temporary *chipería*. Throughout the process, people from neighbouring households stopped by for one reason or another, often commenting to my host about my willingness to work hard and my strength and endurance, even when it was clear that I was not particularly skilled at either grinding maize or shaping *chipa*. In this way, making *chipa* was a public practice: by participating in all the steps, I was signifying more than just my interest in learning about traditional foods, I was also inadvertently demonstrating my willingness to work hard in the pursuit of making food for other people. And in talking about my willingness to do the hard work and give the time associated with making *chipa*, not just partake in the fun "work" of eating it, people were articulating cultural values around hard work, social interactions, and the cooking of food for others.[38]

Concluding Thoughts

Fieldwork is about more than the data that we record—the interviews, the participant observation notes, the demographic data we collect, the community maps or kinship charts we might make, and so on. It is also an embodied experience,[39] about the senses, the everyday experiences of the "sensual aspects of . . . social life."[40] If we work to incorporate this into our writing, it can mean including considerations of tastes, sensations, and sounds rather than privileging only the written and the visual.[41] The inclusion of recipes, tastes, sensations, and the contexts of learning to cook in this chapter is my attempt to integrate aspects of the senses into research writing.

Cooking *chipa* and *mbejú*, and helping in the kitchen in general, became part of a repertoire of everyday acts of reciprocity, an exchange of labour and time, that helped me build relationships in the field. As previously mentioned, Van Esterik discusses the importance of grounding understandings of food systems in "learning by doing."[42] Although her discussion is focused on food activism, her point is also relevant in other food contexts. She asks, "How can we avoid taking discussions of food security and food sovereignty . . . to such a high level of abstraction that the links to local regimes . . . are obscured?" In my case, the processes of learning these recipes by doing them highlighted different social meanings and local regimes associated with foods and ingredients, while also making particularly salient the concerns that villagers were articulating about the loss of locally grown *almidón*. Sitting and listening with people, including "listening" through acts of cooking, helped me avoid overly abstract discussions of food sovereignty and changes to local food systems.[43] Instead, my understanding of these processes became grounded in part through the physicality and sociality of making these two breads. And as I have shown, the relationships and reciprocity that are associated with different foods are not just about learning the recipes but are also about the contexts of how and when these acts of cooking and learning are collectively performed. I therefore encourage fieldworkers, whether new or established, who engage in food-related research or not, to consider the ways that shared acts of making food can shape our understandings of everyday life and experience.[44]

Notes

1 These are not guarded, secret, or otherwise private recipes. Individual cooks add their own flair to the recipes, for example in terms of the relative amounts of different ingredients or flavourings added, but these dishes are part of the broader repertoire of Paraguayan foods made with core ingredients.

2 Messer, "Anthropological Perspectives on Diet"; and Mintz and DuBois, "The Anthropology of Food and Eating."

3 Phillips, "Food and Globalization."

4 Holtzman, "Food and Memory."

5 Sutton, "Food and the Senses."

6 Van Esterik, "Contemporary Trends in Infant Feeding Research."

7 Stone, "The Anthropology of Genetically Modified Crops."

8 Hayden and Villeneuve, "A Century of Feasting Studies."

9 Boas and Hunt, "Ethnology of the Kwakiutl"; Kuper, *The Anthropologists' Cookbook.*

10 For example, Wilk, *Home Cooking in the Global Village.*

11 Typically attributed to Boas, "Ethnology of the Kwakiutl" is also sometimes credited to Boas and Hunt. In recognition of the centrality of Hunt's research role in this work, I attribute the volume to both of them.

12 Codere, "Kwakiutl Society," 476.

13 Kuper, Preface to the Second Edition, in *The Anthropologists' Cookbook*, x.

14 Ibid., xii.

15 Koster, "From the Flocks."

16 Jackson, "Faroese Fare."

17 Ramiaramana, "Malagasy Cooking."

18 Monad-Becquelin, "Three Recipes from the Trumai Indians."

19 Wilk, *Home Cooking.*

20 Keesing and Strathern, *Cultural Anthropology: A Contemporary Perspective*, 8.

21 Van Esterik, "Food Praxis as Method," 119.

22 A pseudonym.

23 While the highway to Piribebuy District is good, the time it takes to get to the community can depend on the state of the side roads. These can be washed out after heavy rains, slowing down most methods of transportation.

24 For example, Finnis et al., "Agricultural and Dietary Meanings."

25 Ritten, "Making Chipas in Paraguay."

26 Ibid.

27 If you prefer clear measurements and smaller amounts, numerous *chipa* recipes can be found online, with variations in ingredients and approaches. Some recipes do not include maize flour, which was key to the *chipa* I helped make, while others include baking powder as a rising agent. Some versions use peanut flour as part of the dry ingredients, others omit the anise. And there are national variations of this *almidón*-based, cheesy bread, for example in Brazil and Argentina. The *chipa* and *mbejú* recipes that I include in this chapter are the result of participant observation and therefore reflect the individual flair, experience, and preferences of my host and her family. In addition, because she made and sold cheese, she owned a food scale. Her baking therefore tended to use weights of ingredients, rather than other measures.

28 Although not the perfect substitute, mozzarella or feta can be used; you can also experiment with other cheeses such as an aged cheddar. If the cheese you choose cannot be crumbled by hand, it will need to be grated.

29 Ritten, "Making Chipas in Paraguay."

30 She would sell (locally) one kilogram of cheese for 10,000 Paraguayan guaraní (which at the time was approximately two Canadian dollars).

31 Finnis et al., "Agricultural and Dietary Meanings of *Mandioca*."

32 Miller and Deutsch, *Food Studies*, 8.

33 Ibid.

34 Stoller and Olkes, "The Taste of Ethnographic Things."

35 Herzfeld, "Senses."

36 Ibid.

37 Stoller and Olkes, "The Taste of Ethnographic Things," 412.

38 Karrebaek, Riley, and Cavanaugh, "Food and Language."

39 Madden, *Being Ethnographic*.

40 Stoller, *The Taste of Ethnographic Things*, 7.

41 Ibid., 9.

42 Van Esterik, "Food Praxis as Method," 119.

43 Stoller, *The Taste of Ethnographic Things*, 128.

44 I am grateful to everyone in Lindo Manantial for welcoming me into their community and their homes. I also wish to thank my Paraguayan research partners Clotilde Benitez, Fatima Candia, Maria Jose Aparicio Meza, Domitila Pereira, Sasha Planas, Noelia Rios, and Daniela Aguero Gomez. This research was funded by the Social Sciences and Humanities Research Council of Canada.

CHAPTER 8

Preparing Rice in Contemporary Japan

Satsuki Kawano

The importance of rice in Japanese foodways has been well documented.[1] Nevertheless, analyzing the continuities and discontinuities of patterns of rice preparation and consumption still provides insights into the persistent cultural importance of rice as well as changes in Japanese society. In this chapter, I explore rice as a significant cultural resource for nourishment through which an enduring sense of Japaneseness and reciprocal relations are enacted.

The findings that I share in this chapter come from my fieldwork on the marketing of rice cookers in 2019 in urban and rural areas, and from more than two decades of anthropological research in urban Japan that focused on diverse themes such as family, religion, aging, ancestor worship and death rites, and childrearing. Though rice was not the main focus of the majority of these projects, my fieldnotes revealed the centrality of rice in (re)shaping a sense of Japaneseness as well as in reciprocal family relations involving children, mothers, seniors, and ancestors. As a Japanese researcher brought up in urban Japan, I also share my personal experiences of rice preparation and consumption.

I begin with how cooking rice constitutes cultural competence. Though Japan is known for a wide circulation of printed recipe books and online culinary sites, rice preparation is often assumed to be naturally learned in daily life and takes an embodied form of "recipe" that is transmitted orally and through practice. People often learn to cook rice by observing and working with their mother or grandmother, and steamed rice is regularly shared by co-resident family members. Rice preparation, therefore, is part of reciprocal family relations.

I then describe how the narratives on the tastes of rice and its patterns of consumption reflect status and identity differences among citizens. White rice consumption became the standard in postwar Japan, signifying the rapidly expanding middle-class urban lifestyle, while the alternative practice of mixing rice and other grains was devalued and tied to a rural way of life. Class and regional differences shaped the manners of sharing homemade rice with guests, and thus an analysis of consuming rice in a complex society such as Japan is incomplete without paying attention to these variations.

Finally, I explore contemporary patterns of rice preparation and consumption by paying special attention to the ages of consumers, the meanings of homemade rice, the availability of socially appropriate alternatives, and technological innovations. Informants noted that homemade rice is considered necessary for certain meals and groups (e.g., school lunches), while delineating what appropriate alternatives (bread, ready-to-eat packaged rice, and store-bought meals) exist. In addition, technological advances have produced diverse rice cookers to serve an increasing number of single people and older couples living away from other kin, while the most advanced rice cookers attempt to recreate the "traditional" method of cooking rice in an old-fashioned metal pot on a wood stove. Thus, I illustrate that the preparation and sharing of rice not only provide a window onto people's changing foodways and lifestyles, but that these culinary processes also constitute a rich cultural resource through which people (re)make their identities and reciprocal relations.

Preparing and Consuming Rice Properly

In my daily life, a recipe is a recorded set of directions found in a cookbook or on a website, and it consists of the types of ingredients and their amounts, a series of written instructions to follow, and possibly a collection of pictures that accompany the stages of preparation. Yet prior to my attempt here to examine the process of rice preparation as a recipe, it never even occurred to me to look for one for steaming rice. As a native Japanese woman brought up

FIGURE 8.1. Polished Japanese rice and a special measuring cup. Photo Credit: Satsuki Kawano.

in urban Japan, thinking about how to steam rice in a Japanese way made me reflect on my own assumptions about what a "recipe" for cooking rice involves.

The aptitude for cooking rice properly is transmitted orally and by demonstration. Yasuda-san, an older woman living in a small town in central Japan, noted that the art of steaming rice properly was acquired naturally while taking part in everyday life. I also do not recall when I learned or who taught me how to steam rice properly; presumably my own mother or a co-resident grandmother taught me. A woman in her forties told me, "My grandmother taught me how to steam rice when I was about ten years old. I remember that the rice that I cooked for the first time was really tasty." She was proud of her accomplishment, and the steamed rice was shared with the other family members that evening. Therefore, the oral recipe for steaming rice as well as the product of labour were both shared within the household. "Eating from the same pot of rice" is a Japanese proverb that denotes a sense of solidarity that stems from routinely sharing rice in a household.

This knowledge of steaming rice is typically gendered, particularly among older generations. An older man who started cooking in his sixties remembers that his wife taught him how to cook rice, indicating the gendered division of labour. Similarly, a woman in her early fifties noted that her husband did not know how to cook rice when they got married. During an interview, she commented on her husband's pitiable existence before marriage; he had been living on boxed meals purchased at a convenience store. He had not been part of common reciprocal relations expected in a family for ten years.

I looked through several Japanese cookbooks that I own and found a recipe for steaming rice in the cookbook that a relative of mine had helped to create.[2] Though I have had the cookbook for at least thirty years and have used a number of the recipes, I do not recall ever looking at the one for steaming rice. The cookbook was designed specifically for those who purchased "no-water" cooking pots (*musui nabe*). Sold by the company that once employed my relative, these pots require much less water than a typical pot. Other middle-class families used electric rice cookers, which became widely available during the 1960s. Yet my family always used the no-water pot over a gas stove to cook rice, believing that doing so produced much tastier rice.

How to Cook Rice

The recipe from my relative's cookbook is only a few lines long and is combined with three other types of rice recipes (red rice mixed with beans, steamed brown rice, and sushi rice). [3]

Wash rice grains and add water (between 110 and 120 percent of the volume of rice). Leave the mixture alone for 30 to 60 minutes.

Start with medium heat. When it begins to boil, let the rice steam for 1 or 2 minutes, and then lower the heat. Wait for 10 to 15 minutes. Then turn off the heat.

Leave the rice steaming for 10 minutes, and then uncover.

Considering that steamed rice is deemed essential in Japanese meals and people frequently discuss whether the rice tastes good or bad, this description provides the bare minimum. The above recipe is also missing some important steps that should be taken before steaming. The brevity and the omitted steps indicate what goes without saying: the taken-for-granted knowledge of cooking rice that is not deemed to require detailed explanations.

In Japan, rice grains are measured by using the units of *gō* and *shō* (one *shō* equals ten *gō*). A special cup (one *go,* or 180 ml) is used for measuring rice and rice wine (see Figure 8.1), though there is also a regular measuring cup for cooking (200 ml). Each *gō* of rice makes two bowls of steamed rice. The unit of *gō* belonged to the measurement system used widely during the Edo period (spanning the sixteenth century to the middle of the nineteenth century), when rice served the role of currency, along with gold and silver. The salaries of samurai warriors who served in the regional and central governments during the Edo period were indicated by the volume of rice. In 1959, the metric system was adopted in Japan,[4] but today rice is still measured using the units of *gō* and *shō*.

Washing rice is important. When explaining the process of preparing rice, informants stressed the significance of aesthetics and sensory experiences. For example, when one first pours cold water into the pot with grains of rice, the water quickly becomes whitish (*shiroku nigoru*), and after mixing the water with rice quickly, the water is discarded and the process is repeated. When the grains are rubbed together with bare fingers, it makes a pronounced rattling noise, similar to the sound that a bag of small dried beans might make. As a child, I used to hear the sound of washing rice that my grandmother made. In winter, washing rice in cold water hurts one's fingers, but warm water should not be used. The task of washing rice is complete once the water is beautifully clear. In contemporary Japan, there are "no-wash rice grains" (*musen mai*). However, as an informant told me, "It feels unsettling (*kimochi warui*) if one does not wash rice with fingers by rubbing them together and does not hear the rattling noise."

Many taboos are involved in rice preparation. One woman recalled that she was criticized whenever the water was left slightly opaque after washing. Though people provided explanations of how breaking taboos led to unsuccessful cooking—for example, interrupting or not completing washing makes the rice smell and taste bad—they more so emphasized the importance of adhering to the appropriate procedure by communicating sensory knowledge and its affective significance. Food collects people's bodies, ideas, memories, and relationships, so learning to cook a valued food means that the learner becomes socialized into a culturally specific way of being in the world (see Elizabeth Finnis, this volume, for a similar point and the implications of learning to cook mundane and special foods during fieldwork).

Cooking rice properly in Japan is often discussed by highlighting the importance of making proper adjustments (*kagen*). Once rice is washed, the right amount of water for cooking is added to the pot. The previous recipe stipulates an amount of water ranging between 110 and 120 percent of the volume of rice for steaming. People may measure the amount of water by using the special measuring cup, using internal lines in a Japanese electric rice cooker, or placing their palm on washed rice in a pot to check the water level on their wrist. The amount of water should be adjusted depending on when the rice was harvested. For example, freshly harvested rice (*shinmai*) in the fall does not require as much water, as the rice grains are still moist. Washed rice is left to soak in the water for at least half an hour or an hour before cooking, as also suggested by the recipe discussed above. If the soaking period is too short, the cooked rice will be hard and taste bad.

The recipe in my cookbook also highlights the importance of adjusting the heat appropriately during the course of steaming. The aforementioned recipe more or less follows an old saying that is widely considered to capture the "traditional" way of cooking rice on a wood stove, which focuses entirely on the adjustments of heat levels while steaming:

Hajime chorochoro	First start with low heat
Naka pappa	Then turn up the heat
Jūjū fuitara	When the content begins to boil and spill over
Hi o hiite	"Pull" or lower the heat
Warashibe hitotaba kubemashite	Add a bundle of straw [which would bring up the heat]
Akago naitemo futa toruna	Do not take the lid away even if a baby cries [keep the lid closed for steaming]

My mother shared this saying with me long time ago, and she believes it came from her own mother. There are variations, and one version is significantly shorter, consisting only of the first two lines and the last line. My mother's version lacked the second-to-last line about adding a bundle of straw. Given that my mother has never cooked rice on a wood stove, that omission is not surprising. Nonetheless, it is noteworthy that this saying is still used to evoke the "traditional Japanese" way, as none of my informants actually had the experience of steaming rice on a wood stove.

The last line of the saying, "Do not take the lid away even if a baby cries," is well known. When discussing the meaning of this line, a woman explained that a crying baby takes a cook's attention away, but one should stay focused on the steps to be followed. Opening the lid lowers the temperature, and rice will not turn out well if the internal temperature is not maintained, yet the effect of opening the lid on the taste of rice is not mentioned in the saying. Interestingly, there is a taboo against checking how rice is coming along during the entire process of steaming, though the saying only makes note of this at the last stage of cooking. The written recipe for steaming rice that I discussed earlier lacks all these prohibitions, illustrating the taken-for-granted cultural competence assumed to exist in those who are steaming rice.

Beyond the process of preparing and steaming rice, the manner of eating rice also involves a number of proper steps and taboos. When eating steamed rice in a rice bowl, one needs to learn how to pick up and hold the bowl, take up and put down chopsticks, and eat all the rice grains. Japanese children are scolded if there are unfinished grains of rice in their bowls and are urged to learn to pick up even the last grain of rice. They are praised for having eaten rice completely through use of the phrase "eaten completely in a beautiful or clean way (*kirei ni zenbu tabeta*)." Children are sometimes reminded that in a single grain of rice there are seven deities, and it should thus not be wasted. This idea of deities residing in each grain of rice conveys the sacredness of this food that demands special attention and respect.

Historically, rice has been a culturally and ritually significant plant in Japan.[5] Rice has been central to Shinto rituals, though the everyday practice of consuming (white) rice regularly on its own, rather than having it mixed with other grains, did not become widely established until the 1950s or 1960s.[6]

When I visited a Shinto shrine in northern Japan in 2019, I learned that in the coming November Emperor Reiwa was scheduled to perform his first Shinto ritual (*daijōsai*) involving an offering of rice to the Sun Goddess. The priest gave me a copy of the newsletter he published for his parishioners, which discussed the role of rice in the reciprocal relations between the Japanese imperial family and the Sun Goddess as well as those between the deity and parishioners. On the first page of the newsletter, it stated, "In our country, the Sun Goddess gave us the gift of the rice plant and we started cultivating rice. . . . We grow rice, offer the harvest at the altar, and then appreciate receiving and consuming that leftover." The priest of the shrine noted that during the upcoming ritual cooked white rice would be offered at the ceremonial altar and then consumed by the emperor, indicating the divine-emperor commensality.

Though contemporary consumers do not necessarily think of the meaning of rice in Shinto or imperial rituals when they consume rice in daily life, rice is still special in subtle ways. The taboos that surround the preparation of rice are not only concerned with producing tastier rice but also denote the moral status of those preparing the rice and the importance of doing it properly. Moreover, cooking rice in a Japanese way is embodied knowledge. The wisdom of proper rice preparation is transmitted orally and through the sharing of aesthetic and sensory facets of cooking and tasting experiences within households.

Preference for White Rice: The Production of Status and Identity Differences

My older informants related their experiences of rice preparation and consumption to good and bad memories of their childhood and changing domestic and social circumstances over their life course. In recounting times when rice tasted terrible as well as when it was splendid, seniors discussed their preference for white rice and its association with urban affluence and a middle-class standard along with their disapproval of the mixture of rice and other grains.

Interestingly, when asked about when they began eating rice regularly for meals, senior informants noted how bad the mix of rice and barley tasted after the war. Born in the late 1930s, Miyako-san survived the period of extreme scarcity and saw the nation's rapid recovery and later years of affluence in the postwar period. He noted, "We didn't have white rice after the war. I was staying with my mother's relatives during the war period, and all we had was barley, millet, and *hie* (barnyard millet). I guess *hie* was given to animals. Foxtail millet (*awa*) cakes were good, but *hie* was terrible. After that we ate white rice mixed with barley for several years."

Another informant in her eighties also recalled the time after the war, when rice mixed with barley "tasted horrible." She stated: "Japan lost the war, and we didn't have white rice anymore. Foxtail millet was tasty, but we had barley or sorghum mixed with rice. I grew up eating white rice, so I really disliked the barley mix. The barley bothered my tongue (*shita ni sawaru*) as it was rough. When I was seven years old, I remember asking my mother to give me just a cup of white rice, rather than two cups of barley mixed with rice. My mother was at a loss what to say, as she didn't have enough rice for the family." The tastiest rice that she had was during this period of deprivation. She told me, "There was a wealthy farming family living across from our residence. The family had an ancestral veneration ritual, and *totally pure white* rice was served with roasted sheets of seaweed. I still clearly remember that it was amazingly tasty." The steamed rice was especially delicious, as white rice was highly valued but largely unavailable during this period. In addition, she had grown up eating white rice—consuming the barley mix daily contradicted her family's urban middle-class identity. In her account, she emphasized the colour difference by comparing the "dark" barley mix with "totally pure white" rice. Other informants were also unenthusiastic when they made note of the "blackish" (*kuroppoi*) colour of the barley mix.

Rice mixed with other grains was devalued among urban Tokyo residents as early as the 1910s,[7] and the barley mix was increasingly associated with poverty and deemed below a socially expected standard in a number of studies on farming and lifestyle conducted during the 1920s and 1930s.[8] By the early 1920s, many urban residents in poverty were also adopting white rice as the staple.[9] In rural areas, mixing rice with other grains continued, but the practice was also considered distasteful there by the 1930s. Embree's classic ethnography of a rural village in southern Japan conducted during the interwar period indicates that villagers mixed barley and wheat with rice, but it was considered unpalatable and not offered to guests.[10] During the late 1950s, villagers in Okayama were still reportedly eating rice mixed with barley,[11] though the consumption of white rice clearly indicated the prominence of a middle-class, urban lifestyle. Regularly eating white rice was a performance of distinction.[12] Informants' recollections of the "poor-quality" rice mixed with other grains thus show the ways in which status and regional differences were made through rice consumption during the 1950s.

Rice today is a crucial part of the traditional Japanese cuisine known as *washoku*, which has been added to the UNESCO Representative List of the Intangible Cultural Heritage of Humanity.[13] Nonetheless, regular consumption of rice is a relatively recent phenomenon in Japanese history.[14] Anthropologist and food studies scholar Katarzyna Cwiertka notes that the "traditional Japanese" cuisine consisting of steamed rice, miso soup, and side dishes registered with the UNESCO list does not reflect Japan's pre-industrial heritage.[15] It was during the 1950s and 1960s that this "traditional" diet became regularly available, "when improving living standards . . . made it possible for all Japanese to indulge in the luxury of eating rice at every meal." White rice, taken for granted in today's Japan, was a sign of consumers' privilege until quite recently.

In addition to how white rice was eaten, the manner around serving rice also signified status and identity differences. The following episode reveals how a host and a guest each had different local expectations regarding sharing rice. An older woman recalled that her husband's cousin came from the countryside to stay with them when they were newlyweds. The cousin asked for a third serving of rice, but she did not have any more to serve the guest. She learned through her marriage, though, that impressing a guest with an abundance of steamed rice was considered an appropriate "rural" quality. The host may not have other foods but should at least offer plenty of rice to guests. She continued, "My family was used to urban ways, and we did not have the custom of making a huge amount of steamed rice for guests. I did not realize that it was so important in my husband's hometown to prepare so much rice that one cannot possibly run out of rice for guests. Our way was more sophisticated—to offer the right amount of rice to guests." When entertaining guests in an urban middle-class setting in postwar Japan, the emphasis lay on the quality of food rather than its volume. Each guest was typically offered a separate serving dish with an individually wrapped sweet.[16] Among rural or working-class families, however, guests were urged to consume a lot, and hosts casually shared crackers and sweets from large serving dishes on the table. During my fieldwork in 1995, an informant and his colleagues recounted being served a massive amount of cold wheat noodles in a bucket-like container for them to share when they landscaped a large garden for an affluent rural family. It was rude to leave the meal unfinished, so they quickly dug a hole in the ground, buried the uneaten noodles, and thanked the client. The previously mentioned informant from an urban middle-class family thus faced a rural subculture when her partner's relative asked for the third serving, taking the availability of an abundance of cooked rice for granted. In this way, not only the type of rice eaten but also the manner of serving rice registered identity distinctions in postwar Japan.

The Cultural Logic of Homemade Rice Preparation and Consumption in Contemporary Japan

In both Tokyo and in a provincial city in northern Japan, informants discussed situations in which homemade rice is necessary or optional. Their accounts illuminated how the culturally constructed need to prepare rice and its meaning as food are embedded in age-specific, gendered relations among family members. Furthermore, informants linked their need to prepare homemade rice to the availability of socially acceptable alternatives at and away from home, such as bread, hot lunches served at school, and store-bought meals.

Children and school lunches: I was told repeatedly that people steam white rice daily in households with children, particularly those in middle and high schools. One woman told me, "During the period when my children were in middle and high school, I cooked rice every morning, because we needed rice for their lunches (*obentō*)." Middle and high schools in Japan usually require students to bring their own lunches, as they typically lack both a kitchen and a cafeteria. However, Japanese public grade schools are required to have a kitchen and serve hot lunches on-site. As a result, homemade rice for lunches is not needed for children in elementary schools. The informant continued, "When my children were in elementary school, they had hot lunches (*kyūshoku*) served at their schools. So, I didn't need to cook rice every morning. We cooked rice, for example, in the evening for the family meal." Another woman in her fifties, who lived with her mother, spouse, and two co-resident unmarried adult children in a provincial city in northern Japan, also explained that she does not cook rice every morning for her own family, as she no longer makes lunches for her daughters. She has rice once a day or so, as she usually has toast for breakfast.

Steamed white rice is typically considered "necessary" for a child's lunch every day, though no such rules exist at school. The unspoken cultural convention is that a child's lunch consists of steamed rice and side dishes. Other starchy foods, such as potatoes and pasta, are not considered culturally equivalent to or a replacement for steamed rice. Potatoes or pasta may be served as a side dish in addition to steamed rice. Common side dishes include a few pieces of sliced egg omelet, stir-fried sliced meat or sausages, steamed or sautéed vegetables, fried chicken, meatballs, and sliced fish cakes.

Once in a while, sandwiches may be given in children's lunches, but this is an exception. Bread came to the urban Japanese middle class during the early twentieth century and was adopted for Sunday breakfasts, indicating "status and style."[17] Today bread is widely consumed by people in diverse classes and regions, and there are even high-status expensive bakeries, often with complicated French names. These stores are extremely popular among the middle class. Meanwhile, domestic mass-produced ordinary (white) bread is also widely available. *Shokupan*, or sliced, fluffy white toasting bread, is extremely inexpensive. The popularity of bread for breakfast among a wide range of groups in both Tokyo and northern Japan indicates the cultural appropriateness of bread for certain meals, though this does not imply that bread is an acceptable replacement for steamed rice in other meals. People sometimes commented that bread was not quite adequate for school lunches, as it does not keep one feeling full for a sufficient period of time. This point was made by using the expression *hara mochi ga ii* (food that sustains one's stomach well). Rice is deemed heavy and sustaining, preventing one from feeling hungry shortly after a meal. This point was specifically made in relation to children who were in school athletic clubs, as they tend to become hungry quickly. Unlike bread, steamed rice was considered to give people more power and energy.[18] The "need" for rice in children's lunches, therefore, was in part shaped by the cultural classification of certain foods as filling.

Homemade rice and mothering: The "necessity" of steamed rice for school lunches is not only tied to the idea of rice as filling but is also linked to the gendered ideal of nourishing children daily through the sharing of homemade rice within the household. An informant stated that it was particularly stigmatizing to buy bread regularly for lunches when she was in middle school. She told me, "My private school had a small store that sold different types of bread and sandwiches. The store was mainly for those who did not or could not bring homemade lunches, and it was pitiable for someone to purchase bread for lunch every day. It indicated that no one made lunches for the student." Buying bread at a store all the time signalled a lack of reciprocity and mothering within the household. This example also highlights the power of homemade rice that nurtures children. Anthropologist Anne Allison observes how homemade *obentō* serves as the state's apparatus; *obentō* preparation is imposed upon mothers through the state's educational framework.[19] Given the state-sanctioned ideal of nurturing children through school lunches and the cultural meaning of homemade rice, it makes sense that students who need to purchase lunches regularly are seen as pitiable.

A middle school student who is forced to buy bread for lunch when no family member makes *obentō* for them, however, is different from a university student who can easily find a school cafeteria or convenience store. University students face no stigma when they purchase lunches. As such, educational institutions powerfully shape the patterns and frequency of rice preparation at home, while indirectly supporting the deservedness of a certain age group to regularly consume homemade rice.

Seniors and vacuum-packed rice: In contrast to middle and high school students, who are expected to be nourished daily by consuming homemade rice, seniors limit their preparation of homemade rice and use alternatives.

Informants in a provincial city as well as in Tokyo told me that seniors today enjoy bread and coffee in the morning. Given the social acceptance of bread noted earlier, a senior consuming bread at home for lunch is not stigmatized if this simply indicates the person's dietary preference. Therefore, "having bread for a meal" must be understood according to the context in which it is consumed.

Tanaka-san, who lives in a provincial city known for rice production, told me, "Older people cook rice less often than those with children. They do not eat very much, and the leftover rice goes bad. They buy rice at a convenience store. They also have vacuum-packed rice, which does not go bad." I was intrigued by her comment, as many families in the area of her residence are rice farmers, though she is not from a farming family and lives in the centre of town rather than near farm fields. The consumption of rice may be different in older persons living in farming families, but unfortunately, I did not have a chance to interview them.

The trends of infrequent rice preparation, the use of purchased rice dishes, and the adoption of bread for breakfast that Tanaka-san described are true for many seniors living in urban areas. One couple told me that they only cook rice twice a week, and that bread is commonly consumed for breakfast. The wife told me, "They sell a package of freshly steamed white rice at a supermarket nearby, but we never buy it. It's silly to pay for that; you can just make white rice at home. Yet we sometimes buy rice dishes, such as sushi [rolls and *inari*, sushi rice packed in stewed fried tofu]." The couple also noted that they always have a supply of vacuum-packed rice at home. According to the wife, "They last forever, and we have these packages for emergencies and when we do not want to cook rice." Her husband needs to go to a hospital in a nearby city every month and stays with his adult child. The night before his departure, they do not want to make a new pot of rice, which typically lasts for a few days, because the wife does not need so much rice while her husband is away. It then makes sense for them to share a package of vacuum-packed rice. Each package consists of steamed rice made from approximately one *gō* of rice. They share the package, each having a bowl of rice with their meal.

Consuming store-bought rice dishes: Forgoing the preparation of steamed rice at home is common in various age groups. Supermarkets, takeout shops, and convenience stores carry steamed rice, rice dishes, and a large collection of *obentō*, or packaged meal boxes, which often consist of steamed white rice and side dishes. Convenience stores typically boast several shelves of rice balls with various toppings, sushi rolls, fried rice, and so on, though these are not considered healthy choices. One woman in her fifties told me, "The rice balls bought at convenience stores do not go bad," indicating that significant levels of preservatives are used in these products. Rice balls sold at convenience stores use steamed rice dipped in oil to prevent them from hardening when they are kept refrigerated. These prepared rice dishes are extremely popular, and an analysis of rice cooking in households does not necessarily predict how many rice and rice-based dishes each person consumes daily.

Unlike the barley mixture discussed earlier, store-bought rice was never described by participants as tasting terrible. Interestingly, however, some told me that packaged rice "tastes just fine" and seemed to defend their use of the product. Nevertheless, vacuum-packed rice is not necessarily considered a replacement for homemade rice for ritual purposes. When participants discussed ancestor veneration, I asked if vacuum-packed rice is ever offered at the ancestral altar. Ancestors are supposed to receive freshly steamed rice. One informant responded, "No. My [deceased] father [enshrined at the altar] would be annoyed and say, 'how lazy (*tenuki*).'" The expression *tenuki* literally means to pull out one's hands; it is the opposite of *te o kakeru*, to use your hands extensively and meticulously to produce something valuable. Though the prepackaged rice "tastes fine," it was not considered a suitable offering by this informant. It is intriguing that using a computerized rice cooker (discussed below) is widely acceptable for steaming rice for the living and the dead, despite the machine managing most of the human labour required to adjust the heat levels appropriately. Manufactured by non-kin at a factory, vacuum-packaged rice may be an unfitting offering because it takes no effort on the part of descendants. Ancestors are thought to watch over the living and ensure their well-being, while in return, descendants are expected to show their gratitude and nourish their ancestors by making offerings. Rice offerings thus speak to the reciprocal relationship between ancestors and descendants. Who prepares the rice, therefore, partly determines the quality and meaning of the valued staple.

Several authors in this volume indicate that people expressed their concerns regarding the quality and meanings of foods and their negative impact on well-being when they switched from home-grown grains to imported or non-local ones (for example, see Gagné, this volume, and Finnis, this volume). Reclaiming Indigenous foods is also seen to promote healing, given the prevalence of unhealthy "colonized carbohydrates" associated with the influences of powerful outsiders in Indigenous communities (see Phillipps and Skinner, and Neufeld, this volume). Though the contexts of these studies differ, anonymity and outside influences that surround food sourcing and processing seem to cause unsettling feelings. In Japan, too, despite the widespread acceptance of purchased rice dishes, these are perceived to qualitatively differ from homemade rice.

In sum, analyzing contemporary rice consumption reveals the cultural logic that makes the preparation of homemade rice "necessary" and its alternatives socially appropriate for certain meals and age groups. I did not discover a linear change, in which older people stick with a rice-based diet and younger people prefer an alternative staple. Rather, informants' accounts show that the culturally constructed need for homemade rice is deeply tied to the meanings of rice embedded in reciprocal care relations.

Contemporary Rice Cookers as Reflections of Cultural Continuities and Social Change

My fieldwork on the marketing of rice cookers, conducted at large electronic stores in 2019, revealed two major trends: traditionalization and diversification. On the one hand, expensive computerized rice cookers were marketed by emphasizing how consumers could easily recreate the "traditional" taste of rice cooked on a wood stove by taking advantage of the latest Japanese technology. On the other hand, inexpensive small rice cookers were advertised to attract a growing number of single people and older couples living on their own, reflecting Japan's contemporary social and demographic trends.

One sunny day in late June, I visited a large electronics store in northern Japan with another anthropologist. I was visiting his field site, as I was interested in contextualizing my data collected in Tokyo. The massive electronics store, set in a suburban mall in a small city, stood near several other stores and well-known chain restaurants along a major road. The shop boasted several aisles of rice steamers of all sizes and prices. I was struck by the prices of high-end rice cookers, ranging from $1,250 to $5,000 (CAD). These products were prominently advertised at the ends of shelves to catch the attention of passersby. When we saw this collection, the anthropologist who had accompanied me to the store, who had doubted that there were such expensive models in his field site, finally believed my claim that some steamers cost as much as $1,250—or more. His reaction made me wonder how commonly these pricy models were purchased in this area.

These costly models were marketed by using the image of rice as an essential Japanese food. For example, one video advertisement stated that "Japan is a nation of rice" (*Nihon wa okome no kuni*). Though no mention was made of Shinto or the emperor, this phrase easily reminded me of the Shinto priest who wrote about Japan as a country of rice in his newsletter for parishioners in 2019. At the electronics store, without referring to that religious idea, rice was still presented as the primordial Japanese food.

The advertisements for high-end products strongly emphasized the "uniquely Japanese" way of preparing rice by using a photo of an old-fashioned metal pot (*kama*) and the blaze of a wood stove. This *kama* image was featured in the pamphlets developed by four major manufacturers of rice cookers; one pamphlet reads, "By returning to the basics, we discovered a new method of steaming rice . . . in the old-fashioned stove, fire burns vigorously, and the moving flame touches the bottom of the stove . . . this creates an energetic dance of rice grains, steaming each grain to achieve the perfect degree of fullness." Another advertisement showed the inner pot of the rice cooker, which was actually shaped like an old-fashioned *kama* pot, though there is no functional need to shape the pot in such a way.

I found this image of cooking rice in a *kama* metal pot on a wood stove all the more interesting given that none of my informants had actually ever had the experience of cooking rice with that method. An older woman, when asked if her mother, born in the early 1910s, ever cooked rice on a wood stove, told me, "I doubt it. Maybe in rural areas people might have had a wood stove then." Even though the actual experiential knowledge of cooking rice in a *kama* pot over a wood stove has been largely lost, this "traditional" image was used to validate the efficacy of some of the most sophisticated and costly contemporary rice cookers enabled by Japan's advanced technology.

It is worth noting that several advertisements cited the old-fashioned saying, or what may be called an oral recipe, that I introduced earlier in this chapter (*Hajime chorochoro / Naka pappa* [First start with low heat / Then turn up the heat]). In one pamphlet, the process of steaming rice described by this saying was mapped onto the steps involved in the computerized program that automatically adjusts the temperature perfectly. The advertisement displayed how the traditional wisdom of cooking rice, including the use of a bundle of straw, was easily managed by the machine. In this way, the old-fashioned saying was used to traditionalize and validate the Japaneseness of mechanized rice preparation.

Several advertisements featured an image of a male artisan. In one advertisement, the artisan was making rice with a *kama* pot over a wood stove, indicating that his skills are applied through the computerized program embedded in the product. Phrases such as "by hand," "cooked carefully," and "each grain is steamed" were employed, as if the manufacturers needed to humanize the mechanized cooking process and assert the cultural authenticity of the steamed rice produced by these machines. The emphasis placed on the careful manual labour in making tasty rice in these advertisements made me reflect on the earlier discussion on the "lack of work by hand" that vacuum-packaged rice represented. Each advertisement displayed a photograph of stunningly shiny, freshly steamed white rice, indicating the result of skilled work.

The high-end rice cookers, however, constituted only a small portion of the displayed models—the majority were family-friendly, medium-priced ones in the rage of 20,000 to 30,000 yen ($250 to $375), accommodating either five or ten *gō* of rice. These rice cookers typically came with the function of timer-based steaming. People can wash and place rice in the machine in the morning and have steamed rice ready when they come home from work, or they can set the timer in the evening and have rice ready in the morning for breakfast. Some of the models had a setting for brown rice, indicating the recent popularity of brown rice among health-conscious consumers.

Then there were some inexpensive, small cookers for around 10,000 yen ($125). The cheapest one cost 7,000 yen and only had space for two *gō* of rice. The advertisement for this model showed a single woman opening the rice cooker, a middle-aged man living away from family because of corporate transfer (*tanshin funin*), and an older couple having a meal together. In 2015 approximately one in three Japanese women and one in two Japanese men between the ages thirty and thirty-four were unmarried.[20] Among those between ages thirty-five and thirty-nine, approximately one in four women and one in three men remained unmarried. Though not all of these single people live away from their families, they constitute a major group of consumers. Salaried workers on corporate transfers, who are likely to be middle-aged married men, are another category of those living alone. Japanese companies often transfer their employees to different locations every few years, and sometimes their spouses and children do not move with them because of, for example, their child's education, the spouse's employment, or the need to care for aging parents living near the original residence. The last group of potential consumers of small rice cookers consists of older couples. In 1990, 36.3 percent of Japanese households that included those over age sixty-five consisted of either couple-only or single-person households, while the figure in 2015 was 57.8 percent.[21] Meanwhile, the percentage of three-generation households declined from 45.9 to 12.2 percent during the same period. The increasing number of smaller households and contemporary patterns of employment have therefore shaped the diversification of rice cookers on the market.

In sum, rice cooker advertisements not only convey the changing patterns of rice preparation in smaller households but also mobilize images of the "traditional" wood stove and a metal *kama* pot to promote the latest rice cookers. Technological innovations are not associated with the loss of Japaneseness; rather, they are marketed to traditionalize steamed white rice as a primordially Japanese food in the midst of social change.

Conclusion

The preparation and consumption of rice in contemporary Japan reveal seemingly contradictory trends of continuity and change. My analysis shows that much of the knowledge around preparing rice is unrecorded and expected to be gained naturally in Japanese social life. The transmission of an oral recipe for steaming rice occurs as younger family members observe and learn to cook with older family members. Despite the advancement of technology that facilitates the steaming of rice, rice preparation is still discussed by emphasizing the following of correct steps and taboos. This ritualistic procedure of rice preparation reveals not only the elevated status of rice in Japanese foodways but also the moral status of those who engage in the preparation of this culturally valued food.

Despite the persistent imagery of rice as essentially Japanese, my analysis also illustrates the diverse ways in which the types of rice consumed and the manners of serving it have shaped status and identity differences. While the rice-and-grain mixture continued to be consumed by rural families and those in poverty in postwar Japan, white rice became established as the normative urban staple. Rice, then, came to register historical, socio-economic, and regional differences among people in postwar Japan.

Contemporary patterns of rice preparation and consumption illustrate more complex relationships between rice and people. Bread is regularly used for breakfast, and thanks to the commercialization of prepared rice and rice products, the "outsourcing" of rice preparation is now widely accepted. Nonetheless, in certain cases, the outsourcing practice is seen as improper, as a lack of homemade rice suggests an absence of nurturing relations in a household. Homemade rice is qualitatively superior and thus "necessary" for children's lunches and ancestral offerings.

Furthermore, Japan's advanced technology supposedly creates a taste of distinction by evoking Japan's timeless past, when rice was steamed in the "traditional Japanese" way by using a wood stove and a metal pot, even though people today have not prepared rice in this way in their lifetimes. Computerized rice cookers not only address social diversification and facilitate rice preparation in a growing number of single-person and couple-only households, but also enable (what is advertised as) the "authentic" way of steaming rice. In sum, despite changing preparation and consumption practices, rice remains a notable register of culturally valued tastes as well as a sheaf of metaphors with which people construct their essence as well as difference.

Notes

1 Allison, "Japanese Mothers and *Obentōs*"; Francks, "Consuming Rice"; and Ohnuki-Tierney, *Rice as Self.*

2 Shibano Sangyō Kabushikigaisha, *Shibano Kicchin*, 5.

3 Ibid.

4 Kotobanku, "Metric System."

5 Ohnuki-Tierney, *Rice as Self.*

6 Cwiertka, "Washoku, Heritage, and National Identity," 385.

7 Francks, "Consuming Rice," 155.

8 Ibid., 160.

9 Uno, "One Day at a Time," 55–56.

10 Embree, *Suye Mura*, 38.

11 Beardsley, Hall, and Ward, *Village Japan*, 106, cited in Francks, "Consuming Rice," 161.

12 Bourdieu, *The Field of Cultural Production.*

13 Cwiertka, "Washoku, Heritage, and National Identity," 377.

14 Ibid., 382–83; Francks, "Consuming Rice," 155–60; and Stalker, "Introduction: Japanese Culinary Capital."

15 Cwiertka, "Washoku, Heritage, and National Identity," 385.

16 See Kondo, *Crafting Selves.*

17 Francks, "Consuming Rice," 159.

18 See also Ohnuki-Tierney, *Rice as Self.*

19 Allison, "Japanese Mothers and *Obentōs*."

20 Cabinet Office of Japan, "*Kōreisha no kazoku to setai.*"

21 Cabinet Office of Japan, "*Mikonka no shinko.*"

CHAPTER 9

Malawian Small Fry

Lauren Classen

> I am wandering through the collection of street vendors recently relegated to the outskirts of a northern Malawian town to find the man who is building my meat smoker from metal scraps and scavenged screws. I plan to use the smoker to lightly smoke duck breasts left over from the ducks I had butchered and rendered to make confit, a part of my effort to make a home in my place of long-term anthropological research. As I move through the area, I run into a fifteen-year-old boy who has played a key role in my research with rural Malawian youth—he prefers to be called Pizza. He represents a large segment of youth who eschew the lives of their parents as subsistence farmers and who strive daily to seem and feel worthy of something else—of *umoyo wachizungu*, or "white life."

Rural youth—who comprise the majority of the population in Malawi and are the most at risk of HIV (and least likely to adhere to antiretroviral regimens), have extremely limited access to school, experience high rates of unemployment,[1] and are often responsible for the care of both younger and older family members[2]—have certainly captured the attention of international donors. The National Youth Council of Malawi (NYCM), which coordinates and monitors the various youth-targeted interventions in Malawi, reported in 2010 that there were 143 youth organizations registered, spanning all 28 districts. According to NYCM, they focus predominantly on two areas of youth development: participation and empowerment, and health. In northern Malawi, where I worked, these organizations frequently host youth clubs in several villages, making youth-targeted interventions more ubiquitous and accessible than secondary schools to rural youth. As Susan Watkins and Ann Swidler have also noted in this context, the youth-targeted programming in northern Malawi is "complex, chaotic, and frenetic." Funded sometimes by international non-governmental organizations (NGOs) and other organizations, including the Global Fund, they are run on the ground by local NGOs, the local hospital, and the Synod of Livingstonia, Church of Central Africa, Presbyterian (CCAP), and a number of individual philanthropists.[3] In the context of their families and villages, however, youth are typically considered incapable of making independent decisions and therefore their opinions are not often sought in planning agriculture, schooling, or their own marriages. This made my own research, which aimed to help youth write their own stories and express their own goals, a popular outlet among young people.

> As I check over my nearly completed smoker, Pizza cocks his head into my line of sight. He knew where to find me when I left the rural villages to stay in town to catch up on work that required electricity—in the market, stocking up on some locally grown foods or engaging in some other food-related project. He asks if I would like to purchase a greeting card he has made so he can buy medicine for his mother and, he adds with a wink, "a [McDonald's] small fry for me." There is no McDonald's in Malawi. Pizza uses food talk as social reference, demonstrating his familiarity with the foods of *umoyo wachizungu*, though he has never eaten these types of foods.

In this chapter I reflect upon how Pizza, his peers, his Elders, and I all used food to mark our identity, to make ourselves belong and feel worthy of our own goals in rural Malawi, as well as to connect with one another even when the meanings we attached to different foods did not quite align. Food has long played an important role in social research. Food marketing, production, and consumption have proved to be a window into broader political, social, economic and environmental changes.[4] Sidney Mintz's famous study among sugarcane workers in the Caribbean,[5] and work examining the history and circulation of sushi,[6] wedding cakes,[7] bananas,[8] and the tortilla[9] are among many key examples of studies that have used food to examine broader social, cultural, and political milieux. And, as James Watson and Jakob Klein point out, "not only may food practices reflect and channel wider social changes, but people also creatively use food as a medium for reflecting upon these changes in all their complexities."[10]

Examples of this were abundant in my own research in Malawi. Later in this chapter, for example, I discuss an impromptu workshop a group of village grandmothers organized to teach me to make *chibama*, a type of steamed bread made from maize flour they say is a traditional food that is no longer popular today. While we cooked together, the grandmothers lamented sourly the ways in which youth both desire store-bought bread over *chibama* and other traditional foods, and choose to eat separately from their rural kin—changes they say are due to the "rights" and "freedoms" that came with the first democratic elections in 1994. Striking in my research, however, was that while Elders used food practices and talk to reflect on the past and the present, youth used food to anticipate and sustain hope for a particular future. Food, as one of the most accessible markers of modernity in this context, is imbued with a kind of power to make young people feel worthy of the futures they desire and sustain hope and anticipation for such futures. In the first part of this chapter, I discuss the anticipatory nature of food consumption and talk among youth and suggest that food studies may be key to understanding not only perceptions of the past and contemporary change but also the goals and desires of young people in similar emerging economies.

In addition to examining food production, circulation, and consumption as a means to glean a deeper understanding of social and political life, food and eating together has also been employed as a way of easing into in-depth conversations with informants in social research. As Watson and Klein put it, "everyone eats and, fortunately for anthropologists, most people like to talk about food."[11] Preparing, eating, and talking about food can all provide gateways into other topics. As other chapters in this volume show, the reciprocity inherent in cooking and eating together builds trust and can even distract from inequalities temporarily, encouraging an openness between researcher and researched in the field (see chapters by Van Esterik, Moffat, and Gagné, for example). Watson's work in south China provides an example of how talking about food can help informants to open up during interviews. "The surest way to break the ice in unfamiliar settings is to broach the topic of food: 'Last year I was in the mountains of western Jiangxi and I had steamed bean curd with catfish.' Or another sure-fire conversation starter: 'Two years ago I was just in time for the harvest of first-crop rice, served with pop-eyed shrimp in the Pearl River Delta.'"[12] In this chapter, I endeavour, however, to pay attention to how my own relationship to food and the pleasure derived from talking about and sharing food similarly encouraged conversation with informants. I am inspired by Sarah Moser[13] and Catherine Wilkinson to go "beyond the key categorical frames of reference including class, gender, sexuality, race and age, to include personality,"[14] and in the latter part of this chapter, I examine my personal relationship with food because it is a particularly salient part of my sense of self at home and in the field. I discuss how my preference for locally grown foods aligned, however awkwardly, with rural diets and what cooking and eating communally revealed and enabled in this context.

I draw on ethnographic research conducted as part of my doctoral thesis, which aimed to understand the goals, challenges and desires of rural Malawian youth (broadly defined as young people between the ages of ten and thirty), as well as my subsequent work with a local development project.[15] During my doctoral fieldwork, I collaborated in part with a local agricultural project, Soils, Food and Healthy Communities (SFHC), which carries out participatory research with smallholder farmers on sustainable agriculture to improve food security and nutrition.[16] The SFHC project aimed to understand the previously identified low level of participation by youth in sustainable agricultural programs, as well as high levels of gender inequality. I learned early on in my research that it was exceedingly difficult to access the thoughts and experiences of rural youth, and of girls in particular. To overcome this, I spent nineteen months staying with rural families, sleeping in their houses and sharing in household chores and activities, including firewood and water collection as well as food preparation and consumption. I also employed a photographic technique I called "photo-LENS" (Life Experience Narratives of Significant concepts), which involved asking youth to take photographs of joy, suffering, love, and health—key or significant concepts identified through ethnographic research. During follow-up interviews the photographers were asked to narrate their experiences, using the photographs as a launching point.

Foodways as a Gateway to the Future

In rural Malawi, where annual food insecurity is endemic, it was inevitable that food would be a central theme in conversations centred on youth suffering and joy. Both Elders and youth told of their immense hardships during the annual hungry season (typically occurring between January and April, when grains stored from the previous harvest have diminished and the new crops are not yet ready to be consumed), and photographs of "suffering" taken by youth provided a painfully visceral picture of the food shortages they faced. They shared photos of empty storage granaries and fertilizer bags; wilting, dying maize crops; families eating what have sometimes been called "survival foods" in the absence of adequate maize, the staple food; and piglets so hungry they had begun to cannibalize one another in their rickety wooden pens. They further told of days spent foraging for something to bring home for dinner, nights spent with hunger, and grandparents begging for food.

Figure 9.1a was taken by a married, twenty-four-year-old woman. She explained, "The main problem to our family is lack of food. We have a very big field but we yield very little, of which half is consumed while the maize is still in the field and the remaining half doesn't even last for more than three months . . . [this makes me suffer] because you can't farm with hunger and the children will be crying with hunger." Figure 9.1b was taken by a nineteen-year-old man. About his "suffering" photo he said, "These pigs are what makes me suffer because, just look at their pen is very poor and they do not have enough food."[17]

Food practices and talk were also windows into broader social and political life in the villages of rural Malawi, given that people "creatively use food as a medium for reflecting upon changes in all their complexities."[18] Elders

FIGURE 9.1A AND 9.1B. The experience of food insecurity. Participant photos (used with permission).

tended to use changes in food practices among youth to reflect on recent political shifts and express discontent with changes in the local economy. In an impromptu focus group, for example, one grandmother danced up to me, gesturing distastefully toward a line of young women dressed for a social occasion (rather than for work) in clean, colourful *chitenji* wrap skirts with cookware on their heads, on their way to visit an *asiki*, or "love friend," as described by the grandmothers. This grandmother chose, as most Elders did, to talk about assertions for independence among youth using food as her lens, stating that "the daughters-in-law and mothers-in-law eat separately today." Another grandmother chimed in, "[This is because] the youth of today are proud. They are undisciplined." When I asked why they felt youth of today were this way, another grandmother said simply, through a mouthful of groundnuts, "Because of school," and another attributed it to "this modern life." I later learned that many Elders blamed democracy, "when everyone got their own rights and freedoms" and youth started to claim their "right" to eat what, where, and with whom they chose. The first president of independent Malawi, Dr. Hastings Kamuzu Banda, headed a strict, thirty-year autocratic regime that mandated military discipline and training of youth. In 1994, the old establishment gave way to the first democratic elections. The concurrent dissemination on a large scale of the concept human rights, often translated and interpreted as "freedom" in Malawi,[19] was employed as a tool for shaping youth into moral leaders of the new democracy. While Elders used food talk and old recipes to reflect nostalgically on the past, youth used food to compare the present to an anticipated future, one characterized by wealth, equality, and *umoyo wachizungu*.

That the imagined future will transpire, however, is very dubious in Malawi. Anticipation of the future emerges amid remarkable uncertainty in rural villages. Access to schooling and employment are highly limited, and even those who are in school or employed feel very insecure about the next year, next term, or even the next day. Hope thus requires sustained, protean efforts to maintain, to keep desired futures perceptible. In particular, it seems necessary to Malawian youth to act as if desired futures will indeed unfold in order to make them a reality. Several researchers have shown how second-hand clothing has been appropriated by youth in African contexts as they articulate their relationship with the West and their ability to "move with fashion."[20] While some Malawian youth also asserted their "freedom" to wear "white/English" clothing, much to the discontent of their Elders, foods considered to be "modern"—in particular, sliced white bread and Fanta, but also sugar more generally, milk and fried foods, oils and margarine—are even more accessible than second-hand clothing in rural villages. Displaying a modern food culture was absolutely central to acting worthy of future desires. In other words, whereas Elders in my research used food as a medium for reflecting on social and political change, a phenomenon that has been identified in many global contexts,[21] rural Malawian youth creatively used food practices and talk to reflect upon and sustain hope for particular kinds of imagined "modern" futures, characterized by *umoyo wachizungu*, an English/white life.

The "joy" photos that youth captured were frequently of houses that they desired. As a typical example, nineteen-year-old Benson's "joy" photo is shown in Figure 9.2.

L: Tell me, why did you take this picture?

B: Okay ah, I took this because my aim is to build a house like this. I think if I can have a house like this I can be at a very good place.

L: Where is this house?

B: In town . . . What I want is to change my life [from the one] at my home there [gesturing to his earthen and thatched natal home, where I had stayed several times since arriving in Malawi]. As you see there the house like my mother is living in, she is living in a very, mm, maybe, I can say it's a dirty house to my heart. As I am looking at my mother, I see she is very shy [embarrassed to live in this house]. So, I want to build a house like that [pointing to the picture] so that I can share a room with my mother.

L: And what is it about this house that you like?

B: I look at town life and I know every part of this life because, sometime back, I was moving around [hanging around] this place and it is a very good place to me. Then the house [in the picture],

FIGURE 9.2. Living in a good place. Participant photo (used with permission).

> it's a very good design. It's not a local design. It's not like a church [pointing to one of the new, plain evangelical churches in the village]. A church, it's like a straight line. The corners are maybe, four. A church doesn't have a veranda like this [pointing to the picture]. It's simply flat.
>
> L: OK, and what else?
>
> B: And I like this house because the toilets are not outside. And the water taps they are inside again. It also has a kitchen [inside] there. . . . I also like it because of the design of the windows. And what I like is the iron sheets, there on the roof. And I want it.

Such houses were also often described as containing nice furniture. One eleven-year-old girl, Stefani, explained that her house in town would have many features that her family home most certainly did not have. The house would be painted, made with timber and glass windows, and, she added, "looking inside . . . like sofas, chairs, beds." Others added, "okay, like, sofa sets, toilets inside, TVs, big radios, beds, mattresses, those things."

Chawanangwa (twenty-nine years old) emphasized the status associated with the "good life" lived in his desired house "on the tarmac near the city." "It has got everything inside the house and when you come with friends to this house, saying 'this is my house,' they are saying you are staying a good life. Just looking at the house [it's obvious] people living in the house are living a good life." He later asked rhetorically about his own mud-and-thatched house in the village, "Can visitors come to this house?" He shook his head is if to say, "Obviously not."

The good life Chawa describes is characterized by wealth and the ability to eat modern foods, the foods of *umoyo wachizungu.*

> L: And why do you say they are living a good life?
>
> C: Because the—just imagine, just looking at the house you know that these people have got money. They can have everything. They can eat good food. A poor person cannot live in such a house—a person who has got no money cannot live in that house. Only those who have got money and have got everything, they are living in this house. So, if you are having money, you enjoy life, yeah.
>
> L: How does money make you to enjoy life, what can you do with money that makes you enjoy life?
>
> C: Okay, money [makes you] enjoy life because you eat good food.
>
> L: Like what kind of food?
>
> C: Ah, bread. Bread, rice, meat. Food that you buy, that we don't even know. That people produce from factory. They are good because they are tested by Malawi Bureau of Standards, those [people] who look to see that the food is good. Yeah, they are safe because you find some are sealed, they are in packets.

New lifestyles determined by access to expensive technologies are another imagined inevitability of the anticipated future among youth. In a discussion with a group of women and men peer educators who ranged in age from nineteen to twenty-six about cellphones, computers, TV, and digital music players in Malawi, the participants argued strongly against the church perspective that this technology does more harm than good.

> L: How do you feel about all this new technology in Malawi?
>
> R1: The church says that technology has brought more bad than good.
>
> R2: But technology in general is good. From TV, we can learn more, more especially we can learn more from preachers internationally, but at the same time we can also watch pornographic. This is the abuse of technology [laughing].
>
> R1: It is the right of the customer to choose how to use the technology.
>
> R3: We will be as prosperous as your country soon. Sometimes keeping our culture clashes with a type of technology, so we must adapt.
>
> R4: In the olden days we used to have a communal dish where we ate together but now because we live in technology advancement with heath issues, each and every person must have a certain plate.
>
> R3: When we are eating *nsima* [maize porridge] we use bare hands, but in the near future we will be eating with forks and spoons.
>
> L: What do you think of this?
>
> R3: That is good because we can have some infection on our hands and we eat with an infection.

The belief that "modern foods" are associated with "advancement," "modernity," and "health" was prevalent, reflecting the fact that youth-targeted health interventions play a significant role in shaping how youth imagine the future and their expectation for its realization. Ironically, the prepackaged, mass-produced, ultra-processed "modern" food that made it to the hands of the villagers was often spoiled and less nutritious than traditional food.

Umoyo wachizungu is characterized by nuclear families, urbanity, certain kinds of loving relations, modern amenities such as electricity and indoor plumbing, eating store-bought foods in modern packaging certified by the

Malawi Bureau of Standards, and, consequently, having many friends, high status, happiness, and good health. These aspirations for lifestyles characterized by particular material standards and consumption practices are increasingly shared by people in many parts of the world, where they represent "membership in the new global order."[22] The consumption and discussion of new and modern foods were the most cited marker of modernity by youth and Elders alike in this context, perhaps because food is one of the most accessible markers of modernity.

While the houses that youth photographed and the material goods in them, including furniture and technology, are solidly future aspirations, youth can to some degree eat "modern foods" in the present in anticipation of imagined futures. A food security and dietary diversity survey I conducted showed, unexpectedly, that youth living with extended families in rural villages tended to eat very differently than the rest of their households.[23] Elders' laments explained this finding. Elders complained persistently about youths' relationship to food and the assertion of their independence through food. "In the past we know only *nsima*," Mary explained. "What else could we eat? Today, they are there, the English [foods], for the ones who have got money, they buy them because they are linked with those [the styles] of nowadays. The English food [youth] say, there is now bread; there are Fanta bottles, Coca Cola, and many things that are eaten today. We were not seeing them during the past days." Speaking of young girls who work in their parents' fields during the day and engage in sex work in town at night, she said, "They bring bread and sugar to the family [in the village]." When I asked if they also bring maize or other staples home, she laughed. "Bread and sugar make them look as though they are working. Workers eat bread and sugar in the morning. It is strange food for us in the village, as though they have taken the highest food." She further described even younger children in the villages exchanging their harvests for "bin Ladens,"[24] the nickname given to a type of sweet bread very popular in Malawi. She complained, "This is not good [because] it is maize porridge that makes children strong [not bread]."

It is at least partly because food is an important marker of modernity and related social and political positionalities that young Malawian boys frequently give themselves food-related nicknames. Examples include

Chicken Pizza, Cheese on Toast, Chicken Nugget, Soft Serve, and Small Fry. I never encountered anyone nicknamed Nsima ya Mphangwe nor its English equivalent, Porridge and Greens. The fast-food names signal to friends and foreigners alike the boys' familiarity with the West and *mzungu* (white or English) commercial foods, or as Chawanangwa put it above, foods "people produce from factory," which are "better because they are [tested]" and not cooked and eaten communally at home in a village. This is particularly significant, because as Chawanangwa's interview also demonstrated, these foods that he believes to be superior include "food that you buy, that [rural Malawians] don't even know." As previously noted, there is no McDonald's serving chicken nuggets or small fries in Malawi, and while some youth knew of these foods from interactions with foreign tourists, media or from locals who migrated temporarily to South Africa for work, most rural Elders, for example, did not. And when I made pizza together with a group of village youth in a clay-brick oven we had spent months designing and building and Pizza, my informant, only gingerly picked at the toppings as he sheepishly nibbled his piece, it was clear he had not given himself that nickname because it was his favourite food. Rather, such names signalled to friends and foreigners in Malawi a readiness for and worthiness of a life characterized by the convenience of such foods, as well as freedom from the social obligations to farm, cook, and eat together in rural villages.

Reflexivity, Misalignments, and Connections in the Field

In the windowless basement of a high-end restaurant in West Toronto, a boombox in the corner vibrates to Katy Perry's "California Gurls" as I rotate the hind leg of a pig in its salt bath, check on my baguette dough rising on the counter and resume my major task for the day—butchering two dozen chickens. The chicken legs will be featured on the evening menu, lightly smoked in-house and then roasted and paired with apple, pumpkin, polenta, chicken liver, and maple butter. The recommendation of our servers will be to start this meal with a smattering of strong cheeses, including Peppato Seco and Goat Tomme, and wine from a vineyard in the

Niagara Region. Every major element of the meal will come from a handful of farms near the city, as the restaurant specializes in local and farm-to-table foods, brings in whole animals to butcher on-site, and prepares all food from scratch, with the menu changing daily to reflect available ingredients. I was offered a position at this prominent, exclusive restaurant in Toronto when I completed my fieldwork, based on my experience butchering and smoking meats and fish in my homemade smoker in Malawi, making pasta from local grains I ground myself, and baking pizza in a mud oven I constructed in my Malawian home's backyard. I drew on my experience in rural villages making *nsima*, or corn porridge, to make soft, perfectly textured polenta (using a traditional Italian recipe) rather than on any professional culinary training.

Farm-to-table food is a contemporary social movement heavily endorsed by environmental activists, authors, and chefs, including Michael Pollan, Wes Jackson, and Dan Barber. It promotes serving locally grown food at restaurants, school cafeterias, and in hospitals, among other facilities. Proponents cite economic, nutritional, food safety, social, and environmental benefits.[25] It is, however, criticized for being economically exclusive—eating at farm-to-table restaurants in Canada and the United States has become a marker of status and a particular version of a modern lifestyle. Whereas eating locally was a marker of poverty in Malawi, it has become a marker of status in the West. The pleasure I took from eating local foods in rural Malawian villages and also from cooking using local ingredients in my little home in town reflected this understanding of local food as an ethical as well as delectable food choice.

In long-term social research, it is inevitable that informants come to know the researcher as more than simply an academic. In my own research, my participants came to see the "researcher as person,"[26] and in some cases, the "researcher as friend."[27] The person they came to know was a single, white female who knew something about agriculture from having been reared on a farm, albeit one with a very different agricultural system, who liked to run long distances and loved to discuss, explore, grow, prepare, and eat food.

While irrelevant to my research in any direct sense, the challenge of making locally produced food into the kinds of delicacies with which I had become familiar at home became critical to my ability to endure the loneliness and unfamiliarity inevitable in conducting fieldwork so far from home.

Capturing the "lived experience" of Malawian young people's narratives of joy and struggle in rural villages was an explicit goal of my research. This required me to live with youth in rural villages through the seasons and periods of struggle, including periods of food insecurity. As other anthropologists have noted, capturing the lived experience in this way comes with its challenges, and there is increasingly a call in the literature for greater attention to the emotionality of fieldwork.[28] Begley argues that we must pay attention to "emotional, psychological, and physical stress that we go through while in the field,"[29] particularly when research takes place in the context of war and violence, and recognize the support anthropologists may need upon returning from the field to deal with this stress. Here, I make explicit some of the challenges I faced and talk about how food and cooking, and in some cases sharing food, helped me to cope with some of the challenges and ultimately make it possible for me to capture the lived experience of youth suffering and aspiration in rural villages.

While I have travelled back and forth to Malawi many times since, my longest stint of fieldwork at one time was nineteen months, during which I missed weddings, births of first children, milestone birthdays, and innumerable small but meaningful experiences at home. I simply could not afford to travel back and forth at that time, and these were sacrifices I wanted to make in pursuit of quality work. During my time in the field, I made close friends and felt immense gratitude and love toward many people. But spending the majority of my time in rural villages, eating "local" foods and drinking local water (despite how careful I tried to be to boil it), and sleeping with local farm animals at my feet, not to mention many mice and rats, meant that I was often sick with various infections, including persistent diarrhea. Engaging in participant observation with youth also meant my days in rural villages were, to my academic sensibilities, characterized by grinding physical labour. But perhaps most difficult was watching the friends I made struggle with food insecurity, AIDS, malaria, and physical abuse.

I took breaks from working in the rural villages, because electricity was required for me to charge cameras, download photos, transcribe fieldnotes and interviews, and so on. On occasions that I caught up on work in my little, electrified home in town, however, I also recovered physically and mentally.

A key to my restoration was experimentation with new recipes based on local foods. I recorded the recipes that worked in my fieldnotes. For example, when on 20 July 2009, I wrote an entry about a workshop I had attended on "Youth in Governance," I then included the recipe for the dinner I had made when I returned to town:

> On my way home I stopped at [the market] to see what meat they had in stock. No fillet beef, but they had pork chops/ribs—the chest ribs, so they are big ones, with lots of meat on them. This is how I prepared them: Rinse and dry ribs and marinate in 3 tablespoons of dark soy sauce for 30 minutes. Meanwhile roughly chop 1 large red onion and 6 cloves garlic. When meat has finished marinating, in a large pot, sauté onion, garlic, and 4 sprigs fresh thyme in 3 tbs oil for 5 minutes adding a pinch of salt. Add meat (working in batches if pot is not large enough) and brown on both sides. When browned, add: rest of soy sauce (4 tbs), 3 tbs tamarind pulp, splash balsamic vinegar, 2 tbs ketchup, 3 tbs brown sugar and ½ cup water. Simmer meat in mixture for 30 mins uncovered and then covered for 1.5 hours until very tender and sauce is reduced to a thick jam. I served this on sticky white rice with a spinach, red onion and egg salad on the side. [The] salad dressing was a variation of my mom's: ¼ cup cream, ¼ cup white sugar and ¼ cup balsamic shaken. Dress salad with this and salt and pepper to taste.

This entry clearly shows how my food explorations in Malawi melded my new environment and local resources with recipes I knew and loved from home. While tamarind was a new ingredient I had never used at home, the rest of the recipe was close to one my mother frequently made by mixing ketchup, brown sugar, and vinegar to make a sweet-and-sour rib sauce. Other entries included recipes for "medium-rare beef fillets in a mulberry compote," "pumpkin ravioli," and "orange and peanut stew," "banana sourdough," "duck confit," and "macadamia nut pie."

My breakfast preference for freshly unearthed sweet potatoes, boiled and eaten whole, over white bread (frequently studded with green and blue mould) sometimes baffled but also suited poor, subsistence households. Quickly my reputation for being easy and even a pleasure to feed preceded my visits, prompting people to prepare proudly their own harvests to share. Conversations around the cooking fire and during meals with families provided some of my most valuable knowledge and insights. I learned how intimate kin relations affected access to resources in rural villages and thus different youths' goals and desires, and how young women creatively asserted gender equality in a context in which they fear retaliation and abuse for taking such stances (both things I address in detail in my dissertation).[30] While our reasons for eating predominantly locally grown foods did not precisely align—I saw them as superior to the processed, store-bought foods, while my informants saw them as inferior but more affordable—they nonetheless connected us.

We similarly shared a mutual understanding of the value of food and food reciprocity. Villagers often made great sacrifices to purchase what they felt were "modern" foods, including white sliced bread and sugar for tea when I visited. I also prepared the dishes I had created for foreigners and locals alike when the opportunity arose. I took great joy in reciprocating the time given to me by my informants by making birthday cakes and wedding cakes when called upon, or helping local organizations organize recipe days aiming to help with the adoption of new crops with particular agro-ecological advantages. And while this personal passion for cooking was critical to my psychological adjustment to living far from home and provided an emotional escape from the hardships endured by my informants and friends in rural Malawi, I came to find that it also helped me immensely in connecting with young men and women in rural villages who spent much of their waking hours nurturing, preparing, and consuming food. While I saw other researchers organize soccer tournaments to connect with young Malawians and development workers play instruments, join local bands, and put on theatre productions with local participants, it quickly became apparent that my love of food provided me unique opportunities for connection.

While I took real pleasure in cooking and sharing food with youth and their families in the villages, there were also several times that it clearly aided my research as well. A kind of trust and friendship was built among young men and women and myself as we engaged in food projects together. For example, there was an enormous fig tree in town that I walked by daily, and it bothered me immensely that the figs were all falling to the ground, unconsumed. I dreamed of fig jams, fig marinades, and ultimately a fig clafouti. On the day I decided I was going to finally make this luscious dessert, I borrowed the tallest ladder I could find and put it up against the tree. Several young people aided me in my efforts, mostly out of curiosity. Since figs were known to be filled with ants, some teased me from the ground by saying I was indeed an anteater (though they all knew that flying ants were my least favourite local food). I had to pick through the figs I harvested thoroughly, for many of them were crawling with the little creatures, but during the weeks that I shared fig clafouti with my accomplices, I received all kinds of local fruits as gifts, made many more desserts, and learned about the wild fruits the youth foraged when they performed tasks away from their natal households (like herding goats or collecting firewood). This data meaningfully informed my understanding of youth food and nutrition.[31]

There were also several instances in which research participants, knowing my interest in cooking, took it upon themselves to organize workshops for me on the preparation of what they called a "traditional" food. These occasions served as invaluable focus group opportunities, as women chatted about their lives while cooking. In the very early stages of my research, I was fortunate that a group of seven *agogos*, or grandmothers, planned a day-long workshop to teach me how to make *chibama*, a bread made from maize flour together with either pounded ground nuts (*chibama cha ntendero*) or mashed bananas (*chibama cha matochi*) and steamed in a banana leaf. The day was relatively cool and so we sat on mats spread on the sunny side of the house and took turns preparing the ingredients for the recipe: pounding maize and groundnuts into flour, grinding salt on a grinding stone, and cutting banana leaves. The reciprocity of labour, knowledge, and food during this day fostered a micro-environment of trust and openness that I had been unable to develop during my research thus far. What I learned from our conversations as we cooked together about how grandmothers felt about youth changed my research approach entirely. Up to that point, I had done a handful of interviews with young people, during which I had elicited almost nothing.

I could barely make out their names, let alone anything else about their lives. Cooking together with the *agogos* taught me that young people were not accustomed to sharing opinions and experiences and not generally considered capable of doing so. This understanding spurred me to find creative ways to engage them. In the end, 103 of the interviews I conducted with young people were structured around photographs they had taken. In the absence of this connection over food, I am not certain I would have recognized the need for such creative methods with youth early enough in my research to make using photography possible.

In my fieldnotes I translated our actions into written recipes as we made them. Here is an example of the recipe for *chibama cha matochi*:

For *chibama*:

16 ripe Zambia *matochi* (a [starchier and sweet] variety of bananas from Zambia)

1½ tsp sea salt, ground

2 cups soaked, white maize flour

1¼ cups water

Banana leaves cut into 1-foot squares and washed

For steaming:

Pieces of *matete* (a hollow reed which is also used to make *mphasa* mats)

2–4 cups water (depending on the size of the pot, more for a bigger pot)

Peel bananas and place in mortar. Add salt and pound until bananas are mashed. Add maize flour and continue mashing. The mixture will be thick and heavy and sweet to the taste. Add 1¼ cups water, all at once, and mash together to create a wet dough. The dough should not stick to the spoon. If it does, add a little more water. Scoop ½ cup of dough into the centre of a banana leaf and fold all four sides over to create enclosed packages.

> Place *matete* sticks on the bottom of a large pot (to prevent leaves from sticking to the bottom) and put wrapped banana leaf packages on top (they can be layered on top of one another). Pour water for steaming down the sides of the pot to cover the sticks but not covering the *chibama* packages. Cover pot with a piece of banana leaf and a lid. Steam over a warm-hot fire for 45 minutes. Remove leaves and unwrap to allow *chibama* to cool. Serve at room temperature. Makes 10–12 bundles.

The transcript from the audio recording I made during this afternoon-long workshop is chaotic. While some grandmothers chatted among themselves, reminiscing about special times with their husbands and children, some quizzed me on wedding and marriage traditions among *mzungu*, some sang songs and danced, some snacked on peanuts, and others shared their frustrations with respect to their grandchildren. They advised me against asking youth their opinions, because "these ones, they are not having any decisions in their minds as of yet. They are guided by parents," and "for those who are still *chinyamata* [youth] you must tell them [what they think] because until they have passed that time of being *chinyamata* they can't have a deciding mind for themselves." While rural youth and children comprise the majority of the population in Malawi, lauded by policy makers as "the leaders of tomorrow" and "foundations of the future," this modernist trope confronts a more powerful trope about generational hierarchies in rural villages, where youth are regarded as unable to contribute valuable ideas and opinions until they reach social adulthood.

In another instance when my fondness for food preparation opened opportunities for me to develop rapport with my informants and access different types of information, I was asked to provide a workshop on making a tiered wedding cake in a rural village. I had no idea how to bake over an open fire, but we agreed that the workshop would have to be a collaborative experiment, and I set forth working on developing a recipe. In the end, days of research and experimentation with recipes using ingredients easily accessible to people living in the village and the budget I had been given to work with resulted in the very unimpressive two-tiered citrus pound cake

FIGURE 9.3. Making a wedding cake in a rural village. Photo by Lauren Classen.

with a pounded sugar and lemon icing pictured in Figure 9.3. I am not sure it was ever repeated in the village, but the process of making it afforded me hours of engagement with young girls about their desires for "white weddings," of which the tiered cake was a symbol, characterized by a particular kind of modern "love" with a partner selected in the absence of involvement from rural kin. I learned that this was a marriage they felt was modern but also "healthy," as women shared experiences of sexual abuse and infidelity in marriages and explained their fear of contracting HIV from their husbands. In addition, making this wedding cake in the village was a lot of fun for all of the participants, taking all of us away from the stresses of everyday life in the village.

Concluding Thoughts

Food was a central topic of conversation in rural Malawi. Annual food insecurity is persistent in rural villages, and much time each day is spent collecting firewood and water, preparing cooking fires, growing, harvesting, cooking, and eating. Sharing in food preparations and consumption in villages, in turn, provided me hundreds of hours of time with young people, especially girls, who are often very shy and unaccustomed to sharing experiences or opinions. Food, however, is also put to work by Malawians to reference broader social issues, and I found it informative from a research perspective to examine changes in diets among rural youth whose dietary consumption is conventionally subsumed in household level analyses.[32] Paying attention to the food consumption patterns and food talk of youth in this context revealed how they use food very differently from their Elders. Whereas Elders used food to reminisce about the past and to respond to social change, for youth food consumption and talk was symbolic of the lives they wanted to lead in the future. Elders used food to express their discontent with youth claiming their newly lauded "rights" as freedoms from family expectations following the shift from the dictatorship to democracy. They lamented the loss of interest among their children and grandchildren in traditional foods and emphasized the health benefits of maize foods over white bread. Youth, instead, used food to demonstrate to themselves and others their readiness for and progress toward desired futures of *umoyo wachizungu*, an English/ white life. They flaunted their "freedom" to eat "modern" food and they emphasized the health of prepackaged bread made in a factory over maize cooked over fire in the village. Given that food has been shown to provide a window into reflections on and responses to social, environmental, and political change, paying attention to how youth in particular put food to use through their consumption and desires, which differ from others in their same households, may reveal a different picture than food studies have shown thus far. Food is used not only to respond to the past but also to anticipate the future and to sustain hope for new, imagined lives.

Like my informants, I hold particular kinds of food as central to my identity at home and in the field, and while my own preference for local foods came from a very different social and political place, it aligned with the means of subsistence farmers who could not afford "white/English foods." My reputation as easy to feed and a pleasure to cook with opened opportunities (and even obligations) for me to stay with many different rural families and both attend and host various food workshops. These in turn enabled a depth of understanding of the tug of war between cultural tradition and an imagined modernity, particularly between Elders and youth, that I am not sure I would have attained otherwise. The alignment between my own food culture and the food culture of *umoyo wachizungu* desired by my young research participants, of course, was less straightforward. But though I preferred local food over bread and Fanta, their requests for a wedding cake workshop and the many wild fruits they delivered to me for my clafoutis demonstrated that they simultaneously did not see me as aligning with their Elders' ideologies. Our food alignments and misalignments were equally informative. Beyond the research benefits, my food journey in Malawi gave me a sense of belonging in a physical and cultural context very different from my own home. My research participants, young and old, and I shared great joy in getting to know one another through food. While this enabled a mutual sense of trust among us, it also facilitated my own endurance for the emotional participation in the sufferings and longings of youth required by my fieldwork in this context.

Notes

1 MDHS, *Malawi Demographic* (2004); MDHS, *Malawi Demographic* (2010).

2 Classen et al., "Revising Conventional Perceptions of Orphanhood."

3 Watkins and Swidler, "Working Misunderstandings," 199.

4 Watson and Klein, "Introduction: Anthropology, Food and Modern Life."

5 Mintz, *Sweetness and Power*.

6 Bestor, "Supply-Side Sushi."

7 Charsley, *Wedding Cakes and Cultural History*.

8 Jenkins, *Bananas*.

9 Lind and Barham, "The Social Life of the Tortilla"; Munoz, *Transnational Tortillas*.

10 Watson and Klein, "Introduction: Anthropology, Food and Modern Life," 5.

11 Ibid.

12 Watson and Klein, "Introduction: Anthropology, Food and Modern Life," 5.

13 Moser, "Personality."

14 Wilkinson, "'Babe, I Like Your Lipstick,'" 115.

15 The Malawian National Youth Policy, written in 1996, defined "youth" as those between fourteen and twenty-five years of age. Later, human rights and HIV programming would be directed at this group,

though in practice youth-targeted programming is frequently extended to young people between ages of ten and thirty or more years. Since young people frequently mistake their ages, other physical characteristics are also sometimes used to identify the appropriateness of various programs for particular young individuals. At a weekend workshop for Life Skills training organized by PEERS (the term I use to refer to both of the two long-term programs targeting youth in the context of my research), one staff member explained, "At Life Skills trainings we sometimes select youth by age but also height to determine the appropriateness of Life Skills maturation material. If they are of medium height then it is OK." I was instructed to expel any attendants who did not fit "medium height," as they were either intended for a more "mature" topic of discussion or were too young to hear about "youth" problems. Other factors sometimes used to determine whether someone was a "youth" included their marital status, their confidence level when speaking to respected adults, and their physical appearance (including the care they took in their cleanliness and the tidiness of their clothing and possessions). For these reasons I intentionally included this broader age range in my research on youth.

16 Msachi, Dakishoni, and Bezner Kerr, "Soils, Food and Healthy Communities."

17 See also see Classen, Bezner Kerr, and Shumba, "Living in the Same Place," for more photos and discussion on youths' experience of food insecurity in this context.

18 Watson and Klein, "Introduction: Anthropology, Food and Modern Life," 5.

19 Englund, *Prisoners of Freedom.*

20 Hansen, "Dressing Dangerously," 174; also see Baden and Barber, *The Impact of the Second-Hand Clothing Trade.*

21 See Watson and Klein, "Introduction: Anthropology, Food and Modern Life."

22 Ferguson, "Of Mimicry and Membership"; Ferguson, *Global Shadows*; and Piot, *Nostalgia for the Future*, 162.

23 Classen, Bezner Kerr, and Shumba, "Living in the Same Place."

24 Just as boys sometimes give themselves food nicknames with social and political significance, modern foods are similarly given political nicknames. Talking to people about the name for the "bin Laden" bun revealed a varied understanding of its significance. One Malawian friend, for example, told me, "It is because they are made in India, and because they are strong breads," meaning sturdy or hard breads. Others also told me they were called bin Ladens because they were dry and hard to chew, and "bin Laden is a hard man." On 10 February 2009, during another fieldwork trip, I wrote in my notes that I'd come across "another political food today." When I purchased my first "Obama" bun today at the bakery, my enquiring look prompted a little laugh from the baker, whom I knew well, and the simple explanation, "Obama is new and this is a new bun, so it is the 'Obama.'" Within weeks of Obama's election, I was told, Obama buns were produced around the country and were even more popular than bin Ladens.

25 Brain, *The Local Food Movement.*

26 Fuller, "Part of the Action, or 'Going Native'?"

27 Wilkinson, "'Babe, I Like Your Lipstick.'"

28 Davies and Spencer, *Emotions in the Field*; Bonet and McWilliams, "'Documenting Tragedy.'"

29 Begley, "The Other Side of Fieldwork," 1.

30 Classen, "Not Just Staying: How Health and Development Programming is Reshaping the Past, Present and Future for Rural Youth in Malawi."

31 Classen, Bezner Kerr, and Shumba, "Living in the Same Place."

32 Ibid.

CHAPTER 10

I Serve You and We Serve Each Other: Honouring the Reciprocity of Métis Relationships in Research

Monica Cyr

Beyond discussions of ingredients, nutrients, and recipes, the *give and take* that comes from the feel-good storytelling when people talk about food and traditions is steeped in the concepts of reciprocity and healing. For me, conducting food research specifically related to Métis cuisine, foodways, and traditions is a way of honouring the cultural capital of Métis women—the vessels of culinary knowledge in the home—and by extension, an opportunity to further learn about my Métisness, a colloquial term I use to describe my personal journey in the pursuit of understanding what it means to be Métis. One of the reasons I sought to do food-related research as part of my graduate work was to learn about my Métis identity. I hoped that by connecting with other Métis women and families I would come to better understand what it means to be Métis, a subject that for half my life was not to be spoken of.

Understanding the dynamic complexities of Métis people, the descendants of European (largely French and British) fur traders and Indigenous women (mainly Cree and Ojibwe), is critical because we possess distinct culture, heritage, language, customs, and art. The negative impacts of colonization, often denigrating us as the "forgotten people,"[1] have dispersed the Métis and sent many into hiding, suppressing our heritage and traditional practices, including our foodways. As a result, there are many cultural aspects of Métis people that are yet to be (re)membered, (re)learned, and (re)vitalized. In recent years, understanding more about the Métis within Canada has piqued the interest of both Indigenous and non-Indigenous scholars. This renewed attention in the domains of research, programming, and policy demonstrates that "Métis cultural restoration has become a priority among Métis organizations and individuals."[2]

For the past number of years, I have focused my research on Métis culture within Manitoba, Canada, with the intent of honouring Métis women in the process. This chapter does not contain Métis recipes and foodways captured within the research I conducted, as that cultural richness can be found elsewhere.[3] Instead, I insert personal entries related to the experiential journey of the research itself, unveiling the reciprocal relationships formed through sharing recipes and gathering food stories. These are pivotal concepts often overlooked but deeply linked to Métis connectedness and identity building. This research forms the context of the reflections in this chapter.

This chapter is broken up into sections that all circle back to a sacred journey that commenced with my search for cultural food knowledge. I first discuss reflexivity as a method used to centre my thinking and capture my thoughts. Following this is a section that provides the reader with personal familial details meant to offer a greater understanding of *who* is writing this chapter, a position many Indigenous scholars embed within their research. I then offer context related to Métis philosophies, because such values centrally guided my research and writing of this chapter. I go on to discuss the concept of insider status, because although I am Métis, that does not automatically privilege me with access to the Métis community. This is an important self-reflection for Indigenous and non-Indigenous scholars alike to consider before conducting community-based research with Indigenous

FIGURE 10.1. Bannock varieties at a Métis gathering in 2019. Image Credit: Monica Cyr.

Peoples. I carve out a section specifically to honour my participants by purposefully using their true identities (names) and sharing journal entries that capture, in part, the essence of my interactions with them. The overall research offers an important contribution, if in small measure, to the literature of the Métis people. I end my chapter with thoughts I am left with and thoughts I hope will make their way to the Manitoba Métis community, to scholars, students, and writers.

Self-Reflexivity

Self-reflexivity is looking inward to explain the outward and is part of understanding the interconnectedness of conducting research. This, according to Fyre Jean Graveline, corresponds to "Nisitohtamowin, a Cree word for 'self-in-relation.'"[4] Early on in my research, I kept a journal of the experiences and associated feelings I was met with during the research process. I kept a journal because journaling adds to the rigour of qualitative research.[5] Within the pages of my journal, it became evident how my research was affecting me and my participants on a personal level, which unveiled the reciprocity of the journey we were engaged in. It was the back and forth of shared childhood memories, similarities of customs, laughter, and heartache that allowed me to outwardly share our experiences, thus further defining and piecing together what it means to be Métis.

Importantly, qualitative research is emotional work and as such has the potential to affect all those involved in it, including the researcher, especially if the research undertaken resonates with a personal issue.[6] In the case of my research, seeking to understand a part of my identity qualifies as a personal issue, which has further allowed me to feel socially connected to the group to which I belong—the Métis Nation. A growing body of social sciences literature on the emotional dimensions of health and well-being draws attention to the self-reflexive inquiry into the interconnectedness between researcher and emotions.[7] Self-reflexivity is the step between analysis and write-up.[8] It is also used to capture the strengths and weaknesses of each stage of the research.[9] The concept of self-reflexivity is itself subject to critique;[10] nonetheless, the method is increasingly used in qualitative work. In the social sciences, qualitative research is a form of scholarship that analyzes data through words rather than the numbers used in quantitative research. Qualitative research captures behaviours and internal cognitions, which in turn inform multiple versions of reality, thus creating new theories. Virginia Braun and Victoria Clarke acknowledge that qualitative research remains subjective and introspective, making it unique.[11] Both characteristics reflect the personal involvement of the researcher in the research process. In my work, qualitative research has enabled a rich understanding of Métis families' food landscapes, food roles and relationships within families, food heritage, identity, and cultural well-being, as well as food-systemic opportunities and barriers. I have been able to convey Métis perspectives as they relate to traditional food practices and protocols in a way that nurtures the concept of perceived thought through sharing stories, which was a priority for my study.

Locating Myself

I am a Métis woman. My family lineage stems from the Red River Métis of Manitoba. Manitoba is the hub of the Métis Nation.[12] Growing up, my brothers and sisters and I were told that we were Métis-French by our father. In fact, that was all we were told. Neither of my parents spoke about our families' heritages and certainly there was no discussion of our Indigenous heritage. This was because many Métis families went into hiding toward the end of the twentieth century. It was only in my adult life and in my university experience that I was propelled to learn about my roots. My ancestors were French and Cree, Manitoba northern Cree specifically. My Métis lineage includes the Lavallees, Mayers, Ducharmes, Deschamps, Beauchamps, and Chartrands. My matriarchal grandmother, Dora Mayer, grew up in Pine Bluff, a Cree community in northern Manitoba. However, Manitoba Hydro flooded the land and so my grandparents eventually relocated south, to Winnipeg. My mother, Rose, who also participated in my research, has been instrumental in my life. I have two brothers and four sisters. I do not know who I would be without them. My life is blessed—simply because I have my siblings by my side. I am the youngest girl in my family. I am also a mother. My daughter is the love of my life and is far brighter than I ever was at her young age of fifteen.

Locating yourself, especially if you are Indigenous, is an essential part of an Indigenous methodology.[13] For example, stating who you are, your objectives, and your epistemological truth as you perceive it, right from the beginning of your research, is a culturally important aspect of conducting research in a good way. According to Shawn Wilson, beyond simply stating biases, locating yourself in the context of Indigenous research means that as a researcher your integrity is on the line and you are held accountable to the people you have asked to embark in research with.[14]

Métis Philosophies and Community

The Métis Centre, a branch under the National Aboriginal Health Centre (NAHO), invited a number of Métis Elders who represented each Métis region within Canada to assist with knowledge gathering over a three-year period, to ensure sustainability of Métis knowledge and protocols. The research project was made into a book, consisting of four chapters that captured the main themes of the project.[15] It is a collection of invaluable stories and quotes from Métis Elders, all underpinning important Métis life lessons and cultural protocols. For my research, I chose to construct a methodology from the quotes, headings, and stories in this book that I felt would best suit my research endeavour. I chose my methodology in this unorthodox way because from within the text of the book, the Elders gave me permission to do so. For instance, the Métis Elders chose to construct their framework in a spontaneous manner, absent of formalities, based on protocols that felt right, were deemed respectful, and made sense in the moment, allowing the moment to guide their decision(s). This approach was conveyed as a truly distinct "Métis" method.[16] Hence, I adopted a similar approach. The methods I selected for my research are a compilation of Métis values and philosophies that immediately, upon first reading, resonated with me. These include sharing knowledge; seeking the knowledge from those who have the knowledge; encouraging Métis to learn the Michif language from oral histories and traditional knowledge; acknowledging the person who shared the knowledge in order to honour that person and their oral traditions; learning and recording the Métis cultural protocols in order to pass the knowledge down; and honouring women as the life force behind the centrality of family.

Indigenous scholars agree that making room for Indigenous frameworks and methodologies, outside of Western world views, is the only way Indigenous cultural perspectives and knowledges can take their rightful place in academic institutions.[17] Indigenous scholars also contend that relationship building is the cornerstone of conducting research in a good way, and therefore taking the time to build such relationships must be woven into research engagement well before and long after the research commences.[18] Being able to gain access to your own cultural group is one of the many documented benefits of conducting research within your own group, community, or Nation. This is often referred to as insider status;[19] however, it is important to note that just because you identify as Indigenous and conduct research within your own Nation does not mean you are automatically granted insider status, nor are you exempt from the protocols tied to conducting Indigenous research in a culturally respectful and safe way. Rather, I would argue that for Indigenous researchers, employing Indigenous epistemological and methodological values is an obligation that must be upheld, especially if you want to maintain cultural integrity and/or be taken seriously as an Indigenous scholar. For example, prior to being granted access to conduct Métis research, I was expected to first garner support, and by extension approval, through a rigorous application and interview process, from the Manitoba Métis Federation (MMF), the official political body that represents Manitoba Métis people.

As part of this process, I was instructed early on that I should connect with Lawrie Barkwell through MMF because he was well respected and highly knowledgeable regarding Métis history and issues. At the time, I referred to this person as the gatekeeper, because his role in my research meant the difference between acceptance or rejection in the larger Métis community. Kelly Devers and Richard Frankel describe gatekeepers as those who have the power to grant meaningful access to potential participants.[20] Lawrie provided guidance, supported my intention to conduct research, which in turn enabled my research to successfully move forward. Although I am Métis, which automatically privileged me to insider access per se, and had been granted "official acceptance" from MMF, I had not yet gained community acceptance, which is what I desired. Cora Weber-Pillwax acknowledges that connections are helpful during the process of recruiting participants but reminds researchers that ultimately "people talk" about you, the researcher.[21] Therefore, being acknowledged as a person of integrity and good intentions is the only way to earn trust within the circles you are trying to penetrate. Lawrie believed in the importance of uncovering Métis food knowledge, which I believe is why he advocated for my research, opening the gate and connecting me to many of the people I would interview. I became indebted to this man for his extended help, and I made a friend.

Feeling Grounded in My Métis Rootedness

In this section, I interweave the voices of Métis with my own personal notes. My goal is to create a rich tapestry of food experiences and food meanings, honouring the experiences and knowledge of participants while also highlighting my own reflections as part of the research process. The use of quote-and-note pairings demonstrates a form of relational accountability. Relational accountability is an Indigenous epistemological view that seeks to understand how we as humans connect to the physical, mental, emotional, and spiritual aspects of life and the cosmos.[22] Relational accountability is a space that has been created to assist researchers who seek to understand self in relation to their research.[23] It outlines the important relationships in a person's life. Wilson describes relational accountability as the interconnected relationships of everything that surrounds and links us together.[24] He goes on to state that predominantly, Indigenous people believe it is the "heart" of being Indigenous, and therefore being accountable to your relations is imperative for researchers.[25] It is in this section where I hold myself accountable.

I am a Métis scholar conducting Métis research. I stand alongside the Métis participants of my research. I am accountable to my participants and to the promise I made to them to share what I have learned, including my personal growth as a result, with others. Furthermore, I will use my participants' names as an act of resistance against dominant institutions and journals that prefer the use of an alias or anonymity, because this is the Métis way, as identified in important Métis philosophies.[26] Quotes from participants are cited, and excerpts from my personal notes are italicized and dated.

Irene MacDonald and Judy MacDonald

"You take a bit for yourself and then I take a bit and I put it in the big bowl for him. And then when they finish going through everybody and then they take that bowl of food and you throw that into the fire." (Judy MacDonald, 2016)

Judy MacDonald is my mom's best friend and Irene MacDonald is Judy's mother. They both are from Tannin in northern Ontario.

> *I interviewed Judy and Irene today. Irene is so cute. She is quite elderly and kept falling asleep during the interview. Judy and I were giggling most of the time. She is so fun. She had a whole spread of*

food for me upon my arrival! It was interesting to learn about their experiences and comparisons from living in Manitoba versus Ontario growing up. I told Judy I had no idea that she was Métis. All these years, it was never brought up nor had I ever asked. I am reminded of how when I was growing up, speaking out about Métis identity was shunned upon and yet as an adult, I am vocal about being a proud Métis woman who is eager to learn from other Métis women. For my daughter, her experience will be different than mine, as I will proudly share with her Métis aspects of our culture as it was shared with me. Praying and showing gratitude for meals and food was a deeply embedded practice for the MacDonald women. Food and ceremonial beliefs unveiled important family cultural food traditions. For example, funerals and wakes included several dishes prepared by family members. Judy recalled the importance of preparing foods that were deemed favourite dishes of the person who had passed. This was understood to be an extension of love and representative of their last meal with their loved one, where the food was then to be burned in a fire that had been lit and continuously burning for three days following the person's death. I appreciated their openness to share with me family tradition.

18 June 2016

Vanessa Kilowkowski

"But I would take everything out that I was going to use, and then I smudge it all—I wash it all and prepare exactly what I was going to use for the feast. And then I had to smudge it all before I cooked it. And then as I was cooking it, I was smudging everything while I am cooking it—I'm praying for all the people who are going to eat it. I'm praying . . . and thanking Creator for the gift of all of food . . . and then, before we ate it, I had to smudge all of it again." (Vanessa Kilowkowski, 2016)

Vanessa Kilowkowski is a dear friend of mine. She is highly knowledgeable with regards to Indigenous cultural protocols. Her family is from the rural community of Peguis, Manitoba. Vanessa identifies as both Métis and First Nations, honouring both aspects of her family's lineage.

> *I don't even think I can count this interview as an interview 'cause all we did was laugh!* OMG *Vanessa is funny! I love the way she explains things. She is so gentle and matter of fact in the way she speaks. Although in my childhood, my family didn't practise Indigenous protocols such as burning medicine, these protocols are very much adhered to in my adult life, traditions that I have picked up along the way in my pursuit of honouring aspects of my First Nations identity. The interview with Vanessa reinstated the importance of smudging (burning sage) throughout the entire process of preparing, cooking, and serving food for family and community, a custom she grew up with. She said that praying while cooking was a way to remain focused on the task of remembering the sacredness of food, nourishment to our bodies, and our connection to land. I am reminded that as Indigenous people our identities are our own and we are defined by our relations to lineage and land, as defined by self, which often leads to rejecting the notion of "one or the other"—Métis or First Nations.*
>
> *26 June 2016*

Barbara Kelich, Candice Kelich, and Shannon Langan

"It was my grandmother who did all the cooking. My mom did cook but when my grandmother was around she would make the bannock, moose meat, and fish." (Candice Kelich, 2016)

Candice (Candi) Kelich, my childhood best friend, along with her sister Shannon Langan and mother Barbara Kelich, have always been my second family—I grew up in their home. When I thought about people to interview, Candi, Shannon, and Barb were at the top of my list. Like me, they grew up in the city of Winnipeg; however, their family is from Duck Bay, Manitoba, and therefore they travel back and forth from the city to their home community.

I interviewed Candi, Shannon, and Barb today. Although the years have passed since we have last seen each other, nothing has changed—SO FUNNY! It's funny when you begin to talk to people about a subject that is focused, the things you learn. I had no idea of the foods they grew up on or the cultural background because I just simply hadn't asked before, wasn't paying attention, or hadn't made the connection that they ate the very similar dishes that my family also made. For example, when Candi told me that her grandmother did all the cooking, especially the traditional cooking, I was immediately reminded that my grandmother did too. I remember my grandma in the kitchen making soup and bannock, despite my mom being around. A shared cultural aspect among my family and theirs was how close Métis families live within proximity to each other, maintaining close ties to the matriarch, allowing us to cook and provide food for one another. When I mentioned that in my family we often made beef bone soup, by boiling the bones of beef legs that was used for broth, and we would then chuck the bones along with the morsels of meat that were hardly worth the energy to eat. The horror expressed from all three of them because for them that was the best part. We had such a good time going back and forth about our soup saga stories and how each family had its "own way." It was being in their kitchen, it was our differences but also similarities, and the fun we were having that I pulled me into the familiar space of family.

1 July 2016

Rose Mayer

"Visiting my Aunty Bernadette and her husband Uncle Salamon in Grand Rapids for the summer . . . we used to go there for summer, sometimes for a month, sometimes two months and we lived on moose meat basically or they had duck, rabbit, and fish. And they used to cook, seemed like they were cooking all day long. I loved the fire thing 'cause I remember with the fire going and they had like a metal thing that hang up on this hook and the potatoes would cook in this open fire. And I thought that was so fascinating 'cause you don't do that in the city. The men were outside doing who knows what but the women were inside always, talking among themselves but nobody ever sat down and did nothing, there was always someone doing something. Peeling potatoes or doing a salad and another one is cooking or making coffee." (Rose Mayer, 2016)

I interviewed my mother, Rose Mayer. She spoke of a place that she and her family would visit as a child. My mom has been through so much, and yet she remains so strong. Her years have made her patient, kind, and gentle.

> *I am very emotional right now because for my whole life my mom has never shared in the way she did during our interview. I came to learn that my family on my mom's side was from a northern community called Pine Bluff, Manitoba. She recalled the location being remote, surrounded by water, and that could only be accessed by boat. There on the island, her mother, aunts, and uncles would hunt and cook on open fires. When my mom described the smell of the open firepit I could see she was describing a place in time that evidently she has long since yearned for. I had no idea about the details of my lineage and the stories about my family. Mom gave me such heartfelt teachings tonight—I didn't even know she possessed such knowledge about food and our ancestral ties to the land. I had heard similar teachings before but only in ceremony. It was as if I was meeting my mother in a new light I had never known of previously. It was as if the teachings were just there living inside her waiting to surface. Thank you so much, Momma!*
>
> *4 July 2016*

Bella and Carl Kraska and Philip Savoie

"Our family had three gardens with all kinds of vegetables and we also had bush berries. We would be on our hands and knees picking all the berries." (Bella Kraska, 2016)

I drove to Lorette, Manitoba, to meet Bella, her husband, Carl, and Bella's brother Philip. Their family lineage stems from Lorette.

From the moment I had met the Kraska family, one evening during a Métis beading workshop held at MMF, *I was embraced. Upon stepping into the room, everyone looked up at me—the stranger—and at that exact moment I was met with a surge of warmth and love that immediately surrounded me. I felt like I was home—it was a feeling I had never quite experienced previously. A woman approached me (Bella) with a big smile and started talking to me as if we were old friends. It was my encounter that evening, surrounded by a large community of Métis people that I knew because I was Métis, I was automatically accepted. I think about that encounter and how grounded I felt. I belonged to something bigger and it changed me.*

13 July 2016

Yesterday, I interviewed Bella, Phil, and Carl. Carl was Bella's husband and he joined in on the interview. They told me Lorette is full of Métis families. Their grandfather had a huge acre farm and so the town named a road after him. Now that's what I call roots. They were offering me sweets and homemade jam! They even gave me recipes! It was so neat to listen to the stories back and forth between all three. The Kraska family spoke of saskatoons, raspberries, low-bush cranberries, mossberries, and strawberries used to make desserts. Gathering berries were the duties assigned to the children, as explained by Bella, and although laborious were well worth the effort. They were easily able to recall which vegetables were grown, which included yellow corn, cucumbers, tomatoes, yellow beans, green beans, beets, peas, carrots, cabbage, Swiss chard, pumpkin, squash, corn, cauliflower, and turnips. Sometimes Bella would correct Phil on his memories and vice versa. At the end of the interview everyone was so happy. Phil said he felt like he had travelled down memory lane and even thanked me for the opportunity.

20 July 2016

Nancy Galliguer

"They wouldn't have had any reason to separate the berries and they were really all about simplicity so the berries definitely would have been mixed together." (Nancy Galliguer, 2016)

Nancy Galliguer is a gifted Métis seamstress and bead worker. Her family grew up in northern Ontario. Nancy possesses a vast amount of knowledge pertaining to Manitoba's Indigenous plants and Métis culture.

> *Nancy has so many stories and is such a gifted storyteller. I spent hours with her this evening! Listening to Nancy talk feels like getting pulled into her story. We spent well over an hour just going through her beautiful wardrobe that she sewed herself and decorated with thousands of beads. Also, she is an actor for Lower Fort Garry (LFG). Apparently, LFG stages a play depicting Métis "historic suppers" for the public. Nancy to me is representative of a strong empowered Métis woman who knows her stuff. For example, she spoke about the Indigenous food sources, including berries, seeds, and nuts that she asserted were most likely used to create "berry mixtures" by our Métis ancestors. Although she was unaware of any literature that could confirm her postulation, to her such a mixture made sense because it would have been a practical food source and berries were so prevalent back then. She asserted that such a mixture was most likely used in recipes such as "trail mix" made with local nuts or mashed into pemmican, a Métis food which sustained the peoples of the fur trade. My interview with Nancy went beyond food talk, where she shared stories related to Métis Voyageurs and their important trading posts in Manitoba. She laid out her vast collection of Métis designs such as vests and dresses, which she explained were intricately sewn with Métis-specific stitching and beading. She also gifted me bear grease with specific instruction to use it in a bannock recipe, a commonly loved bread among Indigenous groups. My encounter with Nancy further contributed to my understanding of our Métis culture. I am incredibly humbled by the knowledge she openly shared.*
>
> *28 July 2016*

Gilbert Bourgeois

"I guess I'm proud and call me red or, I don't care. I'm Métis and if you don't like it, too bad. I'm Métis, I'm sticking to my guns." (Gilbert Bourgeois, 2016)

Gilbert Bourgeois was a connection I made through Lawrie Barkwell. He agreed to meet me in Winnipeg even though he lives in St. Malo, where his family comes from.

> *I love Gilbert's strong French accent. Gilbert is super talented in the beadwork department. His collection of beaded vests and moccasins was so amazing! Gilbert is a bush man and hunter. It is clear to me that Gilbert is a loving pa père. He talked a lot about his grandchildren. I really admire what he said about his Métis identity. He was firm, bold, and proud. He truly embraces his identity. I thought that was really empowering. Like Nancy Galliguer, Gilbert vocalizes his Métis pride and inspired me to do the same. When asked if he would be willing to share his hunting experience with me and/or other interested individuals, he instantly agreed. For Gilbert, it was clear that in large part his identity as a Métis man is attached to his ability to provide food to his family, attributed to his hunting skills.*
>
> *24 September 2016*

The Barton Family

"Right, she would be cooking, she would be planning to cook. She would be cleaning up after cooking. She would be organizing for cooking. She would be writing down what she had cooked. She would write down what she needed to do for cooking. She would be thinking about what she would be cooking three days from then." (Beth Barton, 2016)

The Barton family was another connection I made through Lawrie Barkwell. Brian and Rose-Marie are siblings, and Brian is Beth's father.

> *I am journaling just a few blocks up from where I interviewed Beth, Rose-Marie, and Brian. I had to pull over because I am overwhelmed*

and am emotional right now. I was so touched by this family. The way they were so gentle with discussion and the way they so openly wanted to share their stories to ensure I received everything I needed. I feel like we could have talked for even more than the six hours we had but it's late now and I am exhausted. I think I am particularly emotional right now because I don't feel alone. It's just not the same to "read" about other Métis people who are searching for answers about their identity—it's an entirely other feeling to be face to face with it. There is something to be said about connecting with others who are searching for the same thing you are. Like me, they only now in their adult life are learning about their Métis identity. Brian is the head of the family and he is spearheading the pursuit of discovery regarding their identity. He is literally knocking on doors, talking to people who might know, and researching. I want to do what they are doing. I wonder if we are related, as we have a family connection down the line. Reminiscing, Beth had emotion-filled memories of how hard her mother and grandmother worked to provide food. Her memory of her grandmother was a series of endless all-consuming cooking tasks. Feelings of admiration and empathy were expressed. Rose-Marie and Beth attribute their hard-working ethic as adults to their mother's positive role model behaviour, in their youth. Similarly, I and other participants interviewed attribute the same work ethic to our mothers, clearly outlining a feminine Métis characteristic. We drank tea, shared stories, laughed, and reminisced about family memoires. What began with the discussion of food turned out to be an evening of shared vulnerability in search for answers to better understand our Métis familial lineages.

7 October 2016

The St. Laurent Métis Elders

"Well, they used to make their own hamburger with a grinder, they used to grind deer meat . . . they used to grind their own and make les boulettes.

That's why we had it for special occasions at first. I mean once you start going to the store and buying hamburger, we had it in all kinds of way. But before that they had to grind it . . . so it was a big job . . . so Christmas, New Year's, weddings, everything else." (Lorraine Coutu, 2016)

"And we have our grandma's recipe passed down but when we make it and it doesn't taste the same because Grandma used well water . . . and we try to make it, in the city, and we know it tastes different but we're making the exact same recipe. At first, we don't know why but we figured it out and it was because of the water. But now the hamburger makes sense too because it doesn't taste the same that when Grandma made it, it tastes just a little bit different, it's still good but the taste there's something different." (Andrea Rose, 2016)

The St. Laurent Métis Elders included Patsy Millar, Agatha Chartrand, June Bruce, Lorraine Coutu, and Andrea Rose. Andrea is Lorraine's daughter and not yet an Elder; however, she was instrumental in the knowledge gathering for my research.

My head is spinning! Wow, what an interview! I can't wait to hear this over on the recorder. Oh god, I hope the recorder caught it all! At first, like any encounter with new people things are cordial until the ice breaks and the talking gets going. I feel like I could probably write my entire thesis based on what these ladies have shared alone. It was crazy, when they said they were "Métis-French," I couldn't help but think back to my childhood and remember those were the same words my father used to describe us. They spoke Michif-French and made it a point to tell me not to mix it up with Michif-Cree. Throughout the whole interview they were in and out speaking Michif-French and English. I feel sad yet again that I can't speak my language. I feel left out.

The Métis Elders identified blood sausage, which they referred to in Michif as "boudan," and rabbit brains were not only viewed as Métis dishes but considered delicacies that were reserved primarily for special occasions. Headcheese, pea soup, and tourtière were also mentioned. They reported that Christmas and New Year's Eve including "Jourdri Roway,""King's Day"—the seventh day following

New Year's Day—were all considered important Catholic days which Métis families celebrated, were hosted by an abundance of deliciously prepared foods. Growing up in a strict Catholic family myself, I was curious about these specific Catholic days that we, in my family, did not celebrate. I wonder if those are practices shared solely in rural communities as opposed to urban settings?

25 October 2016

Esther Monkman and Beatrice Chartrand

"Rabbit stew, it was rabbit stew, made with potatoes, onions, and we made like a gravy to mix it up together. We called it ragout served with bannock or we made some homemade bread sometimes too, but we had a lot of bannock. Grandma made bannock. She lived right next door to us so she made bannock." (Beatrice Chartrand, 2016)

Esther Monkman and Beatrice Chartrand were another connection made through Lawrie Barkwell. I met them at their church in Winnipeg and learned that they too grew up in St. Laurent.

Every time I meet someone new I learn something new. A new recipe, a new food term, something. I feel so blessed. I have to remember to touch base with Beatrice because she is going to give me some of her grandmother's recipes. They spoke about similar customs that I had heard from the St. Laurent Elders, which makes sense as they too grew up in St. Laurent. For Esther and Beatrice, defining a traditional home-cooked meal meant it had to be made from scratch, absent of store-bought ingredients, rather naturally from the land. For example, boiled potatoes with onion and boiled or fried fish. Further to discussing foodways and swapping recipes our grandmothers made, Beatrice and Esther spoke about the parish [church] they attend, which combines both Christian and Aboriginal epistemologies, which they explained was an important part of their spiritual health and Métis identity. For me, leaving behind the Catholic religion from my youth, in favour of a natural pull

> *toward my Indigenous ancestral traditions, I was intrigued to learn that such a practice existed and more so, how both women expressed that the equal sharing of spiritual knowledges complemented their understanding of their Métis identity. I am reminded that as Métis people we are diverse and unique, with one foot in both Western and Indigenous worlds, which would no doubt include our spiritual makeup as well.*
>
> *26 October 2017*

Conclusion

If you want to better understand your cultural identity, conduct research within your own cultural group. Even without the physical act of eating food together, my research participants and I through the practice of reciprocity shared stories, memories, and experiences related to family and food. These encounters moved me from a place of psychological dissonance to cultural resonance as the participants I introduced in this chapter helped further mould my Métis identity. I was embraced during these interviews and in following visits, which allowed me to experience firsthand an extension of kindness that made me to feel connected to the larger Métis community. Despite being strangers at first, distant friends, or even acquaintances, knowledge was shared and done so with open arms, as captured in this personal entry:

> *For some of the participants, like me, they too were searching for answers, and together we were piecing [together]aspects of our identity through a vehicle of food research. Evidently, memories surfaced that connected me to them and vice versa. We spoke about our commonalities related to our parents hiding from their identity and how that shame impacted us and the steps we had taken to reaffirm what was hidden. The process was extremely humbling.*
>
> *13 March 2017*

"What does it mean to be Métis?" is a question I am familiar with, and it is from my research journey that I have come to learn that *being* Métis means I am connected to others who are just like me. For me, it begins in the kitchen. It is about listening to the stories and sharing stories of my own, because that's where bonds are formed, lessons are learned, and memories are made. Métis people are proactively searching out their identity and piecing together for themselves who they are. To be Métis means extending kindness, showing leadership, and sharing knowledge about the land and cultural activities. Residing in urban centres does not mean that you are removed from your ancestral ties; rather, it requires more on your part to seek out the information from those who have it, an endeavour that is possible—if you ask. As a Métis woman, I have learned that I am not alone.

Food research has proven to be a protective factor in our cultural continuity. Our knowledge was marginalized on purpose; however, sharing a story or teaching about Métis traditional food knowledge and ensuring the knowledge is mobilized fans the flames of our resilience and becomes a form of Métis sovereignty. Our food stories promote living a healthy life, connecting to the land and one another, and it is for those reasons that participants were eager to contribute to this research. As Indigenous scholarship grows, we as Indigenous scholars pay close attention to the ways in which research embodies our collective understanding of truth, ancestrally based or not, and it is through the impacts of our lived experiences that relationships are formed, identities solidified, and epistemologies articulated. My position as a Métis researcher allowed me to conduct research in a space with other Métis people, which provided a wealth of knowledge. By maintaining a self-reflexive methodology, I was able to go back in my journal entries and see how my research journey had unfolded and how it intersected with food throughout. In this way, I was able to reflect on how research affected me on both a personal and academic level, which has proven to be an emotional journey. It is my hope that other Métis scholars will venture forward in similar pursuits to add to our collective Métis ways of knowing.

Notes

1 Louis Riel, Founding Father of Manitoba, Manitoba Metis Federation website.

2 Préfontaine, Dorion, Young, and Farrell Racette, *Métis Identity*, 8.

3 Cyr and Slater, "Honoring the Grandmothers."

4 Graveline, *Circleworks*, 57.

5 Braun and Clarke, *Successful Qualitative Research*.

6 Dickson-Swift et al., "Researching Sensitive Topics."

7 Ibid.; and Pithouse-Morgan et al., "Letters to Those Who Dare Feel."

8 Charmaz, *Constructing Grounded Theory*.

9 Engin, "Research Diary."

10 Skeggs, "Techniques for Telling the Reflexive Self."

11 Braun and Clarke, *Successful Qualitative Research*.

12 Shore, *The Métis*.

13 Absolon and Willett, "Putting Ourselves Forward."

14 Wilson, *Research Is Ceremony*, 71.

15 Métis Centre, National Aboriginal Health Organization, "In the Words of Our Ancestors."

16 Ibid., 9.

17 Smith, *Decolonizing Methodologies*; and Kovach, *Indigenous Methodologies*.

18 Kovach, *Indigenous Methodologies Characteristics, Conversations, and Contexts*; and Wilson, *Research Is Ceremony*.

19 O'Connor, "The Conditionality of Status."

20 Devers and Frankel, "Study Design in Qualitative Research-2: Sampling and Data Collection Strategies," 266.

21 Weber-Pillwax, "Indigenous Researchers and Indigenous Research Methods."

22 Lavallee, "Practical Application of an Indigenous Research Framework."

23 Kovach, *Indigenous Methodologies*.

24 Wilson, *Research Is Ceremony*.

25 Ibid., 78.

26 All names included in this chapter have been used with written consent.

Bibliography

Abbots, Emma-Jayne. "Introducing a Special Issue on Food Stuffs: Materialities, Meanings, Embodied Encounters." *Gastronomica: The Journal of Critical Food Studies* 16, no. 3 (2016): 1–4. doi.org/10.1525/gfc.2016.16.3.1.

Absolon, Kathy, and Cam Willett. "Putting Ourselves Forward: Location in Aboriginal Research." In *Research as Resistance: Critical, Indigenous and Anti-oppressive Approaches*, edited by L. Brown and S. Strega, 97–126. Toronto: Canadian Scholars Press, 2005.

Abu-Lughod, Lila. "A Tale of Two Pregnancies." In *Women Writing Culture*, edited by Ruth Behar and Deborah A. Gordon, 339–49. Berkeley: University of California Press, 1995.

Allison, Anne. "Japanese Mothers and *Obentōs*: The Lunch-Box as Ideological State Apparatus." *Anthropological Quarterly* 64 (1991): 195–208.

Appadurai, Arjun. "How to Make a National Cuisine: Cookbooks in Contemporary India." *Comparative Studies in Society and History* 30, no. 1 (1988): 3–24.

Baden, Sally, and Catherine Barber. *The Impact of the Second-Hand Clothing Trade on Developing Countries*. Oxfam, 2005.

Banerjee-Dube, Ishita. *Cooking Cultures: Convergent Histories of Food and Feeling*. Cambridge: Cambridge University Press, 2016.

Barker, John. *Ancestral Lines*. Toronto: University of Toronto Press, 2016.

Barron, F.L. "The Indian Pass System in the Canadian West, 1882–1935." *Prairie Forum* 13, no. 1 (1988): 25–42.

Bartlett, Cheryl, Murdena Marshall, and Albert Marshall. "Two-Eyed Seeing and Other Lessons Learned within a Co-learning Journey of Bringing Together Indigenous and Mainstream Knowledges and Ways of Knowing." *Journal of Environmental Studies and Sciences* 2, no. 4 (2012): 331–40.

Beardsley, Robert, John Hall, and Robert Ward. *Village Japan*. Chicago: University of Chicago Press, 1959.

Begly, Larissa. "The Other Side of Fieldwork: Experiences and Challenges of Conducting Research in the Border Area of Rwanda/Eastern Congo." In "Fieldwork Support," special issue, *Anthropology Matters* 11, no. 2 (2009). doi.org/10.22582/am.v11i2.

Bera, Sanjukta. "Food and Nutrition of The Tibetan Women in India." *The Anthropologist* 6, no.3 (2004): 175–80. doi:10.1080/09720073.2004.11890850.

Bestor, Theodore C. "Supply-Side Sushi: Commodity, Market, and the Global City." *American Anthropologist* 103, no. 1 (2001): 76–95.

Bickham, Troy. "Eating the Empire: Intersections of Food, Cookery and Imperialism in Eighteenth-Century Britain." *Past and Present* 198, no. 1 (2008): 71–109. doi:10.1093/pastj/gtm054.

Boas, Franz, and George Hunt. "Ethnology of the Kwakiutl, Based on Data Collected by George Hunt (Part 1 and Part 2)." In *35th Annual Report of the Bureau of American Ethnology to the Secretary of the Smithsonian Institution, 1913–1914*. Washington, DC: Government Printing Office, 1921.

Bolton, Dan. "Nepal's Tea Fortunes on the Rise." *Market Trends, Data and Insights*, 8 July 2019. https://worldteanews.com/market-trends-data-and-insights/nepals-tea-fortunes-on-the-rise.

Bonet, Sally Wesley, and Julia Ann McWilliams. "'Documenting Tragedy': Ethnography and the (Hidden) Costs of Bearing Witness." *Anthropology and Education Quarterly* 50, no. 1 (2019): 114–25.

Bourdieu, Pierre. *La Distinction: Critique sociale du jugement*. Paris: Les Éditions de Minuit, 1979.

———. *The Field of Cultural Production*. Edited by Randal Johnson. New York: Columbia University Press, 1992.

Brain, Roslynn. *The Local Food Movement: Definitions, Benefits and Resources*. Logan, UT: Utah State University, 2012.

Braun, Virginia, and Victoria Clarke. *Successful Qualitative Research: A Practical Guide for Beginners*. London: Sage, 2013.

Breakfast Menu. Feast Café Bistro. http://www.feastcafebistro.com/breakfast-menu/ (accessed 5 August 2019).

Brewer, Tina. "Breaking Bread: A Brief History of Bannock." New Brunswick Community College (website). https://nbcc.ca/indigenous/did-you-know/bannock (accessed 11 September 2019).

Briggs, Rachel V. "The Hominy Foodways of the Historic Native Eastern Woodlands." *Native South* 8 (2015): 112–46.

Brijbassi, Adrian. "How a Newfoundlander Became a Champion for Indigenous Food in BC." *Abbotsford News*, 25 September 2019. https://www.abbynews.com/sip-savour/how-a-newfoundlander-became-a-champion-for-indigenous-food-in-bc/.

Bryson, Bill. *At Home: A Short History of Private Life*. Toronto: Doubleday Canada, 2010.

Burnett, Kristin, Travis Hay, and Lori Chambers. "Settler Colonialism, Indigenous Peoples and Food: Federal Indian Policies and Nutrition Programs in the Canadian

North since 1945." *Journal of Colonialism and Colonial History* 17, no. 2 (2016). doi.org/10.1353/cch.2016.0030.

Cabinet Office of Japan. "*Kōreisha no kazoku to setai.*" *Kōrei Shakai Hakusho* [Annual report on the aging society], 2017. https://www8.cao.go.jp/kourei/whitepaper/w-2017/html/zenbun/s1_2_1.html (accessed 21 May 2020).

———. "*Mikonka no shinkō.*" *Shōshika taisaku* [Policies regarding childlessness]. https://www8.cao.go.jp/shoushi/shoushika/data/mikonritsu.html (accessed 21 May 2020).

Cajete, Gregory. *Native Science: Natural Laws of Interdependence.* Santa Fe: Clear Light Publishers, 2000.

Casagrande, Joseph B. *In the Company of Man: Twenty Portraits by Anthropologists.* New York: Harper, 1960.

Charmaz, Kathy. *Constructing Grounded Theory: A Practical Guide through Qualitative Analysis.* London; Thousand Oaks, CA: Sage, 2006.

Charsley, Simon R. *Wedding Cakes and Cultural History.* London: Routledge, 1992.

Christensen, Julia. "Eskimo Ice Cream and Kraft Dinner Goulash: The Cultural Geographies of Food in Three Cookbooks from the Northwest Territories (NWT), Canada." *CuiZine: The Journal of Canadian Food Cultures* 4, no. 1 (2013). doi.org/10.7202/1015494ar.

Classen, Lauren. "Not Just Staying: How Health and Development Programming is Reshaping the Past, Present and Future for Rural Youth in Malawi." PhD diss., University of Toronto, 2013.

Classen, Lauren, Rachel Bezner Kerr, and Lizzie Shumba. "Living in the Same Place, Eating in a Different Space: Food Security and Dietary Diversity of Youth Living in Rural Malawi." In *Geographies of Health and Development*, edited by Isaac Luginaah and Rachel Bezner Kerr, 151–76. London: Routledge, 2015.

Classen, Lauren, R. Kamanga, C. Khongolo, T. Luhanga, E. Mwale, M. Njikho, and E. Nyambose. "Revising Conventional Perceptions of Orphanhood." *Anthropology News* 49, no. 7 (2008): 15. doi/10.1111/an.2008.49.7.15.

Clifford, James, and George E. Marcus, eds. *Writing Culture: The Poetics and Politics of Ethnography: A School of American Research Advanced Seminar.* Berkeley: University of California Press, 1986.

Cochran, Patricia Longley, and Alyson L. Geller. "The Melting Ice Cellar: What Native Traditional Knowledge Is Teaching Us about Global Warming and Environmental Change." *American Journal of Public Health* 92, no. 9 (2002): 1404–9.

Codere, Helen. "Kwakiutl Society: Rank without Class." *American Anthropologist* 59 (1957): 473–86.

Coleman, Leo. *Food: Ethnographic Encounters.* Oxford: Berg, 2011.

Cornelius, Carol. *Iroquois Corn in a Culture-Based Curriculum.* Albany: SUNY Press, 1999.

Cornet, Candice, and Tami Blumenfield, eds. *Doing Fieldwork in China . . . with Kids! The Dynamics of Accompanied Fieldwork in the People's Republic*. Copenhagen: NIAS Press, 2016.

Counihan, Carole, and Penny Van Esterik. *Food and Culture: A Reader.* 3rd ed. New York: Routledge, 2013.

Crick, Malcom. "Ali and Me: An Essay in Street-Corner Anthropology." In *Anthropology and Autobiography*, edited by Judith Okely and Helen Callaway, 177–89. London: Routledge, 1992.

Cupples, Julie, and Sara Kindon. "Far from Being 'Home Alone': The Dynamics of Accompanied Fieldwork." *Singapore Journal of Tropical Geography* 24, no. 2 (2003): 211–28.

Cwiertka, Katarzyna. "Washoku, Heritage, and National Identity." In *Routledge Handbook of Modern Japanese History*, edited by S. Saaler and C.W.A. Szpilman, 376–88. London: Routledge, 2018.

Cyr, Monica, and Joyce Slater. "Got Bannock? Traditional Indigenous Bread in Winnipeg's North End." In *Indigenous Perspectives on Education for Well-Being in Canada*, edited by Frank Deer and Thomas Falkenberg, 59–73. Winnipeg: Education for Sustainable Well-Being Press, 2016.

———. "Honouring the Grandmothers through (Re)Membering, (Re)Learning, and (Re) Vitalizing Métis Traditional Foods and Protocols." *Canadian Food Studies/La Revue canadienne des études sur l'alimentation* 6, no. 2 (2019): 51–72. doi.org/10.15353/cfs-rcea.v6i2.339.

Daschuk, James. *Clearing the Plains: Disease, Politics of Starvation, and the Loss of Aboriginal Life*. Regina: University of Regina Press, 2013.

Davidson, Sonya. "Exploring Indigenous Cuisine with Chef Bill Alexander." *Toronto Guardian*, 15 May 2019. https://torontoguardian.com/2019/05/indigenous-cuisine-chef-bill-alexander/.

Davies, James, and Dimitrina Spencer. *Emotions in the Field: The Psychology and Anthropology of Fieldwork Experience*. Stanford, CA: Stanford University Press, 2010.

Davis, Heather Greenwood. "'Everyone Is Your Community': Chef Bill Alexander on Bringing Indigenous Food to a Wider Audience." *Globe and Mail*, 18 June 2019. https://www.theglobeandmail.com/life/food-and-wine/article-chef-bill-alexander-on-bringing-indigenous-food-to-a-wider-audience/.

Dawson, Leslie. "'Food Will Be What Brings the People Together': Constructing Counter-Narratives from the Perspectives of Indigenous Foodways." In Settee and Shukla, *Indigenous Food Systems*, 83–100.

Delormier, Treena, Kahente Y. Horn-Miller, Alex M. McComber, and Kayla Marquis. "Reclaiming Food Security in the Mohawk Community of Kahnawà:ke through Haudenosaunee Responsibilities." *Maternal and Child Nutrition* 13, no. 3, e12556. doi.org/10.1111/mcn.12556.

Devers, Kelly J., and Richard M. Frankel. "Study Design in Qualitative Research-2: Sampling and Data Collection Strategies. Education for Health." *Education for Health* 13, no 2 (2000): 263–71.

Devkota, Anurag. "Exploitation in the Hills." *Kathmandu Post*, 1 March 2019. https://kathmandupost.com/opinion/2019/03/01/exploitation-in-the-hills.

DeWalt, Kathleen, and Billie R. DeWalt. *Participant Observation: A Guide for Fieldworkers*. London: Rowman Altamira, 2002.

Dickson-Swift, Virginia, Erika L. James, Sandra Kippen, and Pranee Liamputtong. "Researching Sensitive Topics: Qualitative Research as Emotion Work." *Qualitative Research* 9, no.1 (2009): 61–79.

Dietler, Michael. "Culinary Encounters: Food, Identity, and Colonialism." In *The Archaeology of Food and Identity*, edited by Katheryn C. Twiss, 218–42. Carbondale: Center for Archaeological Investigations Press, Southern Illinois University, 2006.

Dorje, Rinjing. *Food in Tibetan Life*. London: Prospect Books, 1985.

Douglas, Mary. "Deciphering a Meal." In *Myth, Symbol, and Culture*, edited by Clifford Geertz, 61–81. New York: Norton, 1974.

———. Introduction to *The Anthropologists' Cookbook*, rev. ed., edited by Jessica Kuper, 1–7. London: Routledge, 2009.

Draper, Electa. "Native Dilemma." *Denver Post*, 3 August 2005. https://www.denverpost.com/2005/08/23/native-dilemma/.

Egeland, Grace M., Louise Johnson-Down, Zhirong R. Cao, Nelofar Sheikh, and Hope Weiler. "Food Insecurity and Nutrition Transition Combine to Affect Nutrient Intakes in Canadian Arctic Communities." *Journal of Nutrition* 141, no. 9 (2011): 1746–53.

Elliott, Bethany, Deepthi Jayatilaka, Contessa Brown, Leslie Varley, and Kitty K. Corbett. "'We Are Not Being Heard': Aboriginal Perspectives on Traditional Food Access and Food Security." *Journal of Environmental and Public Health* (2012): 1–9.

Embree, John F. *Suye Mura: A Japanese Village*. Chicago: University of Chicago Press, 1939.

Engin, Marion. "Research Diary: A Tool for Scaffolding." *International Journal of Qualitative Methods* 10, no. 3 (2011): 296–306.

Englund, Harri. *Prisoners of Freedom: Human Rights and the African Poor*. Berkeley: University of California Press, 2006.

Evans-Pritchard, Edward Evan. *Witchcraft, Oracles, and Magic among the Azande*. Oxford: Clarendon Press, 1976.

FAO (Food and Agriculture Organization of the United Nations). *Maize in Human Nutrition*. Food and Nutrition Series 25. Rome: Food and Agriculture Organization of the United Nations, 1992. http://www.fao.org/3/t0395e/T0395E00.htm.

Ferguson, James. *Global Shadows: Africa in the Neoliberal World Order*. Durham, NC: Duke University Press, 2006.

———. "Of Mimicry and Membership: Africans and the 'New World Society.'" *Cultural Anthropology* 17, no. 4 (2002): 551–69.

Finnis, Elizabeth. *Reimagining Marginalized Foods*. Tucson: University of Arizona Press, 2012.

Finnis, Elizabeth, Clotilde Benitez, Estela Fatima Candia Romero, and Maria Jose Aparicio Meza. "Agricultural and Dietary Meanings of *Mandioca* in Rural Paraguay." *Food and Foodways* 21, no. 3 (2013): 163–85.

FNIGC (First Nations Information Governance Center). *First Nations Regional Health Survey Phase 3 Volume Two.* https://fnigc.ca/wp-content/uploads/2020/09/53b9881f96fc02e9352f7cc8b0914d7a_FNIGC_RHS-Phase-3-Volume-Two_EN_FINAL_Screen.pdf.

Francks, Penelope. "Consuming Rice: Food, 'Traditional' Products and the History of Consumption in Japan." *Japan Forum* 19, no. 2 (2007): 147–68.

Fricke, Tom. "Imagining Yhebe: Of Friendship and the Field." *Michigan Quarterly Review* 45, no. 1 (2006): 197–218.

Frohlick, Susan E. "'You Brought Your Baby to Base Camp?': Families and Field Sites." *The Great Lakes Geographer* 9, no. 1 (2002): 49–58.

Fuller, Duncan. "Part of the Action, or 'Going Native'? Learning to Cope with the 'Politics of Integration.'" *Area* 31, no. 3 (1999): 221–27.

Gadacz, René R. "Longhouse." *Canadian Encyclopedia*, 8 January 2019. https://www.thecanadianencyclopedia.ca/en/article/longhouse.

Gallani, Barbara. *Dumplings: A Global History*. London: Reaktion Books, 2015.

Ghosal, Sutanuka. "Souring Relationship between India and Nepal May Help Darjeeling Tea Industry." *Economic Times*, 20 June 2020. https://economictimes.indiatimes.com/news/economy/agriculture/souring-relationship-between-india-and-nepal-may-help-darjeeling-tea.

Gibb, Christine. "Not Just Parenting in the Field: Accompanied Research and Geographies of Caring and Responsibility." *Singapore Journal of Tropical Geography* 42, no. 2 (2021): 284–300.

Gilpin, Emilee. "At 'Bigheart Bannock,' Resilience and Resistance in Food Made Well." *Tyee*, 11 July 2017. https://thetyee.ca/Culture/2017/07/11/BigHeart-Bannock-Resilience-Resistance-Food/.

Giroux, Ryan. "Bannock as Medicine." *Canadian Medical Association Journal* 190, no. 11 (2018): E335–E336. doi.org/10.1503/cmaj.170875.

Gordon, Kelly, Adrianne Lickers Xavier, and Hannah Tait Neufeld. "Healthy Roots: Building Capacity through Shared Stories Rooted in Haudenosaunee Knowledge to Promote Indigenous Foodways and Well-Being." *Canadian Food Studies* 5 (2018): 180–95.

Graslie, Serri. "The 'Sioux Chef' Is Putting Pre-colonization Food Back on the Menu." *The Salt*. NPR, 7 October 2014. https://www.npr.org/sections/thesalt/2014/10/07/354053768/the-sioux-chef-is-putting-pre-colonization-food-back-on-the-menu.

Graveline, Fyre Jean. *Circleworks: Transforming Eurocentric Consciousness*. Halifax: Fernwood, 1998.

Grieshop, James. "The Envios of San Pablo, Huixtepec, Oaxaca: Food, Home, and Transnationalism." In *Taking Food Public*, edited by Psyche Williams-Forson and Carole Counihan, 383–92. New York: Routledge, 2012.

Grindal, Bruce T., and Frank A. Salamone. *Bridges to Humanity: Narratives on Fieldwork and Friendship*. Long Grove, IL: Waveland Press, 2006.

Gujar, Bhoju Ram, and Ann Grodzins Gold. "From the Research Assistant's Point of View." *Anthropology and Humanism Quarterly* 17, nos. 3–4 (1992): 72–84.

Haines, Helen R., and Clare A. Sammells. *Adventures in Eating: Anthropological Experiences in Dining from around the World*. Boulder: University Press of Colorado, 2010.

Hanks, Lucien. *Rice and Man*. Chicago: Aldine, 1972.

Hansen, Karen T. "Dressing Dangerously: Miniskirts, Gender Relations and Sexuality in Zambia." In *Fashioning Africa: Power and the Politics of Dress*, edited by Jean Allman, 166–85. Bloomington: Indiana University Press, 2004.

Harjo, Suzan Shown. "My New Year's Resolution: No More Fat 'Indian' Food." *Indian Country Today*, 26 January 2005. https://indiancountrytoday.com/archive/my-new-years-resolution-no-more-fat-indian-food.

Hayden, Brian, and Suzanne Villeneuve. "A Century of Feasting Studies." *Annual Review of Anthropology* 40 (2011): 433–49.

Hayes-Conroy, Allison, and Jessica Hayes-Conroy. *Doing Nutrition Differently: Critical Approaches to Diet and Dietary Intervention*. London: Routledge, 2016.

Heldke, Lisa. "Let's Cook That: Recipes for Colonialism." In *Food and Culture: A Reader*, 3rd ed., edited by Carole Counihan and Penny Van Esterik, 376–406. New York: Routledge, 2001.

Herzfeld, Michael. "Senses." In *Ethnographic Fieldwork: An Anthropological Reader*, edited by Antonius C.G.M Roben and Jeffrey A. Sluka, 431–41. Malden, MA: Blackwell Publishing, 2007.

High, Holly. *Fields of Desire*. Singapore: NUS Press, 2014.

Himalayan Coffee Trading. "Nepal Shows Best Potential in Coffee Farming: Coffee Farming in Nepal." Himalayan Coffee Trading, n.d. https://himalayancoffeetrading.com/coffee-farming-in-nepal/ (accessed 18 September 2020).

Holtzman, Jon D. "Food and Memory." *Annual Review of Anthropology* 35, no. 1 (2006): 361–78.

Hoover, Elizabeth. "'You Can't Say You're Sovereign If You Can't Feed Yourself': Defining and Enacting Food Sovereignty in American Indian Community Gardening." In Mihesuah and Hoover, *Indigenous Food Sovereignty in the United States*, 94–121.

Hoover, Elizabeth, and Devon A. Mihesuah. "Conclusion: Food for Thought." In Mihesuah and Hoover, *Indigenous Food Sovereignty in the United States*, 335–37.

Iacovetta, Franca, Valerie J. Korinek, and Marlene Epp. *Edible Histories, Cultural Politics: Towards a Canadian Food History*. Toronto: University of Toronto Press, 2012.

Ingold, Tim. *Making: Anthropology, Archaeology, Art and Architecture*. London: Routledge, 2013.

Jackson, Anthony. "Faroese Fare." In Kuper, *The Anthropologists' Cookbook*, 37–40.

Jenkins, Sarah Ann. "Assistants, Guides, Collaborators, Friends: The Concealed Figures of Conflict Research." *Journal of Contemporary Ethnography* 47, no. 2 (2018): 143–70.

Jenkins, Virginia Scott. *Bananas: An American History*. Washington, DC: Smithsonian Books, 2000.

Jordan, Jennifer A. "In Search of the Elusive Heirloom Tomato: Farms and Farmers' Markets, Fields, and Fieldwork." In *Food: Ethnographic Encounters*, edited by Leo Coleman, 69–82. Oxford: Berg, 2013.

Karrebaek, Martha Sif, Kathleen C. Riley, and Jillian R. Cavanaugh. "Food and Language: Production, Consumption and Circulation of Meaning and Value." *Annual Review of Anthropology* 47 (2019): 17–32.

Keesing, Roger M., and Andrew J. Strathern. *Cultural Anthropology: A Contemporary Perspective,* 3rd edition. Fort Worth: Harcourt Brace, 1998.

King, Samantha, R. Scott Carey, Isabel Macquarrie, Victoria N. Millious, and Elaine M. Power. *Messy Eating: Conversations on Animals as Food*. New York: Fordham University Press, 2019.

King, Ursula, and Christopher Furgal. "Is Hunting Still Healthy? Understanding the Interrelationships between Indigenous Participation in Land-Based Practices and Human-Environmental Health." *International Journal of Environmental Research and Public Health* 11 (2014): 5751–82.

Kirkness, Verna J., and Ray Barnhardt. "First Nations and Higher Education: The Four R's—Respect, Relevance, Reciprocity, Responsibility." In *Knowledge across Cultures: A Contribution to Dialogue among Civilizations*, edited by R. Hayhoe and J. Pan. Hong Kong, 393–414. Comparative Education Research Centre. Hong Kong: University of Hong Kong, 2001.

Koc, Mustafa, Jennifer Sumner, and Anthony Winson. *Critical Perspectives in Food Studies*. 2nd ed. Don Mills, ON: University of Oxford Press, 2017.

Kondo, Dorinne. *Crafting Selves: Power, Gender, and Discourses of Identity in a Japanese Workplace*. Chicago: The University of Chicago Press, 1990.

Koster, Joan Bouza. "From the Flocks of Greece: *Galopita* (Milk Pie)." In Kuper, *The Anthropologists' Cookbook*, 19–21.

Kotobanku. "Metric System." https://kotobank.jp/word/メートル法-141565(accessed 21 May 2020).

Kovach, Margaret. *Indigenous Methodologies: Characteristics, Conversations, and Contexts*. Toronto: University of Toronto Press, 2009.

Kuhnlein, Harriet V., and Olivier Receveur. "Dietary Change and Traditional Food Systems of Indigenous Peoples." *Annual Review of Nutrition* 16 (1996): 417–42.

Kumar, Nita. *Friends, Brothers and Informants: Fieldwork Memories of Banaras*. Berkeley: University of California Press, 1992.

Kuper, Jessica, ed. *The Anthropologists' Cookbook*. Revised edition. London: Routledge, 2009.

Ladwig, Patrice. "Can Things Reach the Dead?" In *Engaging the Spirit World: Popular Beliefs and Practices in Modern Southeast Asia*, edited by Kirsten Endres and Andrea Lauser, 19–41. New York: Berghahn, 2011.

———. "Feeding the Dead." In *Buddhist Funeral Cultures of Southeast Asia and China*, edited by P. Williams and P. Ladwig, 119–42. Cambridge: Cambridge University Press, 2012.

Lavallee, Lynn F. "Practical Application of an Indigenous Research Framework and Two Qualitative Indigenous Research Methods: Sharing Circles and Anishnaabe Symbol-Based Reflection." *International Journal of Qualitative Methods* 8, no. 1 (2009): 21–40.

LaVeaux, Deborah, and Suzanne Christopher. "Contextualizing CBPR: Key Principles of CBPR Meet the Indigenous Research Context." *Pimatisiwin* 7, no. 1 (2009): 1–16.

Levi, Elisa. "Indigenous Philosophies and Perspectives on Traditional Food Systems Including Food as Cultural Identity: Maintaining Food Security in Elsipogtog First Nation, New Brunswick." In Settee and Shukla, *Indigenous Food Systems*, 39–56.

Lind, David, and Elizabeth Barham. "The Social Life of the Tortilla: Food, Cultural Politics and Contested Commodification." *Agriculture and Human Values* 21 (2004): 47–60.

Lindholm, Melanie M. "Alaska Native Perceptions of Food, Health, and Community Well-Being: Challenging Nutritional Colonialism." In Mihesuah and Hoover, *Indigenous Food Sovereignty in the United States*, 155–72.

Luongo, Gabriella, Kelly Skinner, Breanna Phillipps, Ziwa Yu, Debbie Martin, and Catherine L. Mah. "The Retail Food Environment, Store Foods, and Diet and Health among Indigenous Populations: A Scoping Review." *Current Obesity Reports* 9, no. 3 (2020): 288–306. doi.org/10.1007/s13679-020-00399-6.

Luppens, Lise, and Elaine Power. "'Aboriginal Isn't Just about What Was Before, It's What's Happening Now': Perspectives of Indigenous Peoples on the Foods in Their Contemporary Diets." *Canadian Food Studies/La Revue canadienne des études sur l'alimentation* 5, no. 2 (2018): 142–61. doi.org/10.15353/cfs-rcea.v5i2.219.

Madden, Raymond. *Being Ethnographic: A Guide to the Theory and Practice of Ethnography*. London: Sage, 2010.

Marcus, George E., and Michael M.J. Fischer. *Anthropology as Cultural Critique: An Experimental Moment in the Human Sciences*. Chicago: University of Chicago Press, 1986.

Martin, Aryn, Natasha Myers, and Ana Viseu. "The Politics of Care in Technoscience." *Social Studies of Science* 45, no. 5 (2015): 625–41.

Martin, Debbie. "Nutrition Transition and the Public Health Crisis: Aboriginal Perspectives of Food and Eating." In *Critical Perspectives in Food Studies*, edited by Mustafa Koc, Jennifer Sumner, and Anthony Winson, 208–22. Don Mills, ON: Oxford University Press Canada, 2012.

Mauss, Marcel. "Essai sure le don: Forme et raison de l'échange dans les sociétés archaïques." *L'année sociologique* 1 (1925): 30–186.

McDaniel, Justin. "This Hindu Holy Man Is a Thai Buddhist." *Southeast Asian Research* 21, no. 2 (2013): 191–209.

MDHS. *Malawi Demographic and Health Survey*. Zomba: Government of Malawi, 2004.

———. *Malawi Demographic and Health Survey*. Zomba: Government of Malawi, 2010.

Messer, Ellen. "Anthropological Perspectives on Diet." *Annual Review of Anthropology* 13 (1984): 205–49.

Métis Centre, National Aboriginal Health Organization. "In the Words of Our Ancestors: Métis Health and Healing." Ottawa: National Aboriginal Health Organization, 2008.

Mexico and the United States. Ithaca, NY: Cornell University Press, 2008.

Middleton, Townsend, and Jason Cons. "Coming to Terms: Reinserting Research Assistants into Ethnography's Past and Present." *Ethnography* 15, no. 3 (2014): 279–90.

Mihesuah, Devon. "Indigenous Health Initiatives, Frybread, and the Marketing of Nontraditional 'Traditional' American Indian Foods." *Native American and Indigenous Studies* 3, no. 2 (2016): 45–69. https://www.muse.jhu.edu/article/641379.

———. *Recovering Our Ancestors' Gardens: Indigenous Recipes and Guide to Diet and Fitness*. Lincoln: University of Nebraska Press, 2020.

Mihesuah, Devon A., and Elizabeth Hoover. *Indigenous Food Sovereignty in the United States: Restoring Cultural Knowledge, Protecting Environments and Regaining Health*. Norman: University of Oklahoma Press, 2019.

Miller, Jeff, and Jonathan Deutsch. *Food Studies: An Introduction to Research Methods*. Oxford: Berg, 2009.

Miller, Jen. "Frybread." *Smithsonian Magazine*, July 2008. https://www.smithsonianmag.com/arts-culture/frybread-79191/.

Mintz, Corey. "The History of Food in Canada Is the History of Colonialism." *Walrus*, 12 March 2019. https://thewalrus.ca/the-history-of-food-in-canada-is-the-history-of-colonialism/.

———. "Where Are Canada's Indigenous Restaurants?" *BuzzFeed News*, 27 April 2017. https://www.buzzfeed.com/coreymintz/where-are-canadas-indigenous-restaurants.

Mintz, Sidney. "Food at Moderate Speeds." In *Fast Food/Slow Food: The Cultural Economy of the Global Food System*, edited by Richard Wilk, 3–11. Lanham, MD: Altamira Press, 2006.

———. *Sweetness and Power: The Place of Sugar in Modern History*. New York: Penguin Books, 1985.

———. "Time, Sugar and Sweetness." *Marxist Perspectives* 2, no. 4 (1979): 56–73.

Mintz, Sidney W., and Christine M. DuBois. "The Anthropology of Food and Eating." *Annual Review of Anthropology* 31 (2002): 99–119.

Mishra, Nitu R., Woo Whan Jang, Venecio Ultra, and Sang Chul Lee. "Status of Tea Industry in South Asia and the Potential and Challenges of Nepal's Tea Production and Trade." *Journal of the Korean Society of International Agriculture* 26, no. 1 (2014): 11–19. doi:10.12719/KSIA.2014.26.1.11.

Moffat, Tina. "A Biocultural Investigation of the 'Weanling's Dilemma' in Kathmandu Nepal: Do Universal Recommendations for Weaning Practices Make Sense?" *Journal of Biosocial Science* 33 (2001): 321–38.

———. "Breastfeeding, Wage Labor and Insufficient Milk in Peri-Urban Kathmandu, Nepal." *Medical Anthropology* 21, no. 2 (2002): 207–30.

———. "Diarrhea, Respiratory Infections, Protozoan Gastrointestinal Parasites and Child Growth in Kathmandu, Nepal." *American Journal of Physical Anthropology* 122, no. 1 (2003): 85–97.

———. "Parents' Estimation of Their Children's Body Size Compared to Classification of Children's Status Using the International Growth Reference." *Ecology of Food and Nutrition* 39 (2000): 311–29.

———. "Urbanization and Child Growth in Nepal." *American Journal of Human Biology* 10, no. 2 (1998): 307–15.

Moffat, Tina, and Elizabeth Finnis. "Considering Social and Material Resources: The Political Ecology of a Peri-Urban Squatter Community in Nepal." *Habitat International* 29 (2005): 453–68.

———. "Dietary Diversity, Dietary Transitions, and Childhood Nutrition in Nepal." In *Human Diet and Nutrition in Biocultural Perspective: Past Meets Present*, edited by Tina Moffat and Tracy Prowse, 133–51. Oxford and New York: Berghahn, 2010.

Mol, Annemarie. *The Logic of Care: Health and the Problem of Patient Choice*. New York: Routledge, 2008.

Mol, Annemarie, Ingunn Moser, and Jeannette Pols, eds. *Care in Practice: On Tinkering in Clinics, Homes and Farms*. Bielefeld, Germany: Transcript Verlag, 2010.

Monod-Becquelin, Aurore. "Three Recipes from the Trumai Indians." In Kuper, *The Anthropologists' Cookbook*, 151–55.

Morrison, Dawn. "Reflections and Realities: Expressions of Food Sovereignty in the Fourth World." In Settee and Shukla, *Indigenous Food Systems*, 17–38.

Mosby, Ian, and Tracey Galloway. "'Hunger Was Never Absent': How Residential School Diets Shaped Current Patterns of Diabetes among Indigenous Peoples in Canada." *Canadian Medical Association Journal* 189, no. 32 (2017): E1043–E1045.

Moser, Sarah. "Personality: A New Positionality?" *Area* 40, no. 3 (2008): 383–92.

Msachi, Rodgers, Laifolo Dakishoni, and Rachel Bezner Kerr. "Soils, Food and Healthy Communities: Working towards Food Sovereignty in Malawi." *Journal of Peasant Studies* 36, no. 3 (2009): 700–706.

Mt. Pleasant, Jane. "Food Yields and Nutrient Analyses of the Three Sisters: A Haudenosaunee Cropping System." *Ethnobiology Letters* 7, no. 1 (2016): 87–98.

———. "The Paradox of Ploughs and Productivity: An Agronomic Comparison of Cereal Grain Production under Iroquois Hoe Culture and European Plow Culture in the Seventeenth and Eighteenth Centuries." *Agricultural History* 85 (2011): 460–92.

Muñoz, Carolina Bank. *Transnational Tortillas: Race, Gender, and Shop-Floor Politics in Mexico and the United States.* Ithaca: Cornell University Press, 2008.

Napoleon, Art. "#Next150 Challenge: 'Bannock Challenge.'" Indian Horse Productions. https://next150.indianhorse.ca/challenges/bannock-challenge (accessed 21 August 2019).

NATIFS (North American Traditional Indigenous Food Systems). "Frequently Asked Questions." Indigenous Food Lab, 2020. https://www.natifs.org/faq/.

Neufeld, Hannah. "Socio-Historical Influences and Impacts on Indigenous Food Systems in Southwestern Ontario: The Experiences of Elder Women Living On and Off-Reserve." In Settee and Shukla, *Indigenous Food Systems*, 251–68.

Neufeld, Hannah Tait, Chantelle Richmond, and the Southwest Ontario Aboriginal Health Access Centre (SOAHAC). "Exploring First Nation Elder Women's Relationships with Food from Social, Ecological, and Historical Perspectives." *Current Developments in Nutrition* 4, no. 3 (2020). doi.org/10.1093/cdn/nzaa011.

———. "Impacts of Place and Social Spaces on Traditional Food Systems in Southwestern Ontario." *International Journal of Indigenous Health* 12 (2017): 93–115.

O'Connor, Patricia. "The Conditionality of Status: Experience-Based Reflections on the Insider/Outsider Issue. *Australian Geographer* 35 no. 2 (2004): 169–76.

O'Connor, Richard. "From Fertility to Order, Paternalism to Profits: The Thai City's Impact on the Culture-Environment Interface." In *Culture and Environment in Thailand*, edited by the Siam Society, 393–414. Bangkok: Siam Society, 1989.

Ohnuki-Tierney, Emiko. *Rice as Self: Japanese Identities through Time*. Princeton, NJ: Princeton University Press, 1993.

O'Neill, Tom. *The Heart of Helambu: Ethnography and Entanglement in Nepal*. Toronto: University of Toronto Press, 2016.

Ontario Federation of Indigenous Friendship Centres. *Utility, Self-Voicing, Access, Inter-Relationality (USAI) Research Framework*. Ontario Federation of Indigenous Friendship Centres, 2016.

Phillips, Lynne. "Food and Globalization." *Annual Review of Anthropology* 35 (2006): 37–57.

Piot, Charles. *Nostalgia for the Future: West Africa after the Cold War*. Chicago: University of Chicago Press, 2010.

Pithouse-Morgan, Kathleen, Mathabo Khau, Lungile Masinga, and Catherine van de Ruit. "Letters to Those Who Dare Feel: Using Reflective Letter-Writing to Explore the Emotionality of Research." *International Journal of Qualitative Methods* 11, no. 1 (2012): 41–56.

Préfontaine, Darren R., Leah Dorion, Patrick Young, and Sherry Farrell Racette. *Métis Identity*. Gabriel Dumont Institute, 2003. http://www.metismuseum.ca/resource.php/00726.

Puig de la Bellacasa, María. *Matters of Care: Speculative Ethics in More Than Human Worlds*. Minneapolis: University of Minnesota Press, 2017.

Quaritch Wales, Horace. *Siamese State Ceremonies*. London: Bernard Quaritch, 1931.

Ralat, José R. "The Sioux Chef." *Cowboys and Indians*, 18 December 2015. https://www.cowboysindians.com/2015/12/the-sioux-chef/.

Ramiaramana, Bakoly Domenichine. "Malagasy Cooking." In Kuper, *The Anthropologists' Cookbook*, 104–8.

Ritten, Sanra. "Making Chipas in Paraguay." *Gastronomica* 9, no. 2 (2009): 19–24.

Rosaldo, Renato. "Grief and a Headhunter's Rage." In *Violence in War and Peace: An Anthology*, edited by Nancy Scheper-Hughes and Philippe Bourgois, 150–56. Malden, MA: Wiley-Blackwell, 2004.

Rosendaal, Julie Van. "How a New Guard of Indigenous Chefs Is Sharing Its Traditions." *Globe and Mail*, 14 February 2018. https://www.theglobeandmail.com/life/food-and-wine/food-trends/how-a-new-guard-of-indigenous-chefs-is-sharing-their-traditions/article37974526/.

Ross, J.L. "Adaptation to a Changing Salt Trade: The View from Humla." *Contributions to Nepalese Studies* 10, no. 1 and 2 (1983): 43–49.

Rouse, Carolyn, and Janet Hoskins. "Purity, Soul Food and Sunni Islam: Explorations at the Intersection of Consumption and Resistance." In *Taking Food Public*, edited by Psyche Williams-Forson and Carole Counihan, 175–94. New York: Routledge, 2012.

Saberi, Helen. *Tea: A Global History*. London: Reaktion Books, 2010.

Sagan, Aleksandra. "Canada's Indigenous Restaurants Are on the Rise." *Huffington Post*, 23 September 2018. https://www.huffingtonpost.ca/2018/09/23/mr-bannock-restaurants-indigenous-food_a_23539188/ (accessed 1 August 2019).

Sahlins, Marshall David. *Stone Age Economics*. New York: Aldine de Gruyter, 1972.

Said, Edward W. "Representing the Colonized: Anthropology's Interlocutors." *Critical Inquiry* 15, no. 2 (1989): 205–25.

Sasvari, Joanne. "Redefining Indigenous Cuisine." *Vancouver Sun*, 12 October 2019. https://vancouversun.com/life/food/redefining-indigenous-cuisine.

Sauer, Carl O. *Sixteenth Century North America: The Land and People as Seen by the Europeans*. Berkeley: University of California Press, 1971.

Schaefer, Otto, and Jean Steckle. *Dietary Habits and Nutritional Base of Native Populations of the Northwest Territories*. Yellowknife: Government of the Northwest Territories, 1980.

Settee, Priscilla, and Shailesh Shukla. *Indigenous Food Systems: Concepts, Cases, and Conversations*. Toronto: Canadian Scholars Press, 2020.

Sheikh, Nazneen. *Tea and Pomegranates: A Memoir of Food, Family, and Kashmir*. Toronto: Penguin Canada, 2007.

Sherman, Sean. *The Sioux Chef's Indigenous Kitchen*. Minneapolis: University of Minnesota Press, 2017.

———. *The Sioux Chef.com*, https://sioux-chef.com/owamni-by-the-sioux-chef/.

Shewell, Hugh. *"Enough to Keep Them Alive": Indian Welfare in Canada, 1873–1965*. Toronto: University of Toronto Press, 2004.

Shibano Sangyō Kabushikigaisha (Shibano Industrial Corporation). *Shibano Kicchin Ryōri Bukku* [*Shibano kitchen cookbook*]. Tokyo: Shibano Industrial Corporation, 1982.

Shore, Fred J. *The Métis: Political Maturity and Dispossession*. Aboriginal Information Series, Pamphlet #8, August 2006. Office of University Accessibility, University of Manitoba. https://umanitoba.ca/student/indigenous/media/Pamphlet_08.pdf.

Shukla, Shailesh, and Priscilla Settee. "Revitalizing the Past, Nourishing the Present and Feeding the Future." In Settee and Shukla, *Indigenous Food Systems*, 269–84.

Six Nations Lands and Resources. *Land Rights: A Global Solution for the Six Nations of the Grand River*. Ohsweken, ON: Six Nations Lands and Resources Department, 2019. https://iaac-aeic.gc.ca/050/documents/p80100/130877E.pdf.

Skeggs, Beverley. "Techniques for Telling the Reflexive Self." In *Qualitative Research in Action*, edited by T. May, 350–74. London: Sage, 2002.

Skinner, Kelly, Hannah Tait Neufeld, Emily Murray, Suzanne Hajto, Laurie Andrews, and Anne Garrett. "Sharing Indigenous Foods through Stories and Recipes." *Canadian Journal of Dietetic Practice and Research, eFirst* (2020): 1–5. https://doi.org/10.3148/cjdpr-2020-020.

Smith, Linda Tuhiwai. *Decolonizing Methodologies: Research and Indigenous Peoples*. 2nd ed. London: Zed Books, 2012

Snow, Angela Lilith. "If You Put It in the Oven It's Not Bannock, It's Bread. Change My Mind." Comment on The Arctic Kitchen: Recipes of the North (Facebook group), 8 September 2020. https://www.facebook.com/groups/430157227858562/permalink/736479447226337.

Srinivas, Tulasi, and Krishnendu Ray. *Curried Cultures: Globalization, Food, and South Asia*. Berkeley: University of California Press, 2012.

Stalker, Nancy K. "Introduction: Japanese Culinary Capital." In *Devouring Japan: Global Perspectives on Japanese Culinary Identity*, edited by Nancy K. Stalker, 1–32. New York: Oxford University Press, 2018.

Statistics Canada. "Community Profiles: Oneida Nation of the Thames," 6 February 2013. https://fnp-ppn.aadnc-aandc.gc.ca/fnp/Main/Search/FNMain.aspx?BAND_NUMBER=169&lang=eng.

Steckle, Jean. *Building Partnerships for Heritage and Environmental Education: Strategic Plan*. Kitchener, ON, 1995.

Stewart, Creek. *Pocket Field Guide: Survival Breads, Hard Tacks, Ash Cakes, Biscuits and Bannocks*. Dropstone Press, 2016.

Stoller, Paul. "Ethnography/Memoir/Imagination/Story." *Anthropology and Humanism* 32, no. 2 (2007): 176–91.

———. *The Taste of Ethnographic Things: The Senses in Anthropology*. Philadelphia: University of Pennsylvania Press, 1989.

Stoller, Paul, and Cheryl Olkes. "The Taste of Ethnographic Things." In *Ethnographic Fieldwork: An Anthropological Reader*, edited by Antonius C.G.M. Roben and Jeffrey A. Sluka, 404–16. Malden, MA: Blackwell Publishing, 2007.

Stone, Glenn Davis. "The Anthropology of Genetically Modified Crops." *Annual Review of Anthropology* 39 (2010): 381–400.

Sutton, David E. "Food and the Senses." *Annual Review of Anthropology* 39, no. 1 (2010): 209–23.

Tambiah, Stanley Jeyaraja. *Buddhism and the Spirit Cults in North-East Thailand*. Cambridge: Cambridge University Press, 1970.

Tennant, Zoe. "Does Bannock Have a Place in Indigenous Cuisine?" *Walrus*, 20 May 2016. https://thewalrus.ca/breaking-bread/.

Thapa, Ajit N.S. "Concept Paper on Study of Nepalese Tea Industry: Vision 2020." Nepal Tree Crop Global Development Alliance (NTCGDA). Baneshwor, Kathmandu: Winrock International, 2005. https://web.archive.org/web/20110724190355/http:/www.nepaltea.com.np/VISION-2020.pdf.

Ticktin, Miriam. *Casualties of Care: Immigration and the Politics of Humanitarianism in France*. Berkeley: University of California Press, 2011.

Tiwari, A., K. B. Adhikari, and S.M. Dhungana."Economics of Orthodox Tea Production: A Case of Ilam, Nepal." *The Journal of Agriculture and the Environment* 18 (2017): 1–5.

Treuer, David. "The Sioux Chef Spreading the Gospel of America's First Food." *Saveur*, 9 September 2016. https://www.saveur.com/sean-sherman-sioux-chef/.

Tucker, Catherine M. *Coffee Culture: Local Experiences, Global Connections*. Oxon, UK: Routledge, 2011.

Tye, Diane. *Baking as Biography: A Life Story in Recipes*. Montreal: McGill-Queen's University Press, 2010.

Uno, Kathleen. "One Day at a Time: Work and Domestic Activities of Urban Lower-Class Women in Early Twentieth-Century Japan." In *Japanese Women Working*, edited by Janet Hunter, 37–68. London: Routledge, 1993.

Van den Hoonaard, Deborah K. *Qualitative Research in Action: A Canadian Primer*. Don Mills: Oxford University Press Canada, 2019.

Van Esterik, Penny. "Contemporary Trends in Infant Feeding Research." *Annual Review of Anthropology* 31 (2002): 257–78.

———. "Feeding Their Faith: Recipe Knowledge among Thai Buddhist Women." *Food and Foodways* 1, no. 1 (1986): 198–215.

———. "Food Praxis as Method." In *Food Health: Nutrition, Technology and Public Health*, edited by Janet Chrzan and John Brett, 118–24. Eds. New York: Berghahn, 2017.

———. "Interpreting a Cosmology: Guardian Spirits in Thai Buddhism." *Anthropos* 77 (1982): 1–15.

———. "Nurturance and Reciprocity in Thai Studies." In *State Power and Culture in Thailand*, edited by P. Durrenberger. Yale Southeast Asian Studies 44. New Haven, CT: Yale University Southeast Asian Studies, 1996.

———. "Royal Style in Village Context: Towards a Model of Interaction between Royalty and Commoner." In *Royalty and Commoner: Essays in Thai Administrative, Economic and Social History*, edited by C. Wilson, C. Smith, and G. Smith, 102–17. Contributions to Asian Studies 15. Leiden: Brill, 1980.

Vantrease, Dana. "Commod Bods and Frybread Power: Government Food Aid in American Indian Culture." *Journal of American Folklore* 126, no. 499 (2013): 55–69. doi.org/10.5406/jamerfolk.126.499.0055.

Venkatachalapathy, A.R. "In Those Days There Was No Coffee: Coffee-Drinking and Middle-Class Culture in Colonial Tamilnadu." *Indian Economic and Social History Review* 39, no. 2 and 3 (2002): 301–16.

Wagner, Angie. "Icon or Hazard? The Great Debate over Fry Bread." Associated Press, NBC News, 21 August 2005. http://www.nbcnews.com/id/9022063/ns/us_news-life/t/icon-or-hazard-great-debate-over-fry-bread/.

Wasney, Eva. "A Veritable Feast: Chef Christa Bruneau-Guenther Is Passionate about First Nations Fare." *Winnipeg Free Press*, 31 July 2019. https://www.winnipegfreepress.com/arts-and-life/food/a-veritable-feast-513442902.html.

Wastasecoot, Lorilee. "Bannock: Consuming Colonialism." *Martlet*, 17 March 2016. https://www.martlet.ca/bannock-consuming-colonialism/.

Watkins, Susan C., and Ann Swidler. "Working Misunderstandings: Donors, Brokers, and Villagers in Africa's AIDS Industry." *Population and Development Review* 38 (2012): 197–218.

Watson, James L., and Jakob A. Klein. "Introduction: Anthropology, Food and Modern Life." In *The Handbook of Food and Anthropology,* edited by Jakob A. Klein and James L. Watson, 2–25. London: Bloomsbury Publishing, 2019.

Weber-Pillwax, Cora. "Indigenous Researchers and Indigenous Research Methods: Cultural Influences or Cultural Determinants of Research Methods." *Pimatisiwin: A Journal of Aboriginal and Indigenous Community Health* 2, no. 1 (2004): 77–90.

Wesche, Sonia, Meagan A.F. O'Hare-Gordon, Michael A. Robidoux, and Courtney W. Mason. "Land-Based Programs in the Northwest Territories: Building Indigenous Food Security and Well-Being from the Ground Up." *Canadian Food Studies* 3, no. 2 (2016): 23–48.

White, Rowen. "Planting Sacred Seeds in a Modern World: Restoring Indigenous Seed Sovereignty." In Mihesuah and Hoover, *Indigenous Food Sovereignty in the United States*, 186–97.

Whitehead, Tony L., and Mary E. Conaway. *Self, Sex, and Gender in Cross-Cultural Fieldwork*. Champaign: University of Illinois Press, 1986.

Whelpton, J. "Rana Nepal: A Political History." In *Nepal Rediscovered. The Rana Court 1846–1951*, edited by P.P. Shreshta, 1–17. New Delhi: Time Books International, 1986.

Wild Films in India. *Making Butter Tea: A Tibetan Specialty*. YouTube video, 2:23. Posted 30 April 2013. https://www.youtube.com/watch?v=U6qRMhLeHvA.

Wiley, Andrea. *Cultures of Milk: The Biology and Meaning of Dairy Products in the United States and India.* Cambridge, Massachusetts, London: Harvard University Press, 2014.

Wilk, Richard. *Fast Food/Slow Food: The Cultural Economy of the Global Food System.* Lanham, MD: Altamira Press, 2006.

———. *Home Cooking in the Global Village*. New York, Oxford: Berg, 2006.

Wilkinson, Catherine. "'Babe, I Like Your Lipstick': Rethinking Researcher Personality and Appearance." *Children's Geographies* 14, no. 1 (2016): 115–23.

Wilson, Shawn. *Research Is Ceremony: Indigenous Research Methods.* Halifax: Fernwood, 2008.

Wyatt, David. *Thailand: A Short History*. New Haven, CT: Yale University Press, 1982.

Xavier, Adrianne L. "Longhouse to the Greenhouse." In *Food Leadership*, edited by C. Etaminski, 3–16. International Issues in Adult Education. Rotterdam: Sense, 2017.

Contributors

Lauren Classen holds a PhD in medical anthropology from the University of Toronto and a master's degree in international development from the University of Guelph. Her research has focused on project impact assessment and rural youth in Honduras and Malawi. Using visual and participatory methods, she aims to support participants in telling their own stories and defining their own research.

Monica Cyr is a proud Métis woman born and raised in Winnipeg, Manitoba, homeland of the Métis Nation. She is a mother, a daughter, a sister, and an aunty. Her lineage stems from the Cree and French peoples of the Red River, St. Laurent, and northern regions of Manitoba. At present, Cyr is the Director of Primary Care for the Aboriginal Health and Wellness Clinic of Winnipeg. She also has a master's degree in human nutritional sciences from the University of Manitoba and is best known for her contributions in her community discussing the many roles of food and its impact on health and sovereignty. She is a registered dietitian and believes that food is more than the components of nutrients that are embedded within it. Cyr firmly advocates for the healing and health of her people through the relationship that is built from the reconciliation of lands and ancestral foodways. Recognizing the intimate and powerful relationships formed among women when stories are shared in the presence of food work, she empowers women to be the keepers of culinary knowledge for their families and share what they know. She advocates for women to reclaim the strength that comes with feeding their families.

Elizabeth Finnis is an anthropologist and associate professor in the Department of Sociology and Anthroplogy at the University of Guelph. Her research focuses on agricultural and dietary transitions, environmental change, rural livelihoods, and marginalization, and she has worked in India, Paraguay, and Ontario, Canada. Her work has been published in a range of disciplinary and interdisciplinary journals, as well as in edited volumes.

Karine Gagné is an associate professor in the Department of Sociology and Anthropology at the University of Guelph. Her research work is based in the Indian Himalayas, where she studies a range of issues, including climate change, human-animal relationships, state production, and citizenship. She is the author of *Caring for Glaciers: Land, Animals, and Humanity in the Himalayas*, published by University of Washington Press (2019).

Satsuki Kawano is a professor of anthropology specializing in Japan, ritual, death, and disabilities. She held positions at Harvard University (Center for the Study of World Religions) and the University of Notre Dame (assistant professor) before joining the

University of Guelph in 2004. She has received support from the Andrew Mellon Foundation, the Japan Foundation, the Social Science Research Council of the United States, the Japan Society for the Promotion of Science, and the Social Sciences and Humanities Research Council of Canada (SSHRC). Kawano's publications include *Ritual Practice in Modern Japan* (2005), *Nature's Embrace: Japan's Aging Urbanites and New Death Rites* (2010), *Capturing Contemporary Japan: Differentiation and Uncertainty* (2014), and "Performing Dyslexia in Contemporary Japan" in *DisAppearing: Encounters in Disability Studies* (ed. T. Titchkosky et al., in press). She is currently working on a SSHRC-funded project on academic accommodations in contemporary Japan (2016–22).

Kitty R. Lynn Lickers is a grandma, mother, and a storyteller. She holds a master's degree in social justice and community engagement. Kitty is the community food animator in her community of Six Nations of the Grand River Territory. She is engaged in every kind of food activity that leads toward access and sustainability. Kitty believes in cooking, growing, eating, preserving, and sharing good food. She is always striving toward sovereignty. She is a firm believer in the connections we have and that this is what will save our Mother Earth.

Tina Moffat is an associate professor in the Department of Anthropology at McMaster University who does community-engaged research on maternal-child food and nutrition and food insecurity. She has conducted research in both Nepal and Canada. Recent projects include "Mothers to Babies," which seeks to understand barriers and facilitators of diet and nutrition for healthy pregnancies in Hamilton, and a critical review of youth food programing at the Hamilton Community Food Centre. She is the author of *Small Bites: Anthropological Perspectives on Children's Food and Nutrition* (UBC Press, 2022).

Breanna Phillipps is a recent graduate of the MSc program in the School of Public Health Sciences (formerly the School of Public Health and Health Systems) at the University of Waterloo. She is involved in community-driven transdisciplinary projects with urban and remote Indigenous populations in northern Ontario and the Northwest Territories, spanning aspects of access to traditional foods, food security and sovereignty, wild food policy, climate change, and environmental health. With a background in human kinetics, she is passionate about promoting chronic disease prevention and challenging health inequities through participatory and decolonizing methodologies and the lenses of cultural safety and social and environmental justice.

Kelly Skinner is an associate professor in the School of Public Health Sciences (formerly the School of Public Health and Health Systems) at the University of Waterloo, where she leads and teaches in the online Master of Health Evaluation program. The primary focus of Kelly's research and evaluation practice has been community-based health and social projects related to food, nutrition, food security, health, and risk communication of contaminants in traditional food sources, and the broader context of food systems and environments for Indigenous people in Canada. The majority of this work has a northern focus. Recent evaluation and research projects cover various aspects of northern food environments on the topics of recipes, food costs, food quality, retail food environments, and community food initiatives.

Hannah Tait Neufeld is a nutritionist and associate professor at the University of Waterloo in the School of Public Health Sciences (formerly the School of Public Health and Health Systems). She holds a Tier 2 Canada Research Chair in Indigenous Health, Wellbeing, and Food Environments. Her research focuses on Indigenous health inequalities, taking into consideration community interests, environmental factors influencing maternal health, and Indigenous food systems.

Penny Van Esterik is a nutritional anthropologist, recently retired from York University. She has a long history of research in Southeast Asia, mostly in Thailand and Lao People's Democratic Republic. She also works on maternal and infant nutrition and other food advocacy issues. Since moving to Guelph, she has been affiliated with the anthropologists at the University of Guelph.

Adrianne Lickers Xavier is an Onondaga woman from the Six Nations of the Grand River First Nations Territory. She completed her doctoral degree focusing her research on Indigenous food sovereignty at Royal Roads University in Victoria, British Columbia, and has recently received the Indigenous In-Community Scholar Fellowship from the McMaster Indigenous Research Institute, where she is working with the community to understand and build food sovereignty. Currently she is acting director of the Indigenous Studies Program and an assistant professor in the Departments of Indigenous Studies and Anthropology at McMaster University.

Index